HUMAN RIGHTS AND THE
PRACTICE BEFORE THE TREATY BODIES

Second Edition

NIJHOFF LAW SPECIALS

VOLUME 54

The titles published in this series are listed at the end of this volume

Human Rights and the UN
Practice before the Treaty Bodies

Second Edition

By

Michael O'Flaherty

With a Foreword by

Mr Justice P.N. Bhagwati
Chairman, The Human Rights Committee

MARTINUS NIJHOFF PUBLISHERS
THE HAGUE/LONDON/NEW YORK

Published by:
Kluwer Law International
P.O. Box 85889, 2508 CN The Hague, The Netherlands
sales@kli.wkap.nl
http://www.kluwerlaw.com

Sold and Distributed in North, Central and South America by:
Kluwer Law International
101 Philip Drive, Norwell, MA 02061, USA
kluwerlaw@wkap.com

Sold and Distributed in all other countries by:
Kluwer Law International
Distribution Centre, P.O. Box 322, 3300 AH Dordrecht, The Netherlands

Library of Congress Cataloging-in-Publication Data is available.

Printed on acid-free paper.

ISBN 90-411-1788-1
© 2002 Kluwer Law International

Kluwer Law International incorporates the imprint Martinus Nijhoff Publishers.

Printed and bound in Great Britain by Antony Rowe Limited.

TABLE OF CONTENTS

FOREWORD

Mr. Justice P.N. Bhagwati
Chairman, The Human Rights Committee

The human rights treaty system is the bedrock of international law and practice for the protection of human rights. It provides both the normative framework and the ultimate system of international supervision. The supervision, undertaken, by the six treaty bodies, is an ongoing process of exhaustive review, analysis and dialogue regarding the human rights situation within States Parties. It addresses both system-wide issues and, where the right of petition exists, the plight of individual victims.

Important studies conducted in recent years have demonstrated the actual and potential capacity of the treaty bodies to have real impact in the lives of the people whom the system is designed to protect. We can observe a slow but significant process of heightened respect by Governments for the recommendations of the treaty bodies. However, these same studies also draw attention to the critical need for public and professional awareness regarding the practice and procedure of the Committees.

It is surprising that there continue to be so few reliable and scholarly publications in this area. Much of the available material either focuses on just one treaty body or deals with them all at such a level of generality as to be of the most limited use in practice.

It is fortunate then that we have Michael O'Flaherty's *Human Rights and the UN: Practice Before the Treaty Bodies*. Since the publication of its first edition in 1996 this work has been a most reliable and authoritative point of reference on the subject. Its lucid presentation and analysis charts a path for all those engaging with the Committees: States, non-governmental organisations (NGOs), UN officials, the general public and even treaty body members themselves. For this reason I enthusiastically welcome this second edition, taking account as it does of the quite dramatic changes in practice and procedure that have taken place in recent years.

Perhaps the greatest achievement of this book is its focus on the role of NGOs in the work of the Committees. Without their input, support and national follow-up activities, our work would have only the most limited effect. They serve as eyes, ears and hands – as multipliers of the impact of our efforts. For instance, in the context of the review of State reports, we rely on them to assist States in identifying the forms of human rights violations in society and bringing the issues before the Committees. We rely on them to informally provide information to us to supplement and check the data furnished by Governments. Finally, we call on them to bring the message home, to be our ambassadors in civil society, carrying our message to victims, to carers and to all those in authority who need to hear it.

Above all else, let this book be for them!

INTRODUCTION

Under the auspices of the United Nations, the international community has elaborated a range of internationally binding legal instruments in the field of human rights. The principal of these are:

- The International Covenant on Civil and Political Rights (CCPR)
- The International Covenant on Economic, Social and Cultural Rights (CESCR)
- The International Convention on the Elimination of All Forms of Racial Discrimination (ICERD)
- The Convention on the Elimination of Discrimination Against Women (CEDAW)
- The Convention Against Torture and Other Cruel, Inhuman or Degrading Treatment or Punishment (CAT)
- The Convention on the Rights of the Child (CRC)

International supervision of the implementation by States Parties of the rights in the instruments is undertaken primarily by independent bodies (the Committees/treaty bodies) which, in all but one case, are established pursuant to the provisions of the various instruments. These are:

- The Human Rights Committee (CCPR);
- The Committee on Economic, Social and Cultural Rights;
- The Committee on the Elimination of Racial Discrimination;
- The Committee on the Elimination of Discrimination Against Women;
- The Committee Against Torture;
- The Committee on the Rights of the Child.

In order for the Committees to carry out their tasks effectively it is essential that non-governmental organisations (NGOs) actively contribute to their activities. This involvement can also serve the interests of NGOs by greatly assisting them in their struggles for the protection and promotion of human rights at both national and international levels.

Four of the Committees oversee procedures for the consideration of communications from individuals. In the case of many States these procedures provide the only avenues of international redress for individuals. For those other States which participate in similar regional procedures, such as that under the European Convention on Human Rights, the UN mechanisms have an important complementary or alternative role to play.

All of the Committees are disadvantaged by a lack of public knowledge of their activities or of general understanding of their actual and potential significance for the promotion and protection of human rights. One of the causes of the relative obscurity of the treaty body system has been the ongoing dearth of up-to-date and comprehensive publications on their working methods and on the manner by which NGOs and individuals can be involved in their work. The present volume is intended to redress this lack.

In the following chapters each of the treaty bodies is considered separately and working practices are comprehensively presented. By far the most important activity for NGOs is participation in the procedures for the examination of reports submitted by States Parties. Each of the chapters dealing with specific treaty bodies describes this process, the obligation on the State and all steps of the procedure. The precise status of NGO participation is then identified and a range of practical suggestions proposed. Tables are provided indicating the situation of State Parties with regard to their reporting obligations.

Many of the fundamental issues regarding the participation of NGOs in the reporting procedure, such as promotional work, generation of publicity, the preparation of independent submissions and appropriate forms of lobbying and follow-up, are common to all the treaty bodies. Such matters are explored in Chapter 1.

The Human Rights Committee, the Committee on the Elimination of Racial Discrimination, the Committee Against Torture and the Committee on the Elimination of Discrimination Against Women all administer procedures for the consideration of individual communications. These mechanisms are described in the four respective chapters.

There are a certain number of procedures which are specific to particular treaty bodies and with regard to which NGOs have important roles to play. Among the most important of these are the investigation mechanisms under the Convention Against Torture and Other Cruel, Inhuman or Degrading Treatment or Punishment and the Convention on the Elimination of Discrimination Against Women. Others include the undertaking of missions to States Parties by certain treaty bodies. The various procedures are described as appropriate and the role of NGOs (and individuals) duly indicated.

Finally, the substantive provisions of each of the six instruments are reproduced in the treaty-body-specific chapters. This text is supplemented by brief notes on the General Recommendations or Comments adopted by treaty bodies which elucidate the content of the provisions. Readers wishing to undertake a more thorough examination of the substantive provisions are referred to the select bibliographies contained in the footnotes.

This is the second edition of this work and it has been comprehensively re-written. Since the publication of the first edition in 1996, there have been important innovations in the treaty body system, including the inauguration of the CEDAW procedures for consideration of individual and group communications and the undertaking of investigations. All of the Committees have also undertaken significant revisions to existing procedures, including regarding access for NGOs.

This edition takes full account of these developments as well as comprehensively updating the notes on General Recommendations and Comments, tables and bibliographies.

Responsibility for any errors and omissions is mine alone. That said, a number of experts have kindly commented on drafts of this edition, especially Kitty Arambulo, Ekkehard Strauss, Alessio Bruni, Jane Connors, Wan Hea Lee and Ben Majekodunmi. My special thanks go to Roberta Arnold for her excellent research assistance. I am very grateful to Mr. Justice P.N. Bhagwati, Chairman of the Human Rights Committee, for having written the Foreword.

Unless otherwise indicated the information contained in this volume is accurate as of September 2001.

This second edition would never have seen the light of day without the encouragement and support of Jan Ven. It is dedicated to him.

CHAPTER 1

NON-GOVERNMENTAL ORGANISATIONS AND THE REPORTING PROCEDURES UNDER THE INTERNATIONAL HUMAN RIGHTS INSTRUMENTS

The principal United Nations-sponsored human rights treaties include a mechanism whereby States Parties must submit periodic reports to international supervisory bodies with regard to their implementation of the human rights provisions in the respective instruments. Depending on the terms of the specific treaty (or "instrument"), the periodicity can range from every two to every five years. Reports are considered in public session by the relevant treaty body (or "committee") which then issues a set of observations on the State's compliance with the implementation obligation. Normally, representatives of the State attend the examination and engage in dialogue with the members of the treaty body.

The central purpose of the reporting mechanism is to promote compliance by States with the obligations which arise under the various human rights treaties.[1] All stages of the reporting process can contribute to the achievement of this objective:

(a) The exercise of drafting a report can itself assist a State in identifying and clarifying the extent of its obligations under the instrument in question. The wide-ranging consultations which are required for the drafting of a good text also serve to disseminate throughout the apparatus of government both knowledge of and general sensitivity towards the human rights at issue. The publicity which may surround the preparation of a report can raise the general

---

[1] See P. Alston, "The Purposes of Reporting", in *Manual on Human Rights Reporting*, (United Nations, 1997), pp. 19–24; P. Alston, *Long Term Approaches to Enhancing the Effectiveness of the United Nations Human Rights Treaty Bodies*, United Nations Doc. A/44/668; P. Alston, *Interim Report on Updated Study*, United Nations Doc. A/CONF.157/PC/62/Add.11/Rev.1; P. Alston, *Final Report on Enhancing the Long Term Effectiveness of the United Nations Human Rights Treaty System*, United Nations Doc. E/CN.4/1997/74; A. Bayefsky, *Report: The UN Human Rights Treaty System: Universality at the Crossroads*, (2001); the five papers in section I of *The UN Human Rights System in the 21st Century*, (A. F. Bayefsky, Ed., 2000), pp. 1–62; General Comment 1 of the Committee on Economic, Social and Cultural Rights, United Nations Doc. HRI/GEN/1/1/Rev.5, pp. 12–15; M. O'Flaherty and L. Heffernan, *The International Covenant on Civil and Political Rights: International Human Rights Law in Ireland*, (1995), Chapter 3; M. O'Flaherty, "The Reporting Obligation under article 40 of the International Covenant on Civil and Political Rights: Lessons to be Learned from Consideration by the Human Rights Committee of Ireland's First Report", 16 Hum. Rts. Q. (1994), pp. 515–538.

consciousness in society of the instrument in question and of the ways for individuals and NGOs to contribute towards its effective implementation;

(b) The consideration of a report by an international treaty body can provide the context for an important dialogue between the State and a group of impartial international experts. This dialogue can assist the State in identifying weaknesses in its implementation activities and offer possible ways forward. Occasionally States respond to the process by immediately announcing changes in law or practice or otherwise making commitments for change.[2] The dialogue with the treaty bodies may also contribute to a global understanding of the nature of the range of human rights obligations and offer lessons which can be applied with regard to other States. The ongoing examination of reports equally helps clarify the precise content of the range of human rights provisions in the instruments;

(c) All of the treaty bodies conclude the dialogue with the States Parties by the issuing of Concluding Observations. These typically identify the praiseworthy elements of reports, note matters of concern, draw conclusions and propose recommendations. Concluding Observations constitute authoritative analyses of country situations and can serve as programmatic guidelines. To the extent that they are critical or negative they can be employed to stimulate Governments to make whatever changes may be necessary in law, policy or practice. As well as Concluding Observations, the records of a treaty body's consideration of a report, if skilfully publicised and cited, can also serve to promote compliance with the implementation process.

The reporting process can also have collateral effects:

(a) In order to comply with reporting guidelines, States, either in the reports themselves, or in the oral dialogue with treaty bodies, are constrained to publicly articulate government policy on a range of issues. This is a most important feature of the reporting process in that all those who wish to see change in society or governmental practice must have as a starting point for their advocacy and activities an understanding of the Government position on the matters in question;

(b) If the reporting process is surrounded by adequate publicity it can draw both national and international attention to the human rights record of a country in general and its governmental regime in particular. It can thus contribute to a State's and a Government's image in the minds of its own people and internationally, with all the related consequences for social, economic and institutional well-being and stability;

---

[2] See for example the actions taken by the Irish Government in the context of examination of their initial report under the Covenant on Civil and Political Rights, described in M. O'Flaherty and L. Heffernan, *The International Covenant on Civil and Political Rights: International Human Rights Law in Ireland,* (1995), and M. O'Flaherty. "The Reporting Obligation under article 40 of the International Covenant on Civil and Political Rights: Lessons to be Learned from Consideration by the Human Rights Committee of Ireland's First Report", 16 Hum. Rts. Q. (1994), pp. 515–538.

(c) The reflection on human rights issues in the context of preparation and examination of a State report can contribute to a general raised consciousness with regard to the human rights perspectives of a range of matters which might not previously have been considered in such terms. It thus contributes to the development of a human rights culture in which there is an enhanced respect for the dignity of the person.

The range of immediate and collateral ends which may be achieved are only fully realisable if the protagonists in the report process play their parts in a conscientious and thorough manner.[3] Thus, States must be willing to submit their reports, comply with reporting guidelines, come to the dialogue ready for frank and honest exchanges and follow-through on the actions which prove necessary in order to meet with the implementation obligations under the instruments. The treaty bodies, for their part, must undertake their responsibilities in a thorough manner, deal efficiently with their programme of work and ensure consistent and fair report-examination procedures. Another protagonist in the process is the media. Without public knowledge and attention, the submission and examination of reports is in danger of being little more than a polite diplomatic activity barely impinging on the actual life of a State.

None of these protagonists can play their part adequately without the contribution of the NGO community,[4] a fact which has been repeatedly affirmed by the treaty bodies, the meetings of their chairpersons and the United Nations General Assembly. The crucial tasks of NGOs are as follows:

(a) The channelling of independent information to members of treaty bodies. No State report can be examined adequately without reference to other sources of information against which it can be tested. No matter how good a State report might be, it is going to suffer from oversights and lacunae. Reports may also be misleading whether because of excessive brevity, deliberate misstatement or lack of understanding of the issues involved. Independent information may also simply present an alternative perspective on matters and thus assist a treaty

---

[3] See R. Higgins, "Foreword", in D. Harris and S. Joseph, *The International Covenant on Civil and Political Rights and United Kingdom Law,* (1995); M. O'Flaherty, "The Committee on the Elimination of Racial Discrimination as an Implementation Agency", in *Anti-Discrimination Law Enforcement – A Comparative Perspective,* (MacEwen Ed. 1997) 209–233.

[4] See M. O'Flaherty, "The Reporting Obligation under article 40 of the International Covenant on Civil and Political Rights: Lessons to be Learned from Consideration by the Human Rights Committee of Ireland's First Report", 16 Hum. Rts. Q. (1994), pp. 515–538; S. Guillet, *Nous, Peuples des Nations Unies,* (1995); R. Brett, "The Role and Limits of Human Rights NGOs at the United Nations" *Political Studies* (1995), XLIII, pp. 96–110; L. Theytaz-Bergman, "State Reporting and the Role of Non-governmental Organisations", R. Brett, "State Reporting: An NGO Perspective", the five papers of section IV, all in *The UN Human Rights System in the 21st Century,* (A.F. Bayefsky, Ed., 2000); A. Clapham, "UN Human Rights Reporting Procedures: An NGO Perspective", in *The Future of UN Human Rights Treaty Monitoring,* (P. Alston and J. Crawford, Eds., 2000); A. Edman, "NGOs and UN Human Rights Treaty Bodies: A Case Study of the Committee on the Rights of the Child", in *Human Rights, The United Nations and Nongovernmental Organisations,* (The Carter Center, undated), pp. 102–113; I. Boerefijn, *The Reporting Procedure under the Covenant on Civil and Political Rights: Practice and Procedure of the Human Rights Committee,* (1999), pp. 216–220.

body in forming its own view. Finally, NGOs can channel contemporaneous information to treaty bodies to balance presentations in reports which may have been drafted many months, or even years before.

(b) NGOs have an important role in promoting knowledge and understanding of the reporting process. They can play the lead role in making the general public aware of the significance of the process, in encouraging individuals and groups to reflect on their situation in the context of their rights and in co-ordinating or channelling any submissions they might wish to make to members of treaty bodies. It also falls to the NGOs to convince the media of the newsworthiness of the process and to channel all relevant information to them in a form in which they can and will use it.

(c) NGOs are also crucial to the ongoing effectiveness of the reporting process following the examination by the treaty bodies. Without their constant lobbying and campaigns of public information there is a danger that recommendations of treaty bodies or commitments of Governments may either remain un-implemented or be carried through in an inadequate or misguided manner.

NGO participation in the reporting process may occur at four stages: before submission of a report, following its submission and prior to consideration by a treaty body, in the context of its examination by the treaty body, and following the conclusion of the examination.

1. NGO ACTION BEFORE SUBMISSION OF A REPORT

At this stage the tasks for NGOs include the following: (a) to encourage the State to submit its report in a timely fashion, (b) to explore the role which they might play in the drafting process, (c) to undertake remote planning for the making of independent submissions.

(a) The treaty bodies suffer from a failure of many States to submit their reports in conformity with the periodicity requirements. In response, the treaty bodies have developed a number of procedures such as the regular issuing to Governments of formal reminders[5] and, in extreme cases, the consideration of the situation in States even in the absence of a report.[6] These international responses can be of only limited effect in promoting respect for the reporting obligation.[7] Efforts are also required within the States themselves whereby public awareness is promoted concerning the obligation and the governmental record in that regard. Information might also usefully be disseminated about the actions taken by treaty bodies with regard to

---

[5] See, for example, the practice of the Human Rights Committee, described in Chapter 2.

[6] See, for example, the practice of the Committee on Economic, Social and Cultural Rights, described in Chapter 3.

[7] For example, with regard to their effectiveness in the case of the Committee on the Elimination of Racial Discrimination, see, M. O'Flaherty, "The Committee on the Elimination of Racial Discrimination as an Implementation Agency", in *Anti-Discrimination Law Enforcement – A Comparative Perspective*, (MacEwen Ed. 1997) 209–233.

specific overdue reporting States.[8] Skilful dissemination and employment of all relevant information by NGOs can do much to encourage tardy States in meeting their responsibilities.

Delay in the submission of reports is not, of course, invariably caused by neglect or bureaucratic delay. It will occasionally be the case that a State finds itself overwhelmed in attempting to meet the reporting obligations under a range of instruments. States may also lack the technical expertise to compile reports which adequately meet with the reporting requirements of the various treaty bodies. The United Nations can, on request of a State, provide technical co-operation to assist in overcoming such difficulties. NGOs, also, might wish to explore with Governments the extent to which they might appropriately offer assistance, either through the provision of training or direct participation in the drafting process.

(b) Various models exist for the manner in which NGOs might contribute to the report-drafting process.[9] In many States they simply ignore it or are precluded from involvement. In others, NGOs make submissions to the Government either on their own initiative or at its request. The Government then proceeds with the drafting and may choose to allow them to influence the contents of the reports, append them as annexes or ignore them. Another model is for active participation by NGOs in the drafting process itself, so that the final product is fully representative of the views of the Government and the participating NGOs. Each of the models has both advantages and disadvantages. Involvement in the drafting process can serve to give NGOs an important platform for the influencing of government policy. On the other hand it sharply limits the possibility for the NGOs to subsequently adopt an independent stance in criticising positions taken by the Government. It is, accordingly, for each NGO to assess its own circumstances and to establish an effective and appropriate relationship with Government.

Regardless of whether NGOs do or do not decide to become involved in the report-drafting process, they should, in the exception of threatening circumstances, keep the Government informed of the positions which they intend to take and the types of matters which they propose to include in their own submissions. This approach may encourage the Government to present a more thorough analysis in its report and, more importantly, to rectify problems in anticipation of criticism from treaty bodies. It is also consonant with the common understanding of the reporting process as being of dialogue rather than confrontation.

---

[8] The status of States with regard to the submission of reports is described in the chapters which follow. Information as to action taken by the various treaty bodies with regard to States the reports of which are overdue can be obtained from the respective secretariats or discerned from the Treaty Body Reports and other treaty-body related information on the website of the Office of the High Commissioner for Human Rights (OHCHR), www.unhchr.ch.

[9] See C. Bernard, "The Preparation and Drafting of a National Report" and L. Wiseberg, "Human Rights Information and Documentation", in *Manual on Human Rights Reporting,* (United Nations, 1997); P. Alston, *The Interim Report*, United Nations Doc. A/CONF.157/PC/62/Add.11/Rev.1, 22 April 1993, Chap. III.

(c) In the period prior to the compiling of a report, NGOs can usefully engage in remote preparation for the making of their own submissions. This may include an analysis of the substantive provisions of the international instrument concerned and the putting in place of a systematic programme for the collation of information concerning its implementation. This process will be greatly assisted by a close examination of previous considerations of the State by the respective treaty body, including any Concluding Observations adopted,[10] as well as the summary record of the consideration.[11] The eventual compilation of a submission will also be greatly facilitated by the ongoing assembling of relevant newspaper clippings, parliamentary and other public records, court decisions, scientific research, academic writings, etc. These should be catalogued in a manner whereby they can be related, article by article, to the instrument concerned.

Another important task at this stage is the promotion of knowledge of the procedures within the NGO community and the putting in place of mechanisms for collaboration and co-operation. NGOs will invariably benefit from a mutual sharing of knowledge and from active co-operation in matters of shared concern. Also, in States where a number of NGOs intend to prepare submissions it may be necessary, in effect, to compete for the attention of the Government, the treaty body concerned and the public. In such circumstances, collaborative efforts may enjoy a distinct advantage.[12]

2. NGO ACTION FOLLOWING SUBMISSION OF A REPORT AND PRIOR TO ITS CONSIDERATION

Once a State's report has been submitted it is processed as a United Nations document of general distribution and usually translated into the working languages of the treaty body concerned and placed on the OHCHR website.[13] NGOs may obtain from the website or the Secretariat information as to the likely date for its consideration by the treaty body or, where applicable, by a pre-sessional working group.[14] Armed with this information the preparation of submissions can commence.

What follow in this chapter are some general guidelines which apply for the

---

[10] Available on the OHCHR website. The manner in which these and other documents may be obtained is further described in each of the treaty body-specific chapters.

[11] These records, which are only incompletely available on the OHCHR website, can be ordered from the United Nations Documents Distribution and Sales Section. Symbol numbers can be discerned from the relevant reports of the Committee in question or obtained from the Secretariat.

[12] With regard to the particular significance of coalitions of NGOs in the context of the work of the Committee on the Rights of the Child, see Chapter 7.

[13] Reports can be ordered from the United Nations Documents Distribution and Sales Section. Orders should be accompanied by the document symbol number. This can be indicated by the respective treaty body Secretariat.

[14] Two treaty bodies do not, as a matter of practice, have pre- or post-sessional working groups, the Committee on the Elimination of Racial Discrimination and the Committee against Torture. See Chapters 4 and 6.

preparation of submissions to any of the treaty bodies. Drafters should also take into account the range of specific requirements and working practices of each of the treaty bodies. These are described in subsequent chapters.

Independent submissions are accepted by the members of the treaty bodies as an aid towards the carrying out of the scrutiny of the State reports. The submissions, therefore, should be prepared in the context of the purposes of State reporting. Submissions which stray beyond the boundaries dictated by this context are unhelpful and may have little impact.

To prepare a submission it is essential to study the text of the instrument concerned in order to identify the precise articles which address the issues of concern. The instruments should be read in conjunction with the General Comments or General Recommendations of the treaty bodies.[15] These constitute authoritative interpretations of the provisions and often either expand the understanding of the effective scope of treaty provisions or clarify their relationship to a range of fact situations. It is also very useful to examine the reporting guidelines which each treaty body has adopted to assist States in complying with their obligations.[16] The reporting guidelines are of considerable assistance in further elucidating the scope and application of the substantive articles of the instruments.

In the search for relevant articles of the instrument concerned, care should be taken to take note of the reservations entered by the State.[17] The entering of a reservation does not, however, preclude a treaty body from questioning a State as to the probity of its position.[18] It may, for instance, enquire as to the reason for the maintenance of the reservation or as to any steps being taken towards the withdrawal of a reservation. Accordingly, NGOs can usefully advert to matters which arise under an article which is subject to a reservation.

In preparing submissions it is important to observe how the treaty body last dealt with the country concerned and to identify the key concerns which pre-occupied it on

---

[15] Outlined in the treaty-body-specific chapters. General Comments and Recommendations are reproduced in a document of the United Nations, *Compilation of General Comments and General Recommendations adopted by Human Rights Treaty Bodies.* The current edition, dating from April 2001 has the symbol number, United Nations Doc. HRI/GEN/1/Rev.5. It is available on the OHCHR website and can be ordered from the Documentation Distribution and Sales Service of the United Nations. General Recommendations and Comments adopted subsequently can be found in the reports of the treaty bodies.

[16] See United Nations Doc. HRI/GEN/2/Rev.1. These are summarised in the treaty-body-specific chapters.

[17] Tables of reservations are published by the secretariats of each of the treaty bodies and are available on the OHCHR website. They may also be ordered from the United Nations Publications Distribution and Sales Service. Orders should be accompanied by the document symbol number, which can be indicated by the respective treaty body Secretariat.

[18] The Human Rights Committee has devoted one of its General Comments (No. 24) to an examination of issues relating to reservations. See United Nations Document HRI/GEN/1/Rev.5 at pp. 150–156.

that occasion. Particular attention should be paid to any Concluding Observations which had been adopted. It is also useful to examine the summary record of the previous consideration. Very often, this range of conclusions and records convey a treaty body's central concerns and indicate what might receive priority attention at the forthcoming consideration. They often also contain requests for further information on a range of issues and NGOs may wish, in their own submissions, to address these matters.

Another increasingly important source of guidance regarding issues of most interest to a treaty body may be the record of the manner in which that Committee has followed up with the State after its previous report has been considered. This form of engagement by the treaty body with a State can be observed, to a greater or lesser extent, in the practice of the Committee on the Rights of the Child, the Committee on Economic, Social and Cultural Rights and the Human Rights Committee.[19]

In the drafting of a submission, issues should normally be categorised with reference to articles of the instrument in question. Thus, for instance, if a submission is being made with regard to a particular matter, the approach should not be taken of discussing the issue in general, with inclusion of reference to specific articles only in the body of the text. Instead, it would be advisable to make reference, article by article, to the relevant provisions of the instrument, and to highlight matters as they arise in the context of each of the relevant articles. This approach is very helpful to the treaty bodies and facilitates members in categorising the points which they may wish to raise during the scrutiny. The article by article method of preparation will, of course, give rise to a considerable amount of cross-referencing. This should be kept as clear and simple as possible.

The article by article format should be replaced, in the case of submissions for the Committee on the Rights of the Child, by a format based on the "clusters of rights" style which that treaty body has stipulated for State reports.[20]

A submission will usually require extensive citation of the State report. All references should be made to the version of the report in the form of a United Nations document as it is this which will be considered by the members and it invariably has different page and paragraph numbering to the version submitted by the State. References should, as far as possible, be to paragraphs rather than pages as the pagination will change in the various translations.

Submissions will be most highly valued if they indicate the actual circumstances "on the ground". Thus, discussion of legal or structural injustices should, where possible, be illustrated by evidence of the negative effects on the individual or community. Avoid the anecdotal in the making of points. Submissions should include references to and citation of relevant authorities and sources of information: court cases, official reports, statistics, academic research, scientific research, surveys, etc. It is permissible to make reference to and discuss individual cases which serve to

---

[19] See subsequent chapters.
[20] See further at chapter 7.

illustrate a point being made. This opportunity serves as an informal but valuable way to raise a particular case before a treaty body.

Very often, NGOs may find that positions which they adopt, or assertions which they make are supported by statements of international human rights protection mechanisms. Where such support can be identified it should be cited. Thus, for instance, any pertinent comments of other treaty bodies can, very usefully, be adverted to. Extensive quotation is not always necessary however, as Committee members usually have access to the deliberations of at least the various United Nations treaty bodies. Among the other United Nations mechanisms[21] which may have addressed issues are the range of ad hoc procedures of the Commission on Human rights and its Sub-Commission on Promotion and Protection of Human Rights.[22] In the search for such information, reference might first be made to the reports of mechanisms which deal directly with the issues which concern the treaty body concerned, such as, for instance, the Special Rapporteur of the Commission on Human Rights on Torture, with regard to the Committee on Torture; and the Special Rapporteur of the Commission on Human Rights on Racism, concerning the Committee on the Elimination of Racial Discrimination. However a wide range of mechanisms, both of the type dealing with thematic issues and those which are country-specific, may yield valuable cites.

Submissions should be kept succinct. Elaborate and lengthy submissions may never be read by busy Committee members. Materials should also be bound and otherwise presented in as "user-friendly" and professional a manner as possible. It is useful to attach a one-page summary of the key points – one can be reasonably confident that all members of a Committee will at least acquaint themselves with this.

If it is intended that a submission influence the lists of issues to be drawn up by a working group of a treaty body in preparation for the eventual consideration of a report, it may be useful to include actual questions of a type which might be directly adopted by the working group. In the formulation of such questions or issues care should be taken to avoid the overly confrontational or adversarial. Examples of the types of lists of issues which are adopted by the treaty bodies are to be found in Appendix I.

NGO submissions can also be made which provide further information on matters noted in lists of issues. At present the lists adopted by the Committee on Economic, Social and Cultural Rights, the Human Rights Committee and the Committee on the Rights of the Child are available to the public before the session at which the State report is considered.

---

[21] It is beyond the scope of the present volume to explore these mechanisms in any depth. The reader may wish to refer to *Guide to International Human Rights Practice* (H. Hannum Ed., 1999). Ongoing developments with regard to the non-conventional mechanisms is efficiently reported in the periodical journal of the International Service for Human rights, *The Human Rights Monitor*. Orders for this publication may be made to that organisation at 1 rue de Varembe, PO Box 16, 1211 Geneva 20 cic, Switzerland. See also the OHCHR website.

[22] Formerly known as the Sub-Commission on the Prevention of Discrimination and Protection of Minorities.

The language in which a submission is to be drafted should be chosen with care. In terms of the linguistic skills of Committee members, by far the most useful language is English. It may also, on occasion, be advantageous to target specific members (such as Country Rapporteurs and members of working groups, where applicable) with materials in their own first languages.

The United Nations provides no financial assistance for the preparation of submissions. Some States may, however, be willing to provide funds for this and related purposes.

Except where otherwise indicated in the present volume, completed drafts should be sent to the relevant treaty body secretariats in multiple copies, sufficient for distribution to the targeted treaty body, working group or Country Rapporteurs, and for the placing of a number of reserve copies in the secretariat files. It is advisable, also, to eventually contact the relevant secretariats to confirm that materials have been received, distributed and otherwise brought to the attention of the intended recipients. Electronic versions should also be made available.

As at all other stages of the reporting process, and for the reasons noted above, it may be advisable to make copies of submissions available to the Government concerned. A number of the treaty bodies will, in any case, transmit to Governments copies of those NGO submissions which they have received.

3. NGO PARTICIPATION IN THE REPORTING PROCESS IN THE CONTEXT OF THE EXAMINATION BY A TREATY BODY

The impact of written submissions can be greatly enhanced by the making of direct contact with treaty body members. The range of possibilities for direct encounters with Committee members is surveyed later in this volume. Possibilities range from formal interventions in Committee meetings or pre-sessional working groups to informal encounters outside the sessions. Whatever the form of the meetings, they can prove invaluable in enhancing attention to key issues, providing fuller background briefings, correcting misapprehensions, and otherwise directing thoughts.

Among the other advantages of attending meetings of the treaty bodies are the following:

(a) The possibility is afforded of immediately contesting any inaccurate or misleading statements which may be made by Government representatives. The bringing of such matters to the attention of members in good time may lead to their being pursued vigorously in the ongoing exchanges with the Government representatives and to the inclusion of appropriate references in the Concluding Observations.

(b) NGOs which attend the meetings have the opportunity to make new submissions based on the direction taken by the proceedings. This option may be of most use in attempting to influence the content of the Concluding Observations. Thus, an NGO might consider drafting its own "alternative concluding observations" in the hope that they might be of assistance to the

Committee. Such texts should follow closely the structure of the official documents[23] and, while they will obviously reflect the concerns of the NGOs, they should constitute an honest reflection of the issues which were raised in the examination of the State report. This, then, is an opportunity to ensure adequate attention to a point already made rather than to introduce matters which had so far lain dormant. Submissions should be made within hours of the conclusion of the examination of a report as the drafting of Concluding Observations is often done very speedily.[24] In distributing submissions, NGOs should take care to make copies available to the Country Rapporteur of the Committee (where applicable) and to the Committee Secretariat (in hard copy and on diskette).

(c) For the proceedings before the treaty bodies to be reported adequately in the national media, it is important that information be transmitted to journalists in a speedy and intelligible manner. NGOs must play a central role in this process by ensuring that the media receive information on a daily basis and that it is translated into language and categories which adequately convey its newsworthy quality. This task can be carried out with regard both to journalists who are actually covering the meetings (who may not be particularly well informed of the purposes and practices of the process), and the media at home. In the latter case it is advisable that the NGO representatives at the meetings transmit information through colleagues in the country concerned who are in constant contact with interested journalists and who have the time to devote to the often exhausting and time-consuming process of "selling" the news to sceptical editors and producers. Efforts should also be made to engage the interest and attention of journalists accredited to the United Nations, especially those representing news organisations of the States concerned. Accredited journalists can be contacted through the press rooms at the Palais des Nations in Geneva and United Nations Headquarters in New York. The United Nations Department of Public Information will also assist in establishing contact with accredited journalists.

(d) Attendance at the meetings permits the taking of extensive notes on the proceedings. This is a useful practice in that the official summary records may take some time to issue and then appear only in either English or French, and verbatim reports of the proceedings do not issue in written form.

NGO representatives who wish to make informal contact with members should bear in mind the following considerations:

i. A good opportunity to meet with members is in the minutes prior to the commencement of meetings. However, once a session has begun, it is considered discourteous to attempt to continue the conversation or to otherwise remain in the section of the room reserved for members.

---

[23] Examples of Concluding Observations of all the treaty bodies can be found in Appendix II.
[24] In the case of the Committee against Torture the drafting process had been so swift until recently that there was often no time to make suggestions.

ii.   Many members are willing to have more elaborate meetings with NGOs, and these can be arranged on terms of mutual convenience.
iii. The Secretariat may be willing to perform introductions to members, organise meeting space, publicise informal encounters and provide limited secretarial support (access to photocopy machines, etc.)
iv.   NGO representatives should avoid moving around the meeting room to place documents on member's desks. Instead, documents for distribution can be given to the Secretariat.

NGOs intending to attend treaty body sessions might do well beforehand to explore means of combining forces. Particularly in situations where there are a considerable number of NGOs intending to participate, the impact of submissions can be greatly enhanced by the avoidance of replication, a diminution in the quantity of paper thrust at members and the avoidance of competitive lobbying.

NGOs might find it useful to attempt to organise meetings with the Government delegations. Should the delegations agree to such encounters an opportunity is provided to impress on the Government team the strength of the NGO lobby and the extent to which it will or has already impacted the proceedings. A delegation armed with such impressions may be inclined to moderate positions or to make concessions in the interest of avoiding or mitigating criticism from the treaty body.

Treaty body members may also be willing to travel unofficially to a State to meet with interested groups and to receive information in preparation for a review of a State report.[25] Such missions can do much to clarify the issues and focus attention on priorities. In choosing which members to invite, NGOs may wish to identify those who have shown an interest in the country concerned or otherwise appear to have a particular competence. Where a treaty body has publicly designated a Country Rapporteur that person should certainly be invited. Visits require to be organised with great care, bearing in mind, *inter alia*, that they are private events and that the visitors do not act in any official capacity. Thus the visitors should be fully consulted on any delicate or sensitive aspects of the proposed programmes or related publicity. It is important that the range of interlocutors whom it is intended to present to the visitors be fully briefed as to the nature and context of the visit, the work of the treaty body concerned and the type of information which it would be useful to provide. Where possible, field trips should be organised whereby the visitors can meet directly with victims and observe for themselves the actual situation in the country.

4. NGO ACTION FOLLOWING EXAMINATION OF A REPORT

It is important to speedily obtain copies of the Concluding Observations. If it is not possible to remain at the meetings until their adoption, arrangements can be made to have them transmitted by the Secretariat and they are, in any case, posted on the

---

[25] Certain treaty bodies have particular procedures for the conducting of missions to States Parties. These are discussed in subsequent chapters.

OHCHR website. These texts are usually adopted in English and are eventually translated into the working languages of the treaty body concerned. Immediately on their adoption or transmittal, attempts should be made to obtain media coverage for the Concluding Observations. They should also be copied to organisations and individuals for whom they have immediate relevance, to politicians and all other interested persons. It is no less important to attract attention to those aspects of the examination process beyond the Concluding Observations. Thus there may be a range of comments, observations or questions of Committee members, not to mention remarks of Government representatives, with direct significance for State practice. These dicta can be found in the summary records, the short notes of the proceedings posted daily on the OHCHR website and the official tape-recording.[26] NGOs in possession of tapes may wish to prepare transcripts both for their own use and for distribution to other interested groups.

In the longer term, it is essential for NGOs to ensure that attention continues to be paid to the treaty body proceedings and that these are allowed to play their full part in domestic advocacy campaigns, politics, public affairs and the judicial process. The task of dissemination, promotion, publication and interpretation is therefore an ongoing one requiring the exercise of considerable imagination and ingenuity.

One treaty body, the Committee on Economic, Social and Cultural Rights, has described the role of NGOs regarding the drawing of national attention to Concluding Observations as follows, "NGOs can give publicity to the concluding observations locally and nationally, and monitor the Government's performance in implementing the Committee's recommendations. NGOs reporting back to the Committee on the basis of their local monitoring and awareness-raising activities would contribute to more effective follow-up on the part of the Committee by keeping it informed of developments in the country after the consideration of the State party report. It would also be useful for local and national NGOs actively involved in the monitoring activities of the Committee to prepare a document on their experiences and on the working methods of the Committee, with comments, advice for other NGOs and suggestions for improvement of the system. Such a document, if distributed widely within the country and sent to the Secretariat of the Committee, would serve as a tool for awareness-raising, and would assist the Committee and the Secretariat in improving their performance"[27] To a greater or lesser extent,[28] these comments are helpful in identifying a role for NGOs which is relevant regarding the work of all of the treaty bodies.

Furthermore, one treaty body, the Human Rights Committee, has recently adopted a procedure of follow-up to Concluding Observations, whereby its Bureau,[29] at each session, is charged to observe how the situation with regard to

---

[26] The tapes can be obtained from the United Nations Conference Services Division, on payment of a nominal sum. In case of difficulty in placing an order, the treaty body secretariats may be of assistance.

[27] United Nations Doc. E/C.12/2000/21, Annex V.

[28] For the precise practice and openness to NGO inputs of the various treaty bodies see subsequent chapters.

[29] I.e. the Chairperson, the three vice-chairpersons and the Rapporteur.

serious violations of human rights in a given country may have changed in order to determine whether the possibility of adopting a special decision in plenary could be considered. The Bureau has also been given particular responsibility for the implementation of a decision taken by the Committee at its fifty-second session that, "where the consideration of a report revealed a grave human rights situation, the Committee could request the State party concerned to receive a mission composed of one or more of its members in order to re-establish dialogue with it, explain the situation better and formulate appropriate suggestions or recommendations"[30] NGOs have an obviously important role in alerting the Bureau of the Committee, through the Secretariat, of situations which might warrant the adoption of special decisions or the deployment of a Committee mission to the country.

---

[30] See United Nations Doc. A/51/40 at para. 437.

CHAPTER 2

THE HUMAN RIGHTS COMMITTEE

1. The Substantive Provisions of the International Covenant on Civil and Political Rights[1]

Article 1

1. *All peoples have the right of self-determination. By virtue of that right they freely determine their political status and freely pursue their economic, social and cultural development.*
2. *All peoples may, for their own ends, freely dispose of their natural wealth and resources without prejudice to any obligations arising out of international economic co-operation, based upon the principle of mutual benefit, and international law. In no case may a people be deprived of its own means of subsistence.*
3. *The States Parties to the present Covenant, including those having responsibility for the administration of Non-Self-Governing and Trust Territories, shall promote the realization of the right of self-determination, and shall respect that right, in conformity with the provisions of the Charter of the United Nations.*

Note

In its General Comment 12[2] the Committee states that this article imposes a specific obligation on States Parties, not only in relation to their own peoples but *vis-à-vis* all

[1] M. Nowak, *CCPR Commentary*, (1993); F. Pocar, "The International Covenant on Civil and Political Rights", in *Manual on Human Rights Reporting*, (United Nations, 1997), pp. 171–266; T. Opsahl, "The Human Rights Committee", in *The United Nations and Human Rights* (P. Alston Ed. 1992), pp. 369–443; D. McGoldrick, *The Human Rights Committee: Its Role in the Development of the International Covenant on Civil and Political Rights, (1991);* O. Prounis, "The Human Rights Committee: Towards Resolving the Paradox of Human Rights Law", 17 Colum. Hum. Rts. L. Rev., (1986), pp. 103–109; D. Harris and S. Joseph Eds., *The International Covenant on Civil and Political Rights and United Kingdom Law* (1995); L. Henkin, Ed., *The International Bill of Rights – The Covenant on Civil and Political Rights,* (1981); S. Joseph, J. Schultz, M. Castan, *The International Covenant on Civil and Political Rights, Cases, Materials and Commentary*, (2000); *Fact Sheet 15, Civil and Political Rights: The Human Rights Committee,* (United Nations); S. Pritchard, "The International Covenant on Civil and Political Rights and Indigenous Peoples", in *Indigenous Peoples, the United Nations and Human Rights*, (S. Pritchard, Ed. 1998); G. Cote-Harper, "Le Comité des droits de l'homme des Nations Unies", 28 *Cahiers de droit* (Quebec), (1987), pp. 533–546, pp. 447–477.
[2] UN Doc. HRI/GEN/1/Rev.5, p. 121.

peoples which have not been able to exercise or have been deprived of the possibility of exercising their right to self-determination. Moreover, the Committee invites States to refrain from interfering in the internal affairs of other States and thereby adversely affecting the exercise of the right to self-determination.[3]

Article 2

1. *Each State Party to the present Covenant undertakes to respect and to ensure to all individuals within its territory and subject to its jurisdiction the rights recognized in the present Covenant, without distinction of any kind, such as race, colour, sex, language, religion, political or other opinion, national or social origin, property, birth or other status.*
2. *Where not already provided for by existing legislative or other measures, each State Party to the present Covenant undertakes to take the necessary steps, in accordance with its constitutional processes and with the provisions of the present Covenant, to adopt such laws or other measures as may be necessary to give effect to the rights recognized in the present Covenant.*
3. *Each State Party to the present Covenant undertakes:*
   (a) *To ensure that any person whose rights or freedoms as herein recognized are violated shall have an effective remedy, notwithstanding that the violation has been committed by persons acting in an official capacity;*
   (b) *To ensure that any person claiming such a remedy shall have his right thereto determined by competent judicial, administrative or legislative authorities, or by any other competent authority provided for by the legal system of the State, and to develop the possibilities of judicial remedy;*
   (c) *To ensure that the competent authorities shall enforce such remedies when granted.*

Note

The Committee, in its General Comment 3[4] notes that this article generally leaves it to the States Parties concerned to choose their method of implementation in their territories within the framework set out in the article. However, General Comment 28[5] reminds States that article 2 requires not only measures of protection but also affirmative action to ensure positive enjoyment of rights.

Article 3

The States Parties to the present Covenant undertake to ensure the equal right of men and women to the enjoyment of all civil and political rights set forth in the present Covenant. General comment on its implementation

---

[3] UN Doc. HRI/GEN/1/Rev.5, p. 121.
[4] *Ibid.*

Note

In 2000 the Committee replaced General Comment 4 (13th Session 1981) with General Comment 28,[6] seeking to revise its practice by taking into account the important impact of article 3 on the enjoyment by women of the rights protected under the Covenant. It calls upon States Parties to ensure to men and women equally the enjoyment of all rights provided for in the Covenant, particularly by removing obstacles such as the existence of discriminatory legislation and practices, often rooted in tradition, history and culture, which nevertheless fail to justify the violations of women's right to equality before the law. The Committee invites States to fully report on such matters in their periodic reports to the Committee.[7]

Article 4

1. *In time of public emergency which threatens the life of the nation and the existence of which is officially proclaimed, the States Parties to the present Covenant may take measures derogating from their obligations under the present Covenant to the extent strictly required by the exigencies of the situation, provided that such measures are not inconsistent with their other obligations under international law and do not involve discrimination solely on the ground of race, colour, sex, language, religion or social origin.*
2. *No derogation from articles 6, 7, 8 (paragraphs1 and 2), 11, 15, 16 and 18 may be made under this provision.*
3. *Any State Party to the present Covenant availing itself of the right of derogation shall immediately inform the other States Parties to the present Covenant, through the intermediary of the Secretary-General of the United Nations, of the provisions from which it has derogated and of the reasons by which it was actuated. A further communication shall be made, through the same intermediary, on the date on which it terminates such derogation.*

Note

According to General Comment 5[8] this article has posed a number of problems for the Committee when considering reports from some States Parties. The Committee states that measures taken under the article must be of an exceptional and temporary nature and may only last as long as the life of the nation concerned is threatened and that, in times of emergency, the protection of human rights becomes all the more important, particularly those rights from which no derogations can be made. In its General Comment 18[9] the Committee reminds States that the derogating measures allowed by this article should not involve discrimination on the ground of race, colour, sex, language, religion or social origin.

---

[5] United Nations Doc. HRI/GEN/1/Rev.5, p. 168.
[6] United Nations Doc. HRI/GEN/1/Rev.5, p. 168.
[7] *Ibid.*
[8] United Nations Doc. HRI/GEN/1/Rev.5, p. 114.
[9] United Nations Doc. HRI/GEN/1/Rev.5, p. 134.

Article 5

1. *Nothing in the present Covenant may be interpreted as implying for any State, group or person any right to engage in any activity or perform any act aimed at the destruction of any of the rights and freedoms recognised herein or at their limitation to a greater extent than is provided for in the present Covenant.*
2. *There shall be no restriction upon or derogation from any of the fundamental human rights recognized or existing in any State Party to the present Covenant pursuant to law, conventions, regulations or custom on the pretext that the present Covenant does not recognize such rights or that it recognizes them to a lesser extent.*

Article 6

1. *Every human being has the inherent right to life. This right shall be protected by law. No one shall be arbitrarily deprived of his life.*
2. *In countries which have not abolished the death penalty, sentence of death may be imposed only for the most serious crimes in accordance with the law in force at the time of the commission of the crime and not contrary to the provisions of the present Covenant and to the Convention on the Prevention and Punishment of the Crime of Genocide. This penalty can only be carried out pursuant to a final judgement rendered by a competent court.*
3. *When deprivation of life constitutes the crime of genocide, it is understood that nothing in this article shall authorize any State Party to the present Covenant to derogate in any way from any obligation assumed under the provisions of the Convention on the Prevention and punishment of the Crime of Genocide.*
4. *Anyone sentenced to death shall have the right to seek pardon or commutation of the sentence. Amnesty, pardon or commutation of the sentence of death may be granted in all cases.*
5. *Sentence of death shall not be imposed for crimes committed by persons below eighteen years of age and shall not be carried out on pregnant women.*
6. *Nothing in this article shall be invoked to delay or to prevent the abolition of capital punishment by any State Party to the present Covenant.*

Note

In its General Comment 6[10] the Committee observes that this right is the supreme right from which no derogation is permitted even in time of public emergency, and also, that it is the duty of States to prevent wars. Furthermore, General Comment 14[11] indicates that nuclear weapons are among the greatest threats to the right to life which confront mankind today, and that the production, testing, possession, deployment and use of those weapons should be prohibited and recognized as crimes against humanity.

---

[10] United Nations Doc. HRI/GEN/1/Rev.5, p. 114.
[11] United Nations Doc. HRI/GEN/1/Rev.5, p. 126.

Article 7

No one shall be subjected to torture or to cruel, inhuman or degrading treatment or punishment. In particular, no one shall be subjected without his free consent to medical or scientific experimentation.

Note

The Committee reminds[12] States that this article allows of no limitation and that, even in situations of public emergency such as those referred to in article 4 of the Covenant, no derogations from the provisions of this article is allowed and its provisions must remain in force. In its General Comment 20[13] the Committee states that according to this article, read together with article 2 of the Covenant, States should ensure an effective protection through some control machinery.

Article 8

1. *No one shall be held in slavery; slavery and the slave trade in all their forms shall be prohibited.*
2. *No one shall be held in servitude.*
3. *(a) No one shall be required to perform forced or compulsory labour;*
   (b) Paragraph 3 (a) shall not be held to preclude, in countries where imprisonment with hard labour may be imposed as a punishment for a crime, the performance of hard labour in pursuance of a sentence to such punishment by a competent court;
   (c) For the purpose of this paragraph the term "forced or compulsory labour" shall not include:
      (i) Any work or service, not referred to in subparagraph (b), normally required of a person who is under detention in consequence of a lawful order of a court, or of a person during conditional release from such detention;
      (ii) Any service of a military character and, in countries where conscientious objection is recognized, any national service required by law of conscientious objectors;
      (iii) Any service exacted in cases of emergency or calamity threatening the life or well-being of the community;
      (iv) Any work or service which forms part of normal civil obligations.

Article 9

1. *Everyone has the right to liberty and security of person. N one shall be subjected to arbitrary arrest or detention. No one shall be deprived of his liberty except on such grounds and in accordance with such procedure as are established by law.*
2. *Anyone who is arrested shall be informed, at the time of arrest, of the reasons for his arrest and shall be promptly informed of any charges against him.*

---

[12] General Comment 20, United Nations Doc. HRI/GEN/1/Rev.5, p. 139.
[13] United Nations Doc. HRI/GEN/1/Rev.5, p. 141.

3. *Anyone arrested or detained on a criminal charge shall be brought promptly before a judge or other officer authorized by law to exercise judicial power and shall be entitled to trial within a reasonable time or to release. It shall not be the general rule that persons awaiting trial shall be detained in custody, but release may be subject to guarantees to appear for trial, at any other stage of the judicial proceedings, and, should occasion arise, for execution of the judgement.*
4. *Anyone who is deprived of his liberty by arrest or detention shall be entitled to take proceedings before a court, in order that court may decide without delay on the lawfulness of his detention and order his release if the detention is not lawful.*
5. *Anyone who has been the victim of unlawful arrest or detention shall have an enforceable right to compensation.*

Note
The Committee points out in General Comment 8[14] that paragraph 1 is applicable to all deprivation of liberty, whether in criminal cases or in other cases such as, for example, mental illness, vagrancy, drug addiction, educational purposes, immigration control, etc. Another matter raised by the Committee in its General Comment 8 is the total length of detention pending trial and the conformity of particular categories of criminal cases with the entitlement "to trial within a reasonable time or to release" under paragraph 3. The Committee states that pre-trial detention should be an exception and as short as possible.[15]

Article 10

1. *All persons deprived of their liberty shall be treated with humanity and with respect for the inherent dignity of the human person.*
2. *(a) Accused persons shall, save in exceptional circumstances, be segregated from convicted persons and shall be subject to separate treatment appropriate to their status as unconvicted persons;*
   (b) Accused juvenile persons shall be separated from adults and brought as speedily as possible for adjudication. 3. The penitentiary system shall comprise treatment of prisoners the essential aim of which shall be their reformation and social rehabilitation. Juvenile offenders shall be segregated from adults and be accorded treatment appropriate to their age and legal status.

Note
The Committee, in its General Comments 20,[16] 21[17] and 10,[18] recalls that this article supplements article 7 as regards the treatment of all persons deprived of their liberty.

---

[14] United Nations Doc. HRI/GEN/1/Rev.5, p. 117.
[15] General Comment 8, United Nations Doc. HRI/GEN/1/Rev.5, p. 117.
[16] United Nations Doc. HRI/GEN/1/Rev.5, p. 139 (now replacing General Comment 7).
[17] United Nations Doc. HRI/GEN/1/Rev.5, p. 141 (now replacing General Comment 9).
[18] United Nations Doc. HRI/GEN/1/Rev.5, p. 119.

Moreover, the Committee states[19] that the application of paragraph 1 of this article, as a minimum, cannot be dependent on the material resources available in the State Party and that such considerations should be made in regard of *all* those held under the laws and authority of a State, particularly people hosted in (psychiatric) hospitals.[20] Special considerations should then be taken into account in regard of juvenile offenders.[21]

Article 11

No one shall be imprisoned merely on the ground of inability to fulfil a contractual obligation.

Article 12

1. *Everyone lawfully within the territory of a State shall, within that territory, have the right to liberty of movement and freedom to choose his residence.*
2. *Everyone shall be free to leave any country, including his own.*
3. *The above-mentioned rights shall not be subject to any restrictions except those which are provided by law, are necessary to protect national security, public order (ordre public), public health or morals or the rights and freedoms of others, and are consistent with the other rights recognized in the present Covenant.*
4. *No one shall be arbitrarily deprived of the right to enter his own country.*

Note
Referring to the positions of aliens, the Committee recalls[22] that once an alien is lawfully within a territory, his freedom of movement within the territory and his rights to leave that territory may only be restricted in accordance with this article.

Article 13

An alien lawfully in the territory of a State Party to the present Covenant may be expelled therefrom only in pursuance of a decision reached in accordance with law and shall, except where compelling reasons of national security otherwise require, be allowed to submit the reasons against his expulsion and to have his case reviewed by, and be represented for the purpose before, the competent authority or a person or persons especially designated by the competent authority.

Note
In its General Comment 15[23] the Committee recalls that if the procedure for

---

[19] *Ibid.*
[20] General Comment 21, United Nations Doc. HRI/GEN/1/Rev.5, p. 141.
[21] United Nations Doc. HRI/GEN/1/Rev.5, p. 143.
[22] General Comment 27, United Nations Doc. HRI/GEN/1/Rev.5, p. 163.
[23] United Nations Doc. HRI/GEN/1/Rev.5, p. 127.

expulsion of an alien entails arrest, the safeguards of the Covenant relating to deprivation of liberty (articles 9 and 10) are also applicable.

Article 14

1. *All persons shall be equal before the courts and tribunals. In the determination of any criminal charge against him, or of his rights and obligations in a suit at law, everyone shall be entitled to a fair and public hearing by a competent, independent and impartial tribunal established by law. The press and the public may be excluded from all or part of a trial for reasons of morals, public order (ordre public) or national security in a democratic society, or when the interest of the private lives of the parties so requires, or to the extent strictly necessary in the opinion of the court in special circumstances where publicity would prejudice the interests of justice; but any judgement rendered in a criminal case or in a suit at law shall be made public except where the interest of juvenile persons otherwise requires or the proceedings concern matrimonial disputes or the guardianship of children.*

2. *Everyone charged with a criminal offence shall have the right to be presumed innocent until proved guilty according to law.*

3. *In the determination of any criminal charge against him, everyone shall be entitled to the following minimum guarantees, in full equality:*
   (a) *To be informed promptly and in detail in a language which he understands of the nature and cause of the charge against him;*
   (b) *To have adequate time and facilities for the preparation of his defence and to communicate with counsel of his own choosing;*
   (c) *To be tried without undue delay;*
   (d) *To be tried in his presence, and to defend himself in person or through legal assistance of his own choosing; to be informed, if he does not have legal assistance, of this right; and to have legal assistance assigned to him, in any case where the interests of justice so require, and without payment by him in any such case if he does not have sufficient means to pay for it;*
   (e) *To examine, or have examined, the witnesses against him and to obtain the attendance and examination of witnesses on his behalf under the same conditions as witnesses against him;*
   (f) *To have the free assistance of an interpreter if he cannot understand or speak the language used in court;*
   (g) *Not to be compelled to testify against himself or to confess guilt.*

4. *In the case of juvenile persons, the procedure shall be such as will take account of their age and the desirability of promoting their rehabilitation.*

5. *Everyone convicted of a crime shall have the right to his conviction and sentence being reviewed by a higher tribunal according to law.*

6. *When a person has by a final decision been convicted of a criminal offence and when subsequently his conviction has been reversed or he has been pardoned on the ground that a new or newly discovered fact shows conclusively that there has been a miscarriage of justice, the person who has suffered punishment as a result of such conviction shall be compensate according to law unless it is proved that the*

non-disclosure of the unknown fact in time is wholly or partly attributable to him.
7. *No one shall be liable to be tried or punished again for an offence for which he has already been finally convicted of acquitted in accordance with the law and penal procedure of each country.*

Note
The Committee notes that this article is of a complex nature and that different aspects of its provisions require specific comment.[24] The Committee invites States Parties to provide more detailed information on the steps taken to ensure that equality before the courts is established by law and guaranteed in practice.[25] Moreover, it states that even in cases in which the public is excluded from the trial, the judgement must, with certain strictly defined exceptions, be made public.[26] The Committee also notes that by reason of the presumption of innocence, the burden of proof of the charge is on the prosecution and the accused has the benefit of doubt.[27] The Committee further observers that in considering State reports differing views have often been expressed as to the scope of paragraph 7 (*ne bis in idem*) and that a clear understanding of the meaning of this paragraph may encourage States Parties to reconsider their reservations thereto.

Article 15

1. *No one shall be held guilty of any criminal offence on account of any act or omission, which did not constitute a criminal offence, under national or international law, at the time when it was committed. Nor shall a heavier penalty be imposed than the one that was applicable at the time when the criminal offence was committed. If, subsequent to the commission of the offence, provision is made by law for the imposition of the lighter penalty, the offender shall benefit thereby.*
2. *Nothing in this article shall prejudice the trial and punishment of any person for any act or omission, which, at the time when it was committed, was criminal according to the general principles of law recognized by the community of nations.*

Article 16

Everyone shall have the right to recognition everywhere as a person before the law.

Article 17

1. *No one shall be subjected to arbitrary or unlawful interference with his privacy, family, home or correspondence, nor to unlawful attacks on his honour and reputation.*

---

[24] United Nations Doc. HRI/GEN/1/Rev.5, p. 122.
[25] *Ibid.*
[26] *Ibid.*
[27] *Ibid.*

2. Everyone has the right to the protection of the law against such interference or attacks.

Note

General Comment 16[28] reminds States that the right enshrined in this article is required to be guaranteed against all such interference and attacks whether they emanate from State authorities or from natural or legal persons. Moreover, the Committee invites States to ensure that information on computer, databanks and other devices, concerning a person's private life, does not reach the hands of persons who are not authorised by law to receive, process and use it, and is never used for purposes incompatible with the Covenant.[29]

Article 18

1. Everyone shall have the right to freedom of thought, conscience and religion. This right shall include freedom to have or to adopt a religion or belief of his choice, and freedom, either individually or in community with others and in public or private, to manifest his religion or belief in worship, observance, practice and teaching.
2. No one shall be subject to coercion which would impair his freedom to have or to adopt a religion or belief of his choice.
3. Freedom to manifest one's religion or beliefs may be subject only to such limitations as are prescribed by law and are necessary to protect public safety, order, health, or morals or the fundamental rights and freedoms of others. 4. The States Parties to the present Covenant undertake to have respect for the liberty of parents and, when applicable, legal guardians to ensure the religious and moral education of their children in conformity with their own convictions.

Note

In General Comment 22[30] the Committee states that freedom of thought and freedom of conscience are protected equally with freedom of religion and belief and that these rights are to be distinguished from the freedom to *manifest* religion or belief. It further recalls that the fundamental character of these freedoms is reflected in the fact that this provision cannot be derogated from, even in time of public emergency, as stated in article 4.2 of the Covenant.

Article 19

1. Everyone shall have the right to hold opinions without interference.
2. Everyone shall have the right to freedom of expression; this right shall include freedom to seek, receive and impart information and ideas of all kinds, regardless of

---

[28] United Nations Doc. HRI/GEN/1/Rev.5, p. 129.
[29] United Nations Doc. HRI/GEN/1/Rev.5, p. 129.
[30] United Nations Doc. HRI/GEN/1/Rev.5, p. 144.

frontiers, either orally, in writing or in print, in the form of art, or through any other media of his choice.

3. *The exercise of the rights provided for in paragraph 2 of this article carries with it special duties and responsibilities. It may therefore be subject to certain restrictions, but these shall only be such as are provided by law and are necessary:*
   (a) For respect of the rights or reputations of others;
   (b) For the protection of national security or of public order (ordre public), or of public health or morals.

Note

The Committee notes that the right to freedom of expression has various aspects and that not all States Parties have provided information on these.[31] Moreover, the Committee invites States Parties to take effective measures to prevent forms of control of modern media which would interfere with the right of everyone to freedom of expression in a way not compatible with paragraph 3.[32]

Article 20

1. *Any propaganda for war shall be prohibited by law.*
2. *Any advocacy of national, racial or religious hatred that constitutes incitement to discrimination, hostility or violence shall be prohibited by law.*

Note

In the opinion of the Committee, the prohibitions required by this article are fully compatible with the right of freedom of expression as contained in article 19, the exercise of which carries with it special duties and responsibilities.[33] The Committee further recalls the connection between this article and article 6 of the Covenant.[34]

Article 21

The right of peaceful assembly shall be recognized. No restrictions may be placed on the exercise of this right other than those imposed in conformity with the law and which are necessary in a democratic society in the interests of national security or public safety, public order (ordre public), the protection of public health or morals or the protection of the rights and freedoms of others.

Article 22

1. *Everyone shall have the right to freedom of association with others, including the right to form and join trade unions for the protection of his interests.*

---

[31] General Comment 10, United Nations Doc. HRI/GEN/1/Rev.5, p. 119.
[32] *Ibid.*
[33] United Nations Doc. HRI/GEN/1/Rev.5, p. 120.
[34] United Nations Doc. HRI/GEN/1/Rev.5, p. 114.

2. *No restrictions may be placed on the exercise of this right other than those which are prescribed by law and which are necessary in a democratic society in the interests of national security or public safety, public order (ordre public), the protection of public health or morals or the protection of the rights and freedoms of others. This article shall not prevent the imposition of lawful restrictions on members of the armed forces and of the police in their exercise of this right.*
3. *Nothing in this article shall authorize States Parties to the International Labour Organisation Convention of 1948 concerning Freedom of Association and Protection of the Right to Organize to take legislative measures which would prejudice, or to apply the law in such a manner as to prejudice, the guarantees provided for in that Convention.*

Article 23

1. *The family is the natural and fundamental group unit of society and is entitled to protection by society and the State.*
2. *The right of men and women of marriageable age to marry and to found a family shall be recognized.*
3. *No marriage shall be entered into without the free and full consent of the intending spouses.*
4. *States Parties to the present Covenant shall take appropriate steps to ensure equality of rights and responsibilities of spouses as to marriage, during marriage and at its dissolution. In the case of dissolution, provision shall be made for the necessary protection of any children.*

Note
In its General Comment 19[35] the Committee emphasises that, even if the concept of the family may differ in some respect from State to State, and even from region to region within a State, and that it is therefore not possible to give the concept a standard definition, when a group of persons is regarded as a family under the legislation and practice of a State, it must be given the protection referred to in this article.

Article 24

1. *Every child shall have, without any discrimination as to race, colour, sex, language, religion, national or social origin, property or birth, the right to such measures of protection as are required by his status as a minor, on the part of his family, society and the State.*
2. *Every child shall be registered immediately after birth and shall have a name.*
3. *Every child has the right to acquire a nationality.*

---

[35] United NationsDoc. HRI/GEN/1/Rev.5, p. 137.

Note

General Comment 17[36] reminds States that the implementation of this provision entails the adoption of special measures to protect children, in addition to the measures that States are required to take under article 2 to ensure that everyone enjoys the rights provided for in the Covenant.

Article 25

Every citizen shall have the right and the opportunity, without any of the distinctions mentioned in article 2 and without unreasonable restrictions:
(a) To take part in the conduct of public affairs, directly or through freely chosen representatives;
(b) To vote and to be elected at genuine periodic elections which shall be by universal and equal suffrage and shall be held by secret ballot, guaranteeing the free expression of the will of the electors;
(c) To have access, on general terms of equality, to public service in his country.

Note

In its General Comment 25[37] the Committee reminds States that every citizen's right to take part in the conduct of public affairs, to vote, to be elected and to have access to public service entails a positive obligation of States to adopt such legislative and other measures as may be necessary to ensure that citizens have an effective opportunity to enjoy these rights, whatever form of constitution or government is in force. The Committee further recalls that the rights under article 25 are related to, but distinct from, the right of peoples to self-determination and that these can give rise to claims under the first Optional Protocol.

Article 26

All persons are equal before the law and are entitled without any discrimination to the equal protection of the law. In this respect, the law shall prohibit any discrimination and guarantee to all persons equal and effective protection against discrimination on any ground such as race, colour, sex, language, religion, political or other opinion, national or social origin, property, birth or other status.

Note

The Committee notes that this article requires not only measures of protection but also affirmative action designated to ensure the positive enjoyment of rights, and that this cannot be done simply by enacting laws.[38]

---

[36] United Nations Doc. HRI/GEN/1/Rev.5, p. 132.
[37] United Nations Doc. HRI/GEN/1/Rev.5, p. 157.
[38] General Comment 18, United Nations Doc. HRI/GEN/1/Rev.5, p. 134.

Article 27

In those States in which ethnic, religious or linguistic minorities exist, persons belonging to such minorities shall not be denied the right, in community with the other members of their group, to enjoy their own culture, to profess and practise their own religion, or to use their own language.

Note

In its General Comment 23[39] the Committee observes that this article establishes and recognises a right which is conferred on individuals belonging to minority groups and which is distinct from, and additional to, all the other rights which, as individuals in common with everyone else, they are already entitled to enjoy under the Covenant. Furthermore, the Committee notes that the Covenant draws a distinction between the right to self-determination and the rights protected under article 27, and that the enjoyment of the rights to which this article relates does not prejudice the sovereignty and territorial integrity of a State Party.[40]

2. THE HUMAN RIGHTS COMMITTEE[41]

The Human Rights Committee is established pursuant to the provisions of Part IV of the Covenant. There are 18 members, elected by the States Parties for terms of

---

[39] United Nations Doc. HRI/GEN/1/Rev.5, p. 147.

[40] United Nations Doc. HRI/GEN/1/Rev.5, p. 147.

[41] I. Boerfijn, "Towards a Strong System of Supervision: The Human Rights Committee's Role in Reforming the Reporting Procedure under Article 40 of the Covenant on Civil and Political Rights", 17 Hum. Rts. Q. (1995) pp. 766–793; I. Boerefijn, *The Reporting Procedure under the Covenant on Civil and Political Rights: Practice and Procedure of the Human Rights Committee*, (1999); I. Boerefijn, "The Human Rights Committee's Concluding Observations", in *The Role of the Nation State in the 21st Century, Foreign Policy, Human Rights, International Organisations*, (M. Castermans-Holleman, F. van Hoof, J. Smith, Eds., 1998); R. Higgins, *Ten Years on the UN Human Rights Committee: Some Thoughts Upon Parting*, 1996 European Human Rights Law Review, 570–582; T. Opsahl, "The Human Rights Committee", in *The United Nations and Human Rights* (P. Alston Ed. 1992), pp. 369–443; D. McGoldrick, *The Human Rights Committee: Its Role in the Development of the International Covenant on Civil and Political Rights, (1991);* O. Prounis, "The Human Rights Committee: Towards Resolving the Paradox of Human Rights Law", 17 Colum. Hum. Rts. L. Rev., (1986), pp. 103–109; D. L. Shelton, "Supervising Implementation of the Covenants: The First Ten Years of the Human Rights Committee", 80 Am. Soc. Int.'l L. Proc., (1986), pp. 413–419; J. Gomez del Prado, "United Nations Conventions on Human Rights: The Practice of the Human Rights Committee and the Committee on the Elimination of Racial Discrimination in Dealing with Reporting Obligations of States Parties", 7 Hum. Rts. Q., (1985), pp. 492–513; M.-J. Cote, "Le Recours au Comité des droits de l'homme de l'ONU: Une illusion", 26 *Cahiers de droit* (Quebec), (1985), pp. 531–547; V. Dimitrijevic, "Activity of the Human Rights Committee" , 34 Rev. Int'l Aff., (1983), pp. 24–27; J. A. Walkate, *The Human Rights Committee: Monitoring the Implementation of the International Covenant on Civil and Political Rights*, (1980); D. Harris, "The International Covenant on Civil and Political Rights and the United Kingdom: An Introduction", in *The International Covenant on Civil and Political Rights and United Kingdom Law*, (D. Harris and S. Joseph Eds. 1995), pp. 69–90; *Fact Sheet 15, Civil and Political Rights: The Human Rights Committee,* (United Nations); F. Pocar, "The International Covenant on Civil and

four years.[42] Members, though all nationals of States parties, serve in their private capacities and make a solemn declaration of impartiality upon taking up office. The Committee presently meets three times in each year, in spring, summer and autumn for sessions of three working weeks each. The spring session takes place in New York and the others in Geneva. Secretariat services are provided by the United Nations Office of the High Commissioner for Human Rights.[43]

Three of the activities of the Committee are of particular interest for NGOs and individuals: the periodic reporting procedure, the closely related procedure for the requesting of emergency reports, and the consideration of communications from individuals under the provisions of the Optional Protocol of the Covenant.

3. THE RPORTING PROCEDURE[44]

(a) The obligation on the State

Article 40 of the Covenant obliges States Parties to submit reports to the Human Rights Committee within one year of the Covenant coming into effect for the States concerned and thereafter whenever the Committee so requests.[45] From 1981 until

---

Political Rights", in *Manual on Human Rights Reporting*, (United Nations, 1997), pp. 171–266. See, generally, the following studies by P. Alston, *Long Term Approaches to Enhancing the Effectiveness of the United Nations Human Rights Treaty Bodies*, United Nations Doc. A/44/668; *Interim Report on Updated Study*, United Nations Doc. A/CONF.157/PC/62/Add.11/Rev.1; *Final Report on Enhancing the Long Term Effectiveness of the United Nations Human Rights Treaty System,* United Nations Doc. E/CN.4/1997/74; and, also, A. Bayefsky, *Report: The UN Human Rights Treaty System: Universality at the Crossroads*, (2001); P. Alston and J. Crawford Eds., *The Future of UN Human Rights Treaty Monitoring*, (2000); A. Bayefsky, Ed., *The UN Human Rights System in the 21st Century*, (2000)

[42] Membership as of January 2001: Abdelfattah Amor (Tunisia), Nisuke Ando (Japan), Prafullachandra Natwarlal Bhagwati (India), Christine Chanet (France), Maurice Glele Ahanhanzo (Benin), Louis Henkin (United States of America), Eckart Klein (Germany), David Kretzmer (Israel), Rajsoomer Lallah (Mauritius), Cecilia Medina Quiroga (Chile), Rafael Rivas Posada (Colombia), Nigel Rodley (United Kingdom of Great Britain and Northern Ireland), Martin Scheinin (Finland), Ian Shearer (Australia), Hipolito Solari Yrigoyen (Argentina), Ahmed Twatil Khalil (Egypt), Patrick Vella (Malta), Maxwell Yalden (Canada).

[43] Secretariat of the Human Rights Committee, Support Services Branch, Office of the High Commissioner for Human Rights, UNOG, 1211 Geneva 10, Switzerland (Tel.: 41 22 917 1234; Fax 41 22 917 0099).

[44] Article 40, ICCPR; Rules of Procedures of the Human Rights Committee, Rules, 66–71, United Nations Doc. HRI/GEN/3, pp. 27–60; F. Pocar, "The International Covenant on Civil and Political Rights", in *Manual on Human Right Reporting,* (United Nations, 1997), pp. 171–266; I. Boerefijn, *The Reporting Procedure under the Covenant on Civil and Political Rights: Practice and Procedure of the Human Rights Committee*, (1999); M. O'Flaherty and L. Heffernan, *International Covenant on Civil and Political Rights: International Human Rights Law in Ireland*, (1995), pp. 64–82; S. Joseph, "New Procedures concerning the Human Rights Committee's examination of State reports", *Netherlands Quarterly of Human Rights*, Vol. 13 (1), (1995), pp. 5–23; M. O'Flaherty, "The Reporting Obligation under Article 40 of the International Covenant on Civil and Political Rights: Lessons to be Learned from Consideration by the Human Rights Committee of Ireland's First Report", 16 Hum. Rts. Q. (1994); J. Gomez del Prado, "United Nations Conventions on Human Rights: The Practice of the

1999 the Committee imposed an obligation for the submission of periodic reports every five years. At its sixty-sixth session, in 1999, it decided that, "the submission of a State party's subsequent periodic report is set on a case-by-case basis at the end of the Committee's concluding observations on any report under article 40".[46] In a further refinement to this new approach, as of November 2000, the Committee will request each State party, upon consideration of a report, to produce a focussed follow-up report within a short time-frame (perhaps 18 months) and if it is submitted and satisfactory, a date will be given for the next report which may be many years hence. If the focussed follow-up report is not submitted, then the time set for the next report when the submitted report was considered will apply.[47] Furthermore, pursuant to article 40, the rules of procedure also stipulate that reports can be requested "at any other time the Committee deems appropriate". The provision for the requesting and submission of such reports is discussed below in the context of the Committee's method of addressing emergency situations.

The Committee has provided detailed guidance to States for the preparation of initial and subsequent periodic reports.[48] Reports should indicate measures adopted

---

Human Rights Committee and the Committee on the Elimination of Racial Discrimination in Dealing with Reporting Obligations of States Parties", 7 Hum. Rts. Q., (1985), pp. 492–513; D. D. Fischer, "Reporting under the Covenant on Civil and Political Rights: The First Five Years of the Human Rights Committee", 76 Am. J. Int'l L., (1982), pp. 142–153; O. Schachter, "The Obligation of the Parties to Give Effect to the Covenant on Civil and Political Rights", 73 Am. J. Int'l L., (1979) pp. 462–465; E. Schwelb, "The Nature of the Obligations of the States Parties to the International Covenant on Civil and Political Rights", in *Amicorum Discipulorumque Liber*, (R. Cassin Ed. 1969); D. Harris, "The International Covenant on Civil and Political Rights and the United Kingdom: An Introduction" in *The International Covenant on Civil and Political Rights and United Kingdom Law* (D. Harris and S. Joseph Eds. 1995); I. Boerfijn, "Towards a Strong System of Supervision: The Human Rights Committee's Role in Reforming the Reporting Procedure under Article 40 of the Covenant on Civil and Political Rights", 17 Hum. Rts. Q. (1995), pp. 766–793; E. Klein, "The Reporting System under the International Covenant on Civil and Political Rights", in, *The Monitoring System of Human Rights Treaty Obligations: Colloquium, Potsdam, 22–23 November 1996*, (E. Klein Ed. 1998), pp. 17–30; E. Evatt, "Periodic Reporting: The International Covenant on Civil and Political Rights and the Convention on the Elimination of All Forms of Discrimination Against Women", in *Indigenous Peoples, the United Nations and Human Rights*, (S. Pritchard, Ed. 1998).

[45] See F. Pocar, "The International Covenant on Civil and Political Rights", in *Manual on Human Rights Reporting*, (United Nations, 1997), pp. 171–266.

[46] United Nations Doc. A/55/40 (Vol. I), para 55.

[47] See Rule 70A of the Rules of Procedure, "Where the Committee has specified for priority, under rule 70.5, certain aspects of its concluding observations on a State party's report, it shall establish a procedure to consider replies by the State party on those aspects and to decide what consequent action, including the date set for the next periodic report, may be appropriate", United Nations Doc HRI/GEN/3 at page 50, and United Nations Doc CCPR/C/70/INFORMAL/2.

[48] United Nations Doc. HRI/GEN/2/Rev.1, pp. 26–31. The first part of reports should also comply with the consolidated guidelines relating to the preparation of the initial part of reports under the various international human rights instruments. See United Nations Doc. HRI/CORE/1. For an elucidation of the reporting requirements under each of the articles, see F. Pocar, "The International Covenant on Civil and Political Rights", in *Manual on Human Rights*, (United Nations, 1997), pp. 171–266.

to give effect to rights in the Covenant and on the progress made in the enjoyment of those rights. In preparing reports it is necessary that attention be paid both to the articles of the Covenant and the General Comments thereon which have been adopted by the Committee. Reference should be made to any reservations, declarations or derogations which have been made by the State party and these should be fully explained and justified. Reports should indicate the factors and difficulties, as well as restrictions or limitations, affecting the implementation of the rights. The situation regarding the equal enjoyment of Covenant rights by men and women should be specifically addressed.[49]

Initial reports, since they constitute a State party's first opportunity to indicate to the Committee the extent to which its laws and practices comply with the Covenant, should include information on the constitutional and legal framework for the implementation of Covenant rights, explain the legal and practical measures adopted to give effect to the rights and demonstrate progress made in ensuring their enjoyment. The Committee has stipulated that reports should not just refer to legal norms and that the practical situation and the practical availability, effect and implementation of remedies for violation of rights should be explained and illustrated. Reports should be accompanied by copies of all relevant principal constitutional, legislative and other texts which guarantee and provide remedies in relations to Covenant rights.

With regard to all reports other than initial reports, the primary drafting reference points are, (a) the Concluding Observations on the previous report and the summary records of the Committee's consideration thereof, and (b) an examination by the State party of the progress made towards and the current situation concerning the enjoyment of Covenant rights by persons within its territory or jurisdiction. The reports should, to the extent possible, be structured to follow the articles of the Covenant.

Where a State Party is also party to the Optional Protocol and the Committee has issued Views entailing provision of a remedy or expressing any other concern, relating to a communication received under the Protocol, a report should include information about the steps taken to provide a remedy, or meet such a concern, and to ensure that any circumstances thus criticised do not recur. If a State party has abolished the death penalty the situation relating to the Second Optional Protocol should be explained.

(b) The procedure

i. The scheduling process
Reports are generally scheduled for consideration by the Committee within two years of their submission and information regarding the session at which a report will be considered is usually posted one year in advance on the web site of the United

---

[49] United Nations Doc. HRI/GEN/2/Rev.1; for detailed examination of the reporting requirement regarding equality of rights between men and women see General Comment 28, reported in United Nations Doc. A/55/40 (Vol. I) pp. 128–132.

Nations High Commissioner for Human Rights.[50] Scheduling arrangements may be subject to change at short notice, particularly with regard to the exact dates for consideration within a session. Full details of scheduling and any changes which might occur can be obtained from the Secretary of the Committee. State party reports, once published as United Nations documents, can be ordered from the United Nations Documents Distribution and Sales Section. The symbol number can be obtained from the Secretariat. Reports are usually available in all of the working languages of the Committee (English, French and Spanish). Reports are also posted on the OHCHR website.

ii. Before the session
Reports receive pre-session scrutiny by a Working Group, which meets in private session in the week immediately preceding the session of the Committee prior to that during which it is intended to take up the report, in other words some four months in advance of that consideration. The purpose of this preliminary scrutiny is to finalise lists of issues[51] to be put to the representatives of the State. In the course of its work the Working Group may receive oral and written representations of UN Agencies, OHCHR, NGOs and others[52] (see further below). When considering a periodic report the Working Group also makes reference to a "Country Profile" drawn up by the Secretariat on the basis of previous concluding observations of the Committee and previous reports of the State party.

The first draft of each list is prepared by a Working Group member who is designated as Country Rapporteur. The questions are grouped into a number of categories, each encompassing a range of the articles of the Covenant. Questions focus on perceived *lacunae* in the report, follow-up to previous consideration by the Committee of the State concerned, and any other preoccupations which working group members may have about implementation of the Covenant. The list of issues is transmitted to the State party and made available on the OHCHR website. The State party is not expected to submit written replies to the list of issues but rather to use it to prepare for a constructive oral dialogue with the Committee.[53]

iii. Consideration by the Committee
The actual scrutiny of the report by the Committee takes place over two (periodic reports) or three (initial reports) meetings held in public. The report is usually introduced by a Government representative who may take the opportunity to state government policy on a range of issues and to update material in the report.

---

[50] www.unhchr.ch.

[51] A sample list of issues (for The Netherlands) is reproduced in Appendix 1.

[52] For example, in 2000, the Committee reported that its Working Groups considered oral and written presentations by representatives of "non-governmental organisations, including Amnesty International, Equality Now, Human Rights Watch, the International Federation of Human Rights Leagues, the International Service for Human Rights, the Lawyers' Committee for Human Rights, and several local organisations. The Inter-Parliamentary Union also provided information for Committee members", United Nations Doc A/55/40 (Vol. I) para 17.

[53] United Nations Doc., A/55/40 (Vol. I) at para 48.

32

Following a general introduction by the State representative the groups of questions/issues posed by the pre-sessional Working Group are taken one by one. Thus, the representative proceeds to answer separately the questions posed in each part of the questionnaire. Members then ask supplementary questions and the representative endeavours to give immediate replies. This procedure is repeated for each of the sections of the questionnaire.

Following the consideration in public meetings, the Committee proceeds to draft and, in closed session, adopt its Concluding Observations.[54] The Concluding Observations comprise a critique of the State report and of the response of the State representative to the scrutiny of the Committee, noting positive factors, drawing attention to subjects of concern and making recommendations. Concluding Observations are issued as public documents at the end of each session of the Committee, posted on the OHCHR website (initially solely in the language of adoption), transmitted to NGOs which have submitted information to the Committee, and included in the Committee's annual report to the General Assembly of the United Nations.

As a form of follow-up to the consideration of State reports, the Committee has charged its Bureau,[55] at each session, to observe how the situation with regard to serious violations of human rights may have changed in order to determine whether the possibility of adopting a special decision in plenary should be considered. The Bureau has also been given particular responsibility for the implementation of the decision taken by the Committee at its fifty-second session that, "where the consideration of a report revealed a grave human rights situation, the Committee could request the State party concerned to receive a mission composed of one or more of its members in order to re-establish dialogue with it, explain the situation better and formulate appropriate suggestions or recommendations"[56]

(c) The role of non-governmental organisations[57]

NGOs and other non-State actors do not have formal standing under the reporting procedure. Thus, they may not have their documents received and processed as "United Nations documents" and they may not formally address the proceedings of the Committee. NGOs and others do however have a wide range of opportunities to convey information to the pre-sessional Working Group as well as informally to Committee members and thus to influence proceedings.[58]

---

[54] A sample set of concluding observations (for The Netherlands) is reproduced in Appendix II.
[55] I.e. the Chairperson, the three vice-chairpersons and the Rapporteur.
[56] See United Nations Doc. A/51/40 at para 437.
[57] See further at Chapter 1.
[58] See, *inter alia*, United Nations Doc. A/55/40 (Vol. I) para. 17, where it is indicated that the Committee welcomes information provided by NGOs, see also, F. Pocar, "The International Covenant on Civil and Political Rights" in *Manual on Human Rights,* (United Nations, 1997), pp. 171–266; I. Boerefijn, *The Reporting Procedure under the Covenant on Civil and Political Rights: Practice and Procedure of the Human Rights Committee,* (1999), pp. 216–220.

Once a State's report has been scheduled for consideration, NGOs should indicate their interest to the Secretariat and send as much preliminary material as possible for transmission to the members of the Working Group and the Committee in general.

In drafting written submissions, NGOs should bear in mind the significance of articles 2 and 26 of the Covenant. These articles, which demand non-discrimination and equality before the law, have a very wide scope. It will often be possible to cite them in a submission together with other articles which deal more directly with issues which an NGO may wish to raise. This is because many human rights violations also contain within them an element of discrimination or inequality. Also, article 26 demands equality before the law in all matters. Thus, it can be invoked against a very wide range of inequalities and instances of discrimination, and it matters not whether the particular issues are dealt with explicitly in the Covenant. It is in this context, for instance, that a range of social or economic matters might be raised. Treatment of such matters should always, however, be couched in the language of discrimination and inequality.

Some weeks before the meeting of the pre-sessional Working Group, NGOs should send to the Secretariat a written submission with the request that it be distributed to members. Multiple hard copies should be provided as well as an electronic version.

The pre-sessional Working Group meets in private and is willing to receive the oral and written submissions of NGOs. These submissions can significantly influence the form of questions drafted by the Group. NGOs considering the making of oral submissions are advised to co-ordinate their activities to ensure that they make the best use of the very limited time available. It should also be borne in mind that at these meetings no interpretation facilities will be provided and no records will be kept.

In the period of some four months between the consideration of a report by the Working Group and the actual meeting of the Committee, NGOs have the opportunity to finalise any further submission they wish to make taking account of both changed circumstances and the contents of the Working Group's list of issues. Such submissions should be sent to the Secretariat, in both hard copy and electronic versions, in good time for distribution to members prior to the session.

If at all possible, NGOs should send representatives to attend the Committee meetings. Presence at the meetings permits informal contact with members, provision of updated submissions and other documentation, the channelling of information back to the country and the making of a comprehensive record of the proceedings. Opportunities may also arise for useful meetings with the Government representatives, with international media in Geneva (and New York), OHCHR staff and with the international human rights NGOs.

Access to the United Nations buildings in Geneva and New York can be arranged in advance with the Secretary of the Committee.

The role of NGOs following the conclusion of the Committee proceedings is described in chapter one. It is particularly important to acknowledge the manner in which NGOs may influence the operation of the new follow-up procedure (described above) whereby the Committee's Bureau is tasked to monitor situations of grave human rights violations with a view to proposing special decisions of the Committee or the deployment of a mission to the country concerned.

4. TABLE OF STATES PARTIES INDICATING WHEN A REPORT WAS LAST CONSIDERED AND IS NEXT DUE[59]

State Party	Entry into force	Last report considered (year)	Next report due	Date due or overdue since
Afghanistan	24.04.83	Initial (1985)	3rd–4th periodic	23.04.94
Albania	04.01.92		Initial–2nd periodic	03.03.93
Algeria	12.12.89	2nd periodic (1998)	3rd periodic	01.06.2000
Angola	10.04.92		Initial–2nd periodic	31.12.97
Argentina	08.11.86	3rd periodic (2000)	4th periodic	31.10.05
Armenia	23.09.93	Initial (1998)	2nd periodic	01.10.01
Australia	13.11.80	4th periodic (2000)	5th periodic	31.07.05
Austria	10.12.78	3rd periodic (1998)	4th periodic	01.10.02
Azerbaijan	13.11.92	2nd periodic (2001)*		
Barbados	23.03.76	2nd periodic (1988)	3rd–5th periodic	11.04.91
Belarus	23.03.76	Add. inf. to 4th periodic (1997)	5th periodic	07.11.01
Belgium	21.07.83	3rd periodic (1998)	4th periodic	01.10.02
Belize	10.09.96		Initial	09.09.97
Benin	12.06.92		Initial–2nd periodic	11.06.98
Bolivia	12.11.82	2nd periodic (1997)	3rd periodic	31.12.99
Bosnia and Herzegovina	06.03.92	Special (1992)	Initial–2nd periodic	05.03.93
Botswana	08.12.00		Initial	08.12.01
Brazil	24.04.92	Initial (1996)	2nd periodic	23.04.98
Bulgaria	23.03.76	2nd periodic (1993)	3rd–4th periodic	31.12.94
Burkina Faso	04.06.99		Initial	03.04.00
Burundi	09.08.90	Initial (1992)	2nd periodic	08.08.96
Cambodia	26.08.92	Initial (1999)	2nd periodic	31.07.02
Cameroon	27.09.84	3rd periodic (1999)	4th periodic	31.10.03
Canada	19.08.76	4th periodic (1999)	5th periodic	30.04.04
Cape Verde	06.11.93		Initial–2nd periodic	05.11.94
Central African Republic	08.08.81	Initial (1988)	2nd–4th periodic	09.04.89
Chad	09.09.95		Initial	08.09.96
Chile	23.03.76	4th periodic (1999)	5th periodic	28.04.02
China	Signature only	Initial on Hong Kong (1999)	Initial–2nd periodic	31.10.01
Colombia	23.03.76	4th periodic (1997)	5th periodic	02.08.00
Congo	05.01.84	2nd periodic (2000)	3rd periodic	31.03.03
Costa Rica	23.03.76	4th periodic (1999)	5th periodic	30.04.04
Croatia	08.10.91	Initial (2001)	2nd periodic	01.04.05
Cyprus	23.03.76	3rd periodic (1994)	4th periodic	01.06.02
Czech Republic	01.01.93	Initial (2001)*		

---

[59] As of July 2001

State Party	Entry into force	Last report considered (year)	Next report due	Date due or overdue since
Cote d'Ivoire	26.06.92		Initial–2nd periodic	25.06.93
Democratic People's Republic of Korea	14.12.81	2nd periodic (2001)*		
Democratic Republic of the Congo	01.02.77	2nd periodic (1990)	3rd–5th periodic	31.07.91
Denmark	23.03.76	4th periodic (2000)	5th periodic	31.10.05
Dominica	17.09.93		Initial–2nd periodic	16.09.94
Dominican Republic	04.04.78	4th periodic (2001)	5th periodic	01.04.05
Ecuador	23.03.76	4th periodic (1998)	5th periodic	01.06.01
Egypt	14.04.82	2nd periodic (1993)	3rd–4th periodic	31.12.94
El Salvador	29.02.80	2nd periodic (1994)	3rd–5th periodic	31.12.95
Equatorial Guinea	25.12.87		Initial–3rd periodic	24.12.88
Estonia	21.01.92	Initial (1995)	2nd periodic	20.01.98
Ethiopia	11.09.93		Initial–2nd periodic	10.09.94
Finland	23.03.76	4th periodic (1995)*	5th periodic	01.06.03
France	04.02.81	3rd periodic (1997)	4th periodic	31.12.00
Gabon	21.04.83	2nd periodic (2000)	3rd periodic	31.10.03
Gambia	22.06.79	Initial (1984)	2nd–5th periodic	21.06.85
Georgia	03.08.94	2nd periodic (2001)*		
Germany	22.03.76	4th periodic (1996)	5th periodic	03.08.00
Greece	05.08.97		Initial	04.08.98
Grenada	06.12.91		Initial–2nd periodic	05.12.92
Guatemala	05.08.92	2nd periodic (2001)*		
Guinea	24.04.78	2nd periodic (1993)	3rd–4th periodic	30.09.94
Guyana	15.05.77	2nd periodic (2000)	3rd periodic	31.03.03
Haiti	06.05.91		Initial–2nd periodic	31.12.96
Honduras	25.11.97		Initial	24.11.98
Hungary	25.03.76	4th periodic (2000)*	5th periodic	02.08.00
Iceland	22.11.79	3rd periodic (1998)	4th periodic	30.10.03
India	10.07.79	3rd periodic (1997)	4th periodic	31.12.01
Islamic Republic of Iran	23.03.76	2nd periodic (1993)	3rd–4th periodic	31.12.94
Iraq	23.03.76	4th periodic (1997)	5th periodic	04.04.00
Ireland	23.03.76	2nd periodic (2000)	3rd periodic	31.07.05
Israel	03.01.92	Initial (1998)	2nd periodic	01.06.00
Italy	15.12.78	4th periodic (1998)	5th periodic	01.06.02
Jamaica	23.03.76	2nd periodic (1997)	3rd periodic	07.11.01
Japan	21.09.79	4th periodic (1998)	5th periodic	31.10.02
Jordan	23.03.76	3rd periodic (1994)	4th periodic	22.01.97
Kenya	23.03.76	Initial (1981)	2nd–5th periodic	11.04.86
Kuwait	21.08.96	Initial (2000)	2nd periodic	31.07.04
Kyrgyzstan	07.01.95	Initial (2000)	2nd periodic	31.07.04
Latvia	14.07.92	Initial (1995)	2nd periodic	14.07.98
Lebanon	23.03.76	2nd periodic (1997)	3rd periodic	31.12.99

State Party	Entry into force	Last report considered (year)	Next report due	Date due or overdue since
Lesotho	9.12.92	Initial (1999)	2nd periodic	30.04.02
Libyan Arab Jamahiriya	23.03.76	3rd periodic (1998)	4th periodic	01.10.02
Liechtenstein	10.03.99		Initial	11.03.00
Lithuania	20.02.92	Initial (1997)	2nd periodic	07.11.01
Luxembourg	18.11.83	2nd periodic (1992)	3rd–4th periodic	17.11.94
Madagascar	23.03.76	2nd periodic (1991)	3rd–5th periodic	31.07.92
Malawi	22.03.94		Initial–2nd periodic	21.03.95
Mali	23.03.76	Initial (1981)	2nd–5th periodic	11.04.86
Malta	13.12.90	Initial (1993)	2nd periodic	12.12.96
Mauritius	23.03.76	3rd periodic (1996)	4th–5th periodic	04.11.93
Mexico	23.06.81	4th periodic (1999)	5th periodic	31.07.02
Monaco	28.11.97	Initial (2001)*		
Mongolia	23.03.76	4th periodic (2000)	5th periodic	31.03.03
Morocco	03.08.79	4th periodic (1999)	5th periodic	31.10.03
Mozambique	21.10.93		Initial–2nd periodic	20.10.94
Namibia	28.02.95		Initial–2nd periodic	27.02.96
Netherlands	11.03.79	3rd periodic (2001)*	4th periodic	31.10.96
New Zealand	28.03.79	4th periodic (2001)*		
Nicaragua	12.06.80	2nd periodic (1990)	3rd–4th periodic	11.06.91
Niger	07.06.86	Initial (1993)	2nd–3rd periodic	31.03.94
Nigeria	29.10.93	Initial (1996)	2nd periodic	28.10.99
Norway	23.03.76	4th periodic (1999)	5th periodic	01.08.01
Panama	08.06.77	2nd periodic (1991)	3rd–5th periodic	31.03.92
Paraguay	10.09.92	Initial (1995)	2nd periodic	09.09.98
Peru	28.07.78	4th periodic (2000)	5th periodic	31.10.03
Philippines	23.01.87	Initial (1989)	2nd–3rd periodic	22.01.93
Poland	18.06.77	4th periodic (1999)	5th periodic	31.07.03
Portugal	15.09.78	4th periodic (1999)	4th periodic	01.08.96
Republic of Korea	10.07.90	2nd periodic (1999)	3rd periodic	31.10.03
Republic of Moldova	26.04.93	Initial (2001)*		
Romania	23.03.76	4th periodic (1999)	5th periodic	28.04.99
Russian Federation	23.03.76	4th periodic (1995)	5th periodic	04.11.98
Rwanda	23.03.76	2nd periodic (1987)	4th periodic	10.04.97
Saint Vincent and the Grenadines	09.02.82	Initial (1990)	2nd–4th periodic	31.10.91
San Marino	18.01.86	Initial (1989)	2nd–3rd periodic	17.01.92
Senegal	13.05.78	4th periodic (1997)	5th periodic	04.04.00
Seychelles	05.08.92		Initial–2nd periodic	04.08.93
Sierra Leone	23.11.96		Initial	22.11.97
Slovakia	01.01.93	Initial (1997)	2nd periodic	31.12.01
Slovenia	25.06.91	Initial (1994)	2nd periodic	24.06.97
Somalia	24.04.90		Initial–3rd periodic	23.04.91
South Africa	10.03.99		Initial	09.03.00

State Party	Entry into force	Last report considered (year)	Next report due	Date due or overdue since
Spain	27.07.77	4th periodic (1996)	5th periodic	28.04.99
Sri Lanka	11.09.80	3rd periodic (1995)	4th periodic	10.09.96
Sudan	18.06.86	Initial (2000)	2nd periodic	30.06.03
Suriname	28.03.77	Initial (1980)	2nd–5th periodic	02.08.85
Sweden	23.03.76	4th periodic (1995)	5th periodic	27.10.99
Switzerland	18.09.92	2nd periodic (2001)*		
Syrian Arab Republic	23.03.76	2nd periodic (2001)	3rd periodic	01.04.03
Tajikistan	04.04.99		Initial	03.04.00
Thailand	29.01.97		Initial	28.01.98
Togo	24.08.84	2nd periodic (1994)		
Trinidad and Tobago	21.03.79	3rd, 4th periodic (2000)		5th periodic
odic	31.10.03			
Tunisia	23.03.76	4th periodic (1994)	5th periodic	04.02.98
Turkmenistan	01.08.97		Initial	31.07.98
Uganda	21.06.95		Initial	20.09.96
Ukraine	23.03.76	5th periodic (2001)*		
United Kingdom of Great Britain and Northern Ireland	20.08.76	5th periodic on (2001)*		
United Republic of Tanzania	11.09.76	3rd periodic (1998)	4th periodic	01.06.02
United States of America	08.09.92	Initial (1995)	2nd periodic	07.09.98
Uruguay	23.03.76	4th periodic (1996)	5th periodic	21.03.03
Uzbekistan	28.12.95	Initial (2001)	2nd periodic	01.04.04
Venezuela	10.08.78	3rd periodic (2001)	4th periodic	01.04.05
Vietnam	24.12.82	Initial (1990)	2nd–4th periodic	31.07.91
				23.12.93
				23.12.98
Yemen	09.05.87	2nd periodic (1995)	3rd periodic	08.05.98
Yugoslavia	23.03.76	4th periodic (1999)	5th periodic	03.08.98
Zambia	10.07.84	2nd periodic (1996)	3rd periodic	30.06.98
Zimbabwe	13.08.91	Initial (1996)	2nd periodic	01.07.02

(An asterisk indicates that a report has been submitted but has not yet been considered by the Committee)

5. THE EMERGENCY PROCEDURE[60]

The Committee has, since 1991, developed a procedure to respond to what it perceives as emergency situations. The procedure is clearly based on the provisions

---

[60] S. Joseph, "New Procedures Concerning the Human Rights Committee's Examination of State Reports", N.Q.H.R. 1995, 13 (1), 5–23; I. Boerfijn, "Towards a Strong System of Supervision: The Human Rights Committee's Role in Reforming the Reporting Procedure under Article 40 of the

of article 40 of the Covenant and is reflected as follows in the Committee's Rules of Procedure:

> Requests for submission of a report under article 40, paragraph 1 (b) of the Covenant may be made in accordance with the periodicity decided by the Committee or at any other time the Committee may deem appropriate. In the case of an exceptional situation when the Committee is not in session, a request may be made through the Chairman, acting in consultation with the members of the Committee.[61]

Under the procedure, the Committee had, by the end of 2000, requested urgent reports from twelve States Parties.[62] In most cases, the States Parties have been requested to submit the reports within three months. Many of the decisions requesting urgent reports indicate that such reports should provide detailed information concerning specified articles of the Covenant.

Reports which have been submitted under the emergency procedure have been considered by the Committee as soon as possible, usually at the next scheduled session. Emergency reports have not received the attention of a pre-sessional Working Group, lists of issues are not prepared and the members put all their oral comments and questions successively. Usually, no more than two meetings are scheduled for consideration of emergency reports. Concluding observations may include a provision whereby the Secretary-General of the United Nations is requested to bring grave human rights situations to the attention of the "competent organs of the United Nations, including the Security Council".[63]

Closely related to the emergency procedure is the practice whereby the Committee's Chairman may choose to send letters to States Parties in circumstances where they are seriously overdue in submitting reports and the human rights situation in the country gives cause for serious concern.[64]

NGOs have an important role in bringing emergency situations of human rights violations to the attention of the Committee. During sessions approaches might be made to all members, whereas inter-sessionally, NGOs might choose to direct their attention directly to the Chairman, through the Secretariat. Once reports are scheduled for consideration, the role of NGOs is as with regard to the normal reporting procedure. In preparing submissions and otherwise bringing information to the attention of Committee members, NGOs should, however, pay close attention

---

Covenant on Civil and Political Rights", 17 Hum. Rts. Q. (1995), 766–793; I. Boerfijn, *The Reporting Procedure Under the Covenant on Civil and Political Rights*, (1999), pp. 255–283; M. O'Flaherty, "Treaty Bodies Responding to States of Emergency: The Case of Bosnia and Herzegovina", *in The Future of UN Human Rights Treaty Monitoring*, (P. Alston and J. Crawford, Eds., 2000).

[61] Rules of Procedure of the Human Rights Committee, Rule 66, para. 2, United Nations Doc. HRI/GEN/3, page 47.

[62] Albania, Angola, Bosnia and Herzegovina, Burundi, Croatia, Haiti, Iraq, Nigeria, Peru, Rwanda, United Kingdom (Hong Kong), Federal Republic of Yugoslavia.

[63] See United Nations Doc. A/49/40, para. 47.

[64] See S. Joseph, "New Procedures Concerning the Human Rights Committee's Examination of State Reports", N.Q.H.R. 1995, 13 (1), 17–18.

to the concerns of the Committee, as reflected in the form of its request to the State Party for submission of the report. Finally, NGOs can draw public attention to whatever actions have been taken by the Committee and use this information in their own activities.

6. THE INDIVIDUAL COMMUNICATIONS PROCEDURE[65]

The procedure permits individuals to complain directly or through representatives, to the Committee about a State Party in circumstances where they are the alleged victims of violations of the Covenant and the State Party has ratified or otherwise acceded to the Optional Protocol to the Covenant.

The function of the Committee is to gather all necessary information, by means of written exchanges with the parties (the State and the complainant), to consider the admissibility and merits of complaints and to issue its "Views" or "Decisions" accordingly. It should be noted that the Committee is not a court, does not issue "judgements" and has no means to enforce any views which it might adopt.[66] Furthermore, all exchanges with the Committee take only written form. There is no provision for the awarding of any financial assistance to needy applicants to assist them in taking a case to the Committee.

All steps of the procedure under the Optional Protocol are confidential until the point where the Committee adopts its Views or otherwise concludes a case. However, unless the Committee (itself or through its Special Rapporteur on New Communications or the Working Group on Communications) requests otherwise, a

---

[65] See generally: M. Nowak, *CCPR Commentary*, (1995), pp. 647 *et seq.*, D. McGoldrick, *The Human Rights Committee: Its Role in the Development of the International Covenant on Civil and Political Rights*, (1991); L. Zwaak, *International Human Rights Procedures: Petitioning the ECHR, CCPR, and CERD*, (1991); M. O'Flaherty and L. Heffernan, *The International Covenant on Civil and Political Rights: International Human Rights Law in Ireland*, (1995), pp. 86–122; P. R. Ghandi, "The Human Rights Committee and the Rights of Individual Communication", 57 British YB Int'l L., (1986); A. de Zayas, "Application of the International Covenant on Civil and Political Rights" under the Optional Protocol by the Human Rights Committee", 28 German YB Int'l L., (1985); E. Mose and T. Opshal, "The Optional Protocol to the International Covenant on Civil and Political Rights", 21 Santa Clara L. Rev., 1981; C. Tomuschat, "Evolving Procedural Rules: The United Nations Human Rights Committee's First Two Years in Dealing with Individual Communications", 1 Hum. Rts. LJ (1980); D. Harris, "The International Covenant on Civil and Political Rights and the United Kingdom: An Introduction" and M. Schmidt, "The Complementarity of the Covenant and the European Convention on Human Rights – Recent Developments" in *The International Covenant on Civil and Political Rights and United Kingdom Law* (D. Harris and S. Joseph Eds. 1995); N. Schriffrin, "Bringing a Complaint Before the UN Human Rights Committee under the First Optional Protocol", Interights Bulletin, 1996, 10(1), 6–7; D. Kretzmer, "Commentary on Complaint Processes by Human Rights Committee and Torture Committee Members", and A. Byrnes, "An Effective Complaints Procedure in the Context of International Human Rights Law", in *The UN Human Rights Treaty System in the 21st Century*, (A.F. Bayefsky Ed.), 163–167 and 139–162; E. Evatt, "Individual Communications under the Optional Protocol to the International Covenant on Civil and Political Rights", in, *Indigenous Peoples, the United Nations and Human Rights*, (S. Pritchard, Ed. 1998).

[66] However, since 1994, the Committee has implicitly suggested in its Views on individual communications that the decisions of the Committee are of a binding nature.

complainant or the State party may make public any submission or information bearing on the proceedings.[67] Views are reported in the Committee's annual report and posted on the OHCHR website. Decisions on non-admissibility and discontinuance are also reported. In exceptional cases decisions on admissibility may be made public by the Committee.[68] Information furnished by the parties and decisions of the Committee within the framework of follow-up to the Committee's views are not subject to confidentiality, unless the Committee decides otherwise.[69]

By the end of March 2001, ninety-eight States had ratified or otherwise acceded to the Optional Protocol.[70] In 2000 the Committee indicated the status of all communications under the Optional Protocol as follows:[71]

i.   936 communications have been registered.
ii. Views have been adopted concerning 346 communications (including 268 in which violations of the Covenant were found).
iii. 283 communications have been declared inadmissible.
iv. 134 communications have been discontinued or withdrawn.
v.   28 communications have been declared admissible but not yet concluded.
vi. 145 communications were at the pre-admissibility stage.

A communication must negotiate two stages, those of consideration for admissibility and on the merits. However, since 1997, the Committee, as a rule and in order to expedite its work, decides on the admissibility and merits of a communication together. Only in exceptional circumstances will the Committee request a State to address admissibility only. On average, a case can take from two and a half (in situations of decisions on inadmissibility) to four years (adoption of Views on the merits) to negotiate its way through the process. At any stage in the process, the

---

[67] Rules of Procedure of the Human Rights Committee, Rule 96; United Nations Doc. HRI/GEN/3, page 59.

[68] *Kennedy v Trinidad and Tobago* Comm No. 845/1999, as discussed in United Nations Doc., A/55/40 (Vol. I) at para 537.

[69] Rules of Procedure of the Human Rights Committee, Rule 97; United Nations Doc. HRI/GEN/3, page 60.

[70] As of March 2001: Algeria, Angola, Argentina, Armenia, Australia, Austria, Barbados, Belarus, Belgium, Benin, Bolivia, Bosnia and Herzegovina, Bulgaria, Burkina Faso, Cameroon, Canada, Central African Republic, Chad, Chile, Colombia, Congo, Costa Rica, Cote d'Ivoire, Croatia, Cyprus, Czech Republic, Democratic Republic of the Congo, Denmark, Dominican Republic, Ecuador, El Salvador, Equatorial Guinea, Estonia, Finland, France, Gambia, Georgia, Germany, Greece, Guinea, Guyana, Hungary, Iceland, Ireland, Italy, Kyrgyzstan, Latvia, Libyan Arab Jamahiriya, Liechtenstein, Lithuania, Luxembourg, Madagascar, Malawi, Malta, Mauritius, Mongolia, Namibia, Nepal, Netherlands, New Zealand, Nicaragua, Niger, Norway, Panama, Paraguay, Peru, Philippines, Poland, Portugal, Republic of Korea, Romania, Russian Federation, Saint Vincent and Grenadines, San Marino, Senegal, Seychelles, Sierra Leone, Slovakia, Slovenia, Somalia, Spain, Sri Lanka, Suriname, Sweden, Tajikistan, The former Yugoslav Republic of Macedonia, Togo, Turkmenistan, Uganda, Ukraine, Uruguay, Uzbekistan, Venezuela, and Zambia. The Optional Protocol has been denounced and not reacceded to by Jamaica and Trinidad and Tobago. Current information on the status of ratification of human rights instruments can be found at the OHCHR website: www.unhchr.ch.

[71] United Nations Doc A/55/40 (Vol. I) paras. 531–532.

Committee, or delegated Working Groups or Special Rapporteurs, may request that the State take interim measures to safeguard the alleged victim.[72] Such a request has no binding force.

The first step in bringing a communication to the attention of the Committee is to contact the Secretariat.[73] The Secretariat will respond by sending the complainant a model form to be filled out concerning the case.[74] It is not necessary to use this form but it may constitute a useful way to indicate the key elements of a case. At this or any other stage, complainants are free to maintain contact with members of the Secretariat to obtain advice and guidance.

Once the model form is returned to the Secretariat (or all the key details have been otherwise supplied in writing) the communication is assigned to a member of the Committee known as the Special Rapporteur on New Communications, who has the task of preparing the case for consideration on admissibility and on the merits.

At any time the Special Rapporteur may decide either not to register a communication or to send a recommendation of inadmissibility directly to the Committee for its consideration.

Once the Special Rapporteur is satisfied that the communication is not anonymous, an abuse of the right of petition or incompatible with the Covenant,[75] or otherwise inadmissible, it is sent to the State for comment on the issues of admissibility and the merits. The State has six months in which to reply. However, if the State wishes the communication to be dismissed as inadmissible it must present its argument in writing within two months. While this two-month requirement does not normally extend the six-month time limit for reply by the Government, there is provision for the granting of extensions in light of special circumstances. Additional requests for information on both admissibility issues and the merits, with fixed-time limits for reply, may be made of the State or the complainant. All exchanges are shared with the other party, who has the opportunity to comment thereon subject to fixed time limits.

Following these exchanges, the case is referred to the Working Group on Communications, comprised of five members of the Committee, which is authorised to consider both issues of admissibility and the merits. The Working Group may decide unanimously that a communication meets the requirements for admissibility.[76] A lack of unanimity on admissibility or a decision on inadmissibility must be referred for final consideration to the Committee itself. Similarly, regarding all issues

---

[72] Rules of Procedure of the Human Rights Committee, Rule 86, United Nations Doc., HRI/GEN/3 at page 55. See, also, *Mansaraj et al.; Gborie Tamba et al.; Sesay et al. v Sierra Leone* Comm No 839/1998; 840/1998 and 841/1998.

[73] Where the matter will be dealt with by a dedicated "petitions team" which handles all communications under the Optional Protocol, the Convention Against Torture and the Convention on the Elimination of All Forms of Racial Discrimination.

[74] The model communication form is reproduced in Appendix III.

[75] Article 3 of the Optional Protocol of ICCPR.

[76] Rules of Procedure of the Human Rights Committee, Rule 87, para. 2. United Nations Doc. HRI/GEN/3 at page 55.

of the merits of a case, the Working Group may only make recommendations to the Committee.

During the period of consideration by the Working Group additional requests for information on both admissibility issues and the merits, with fixed-time limits for reply, may be made of the State party or the complainant. All exchanges are shared with the other party, who has the opportunity to comment thereon subject to fixed time limits.

Decisions on inadmissibility may be reconsidered on application and in the light of changed circumstances.[77]

The admissibility requirements are as follows:[78]

(a) Communications may only be made by an individual who claims to be a victim of violation of right under the Covenant. Groups, bodies corporate, etc., may not take cases. The alleged victim may nominate a representative to handle the matter before the Committee. In certain cases where the alleged victim is impeded the Committee may permit a third party to take a case on his/her behalf.[79]

(b) For a communication to be admissible the alleged victim must have been subject to the jurisdiction of the State Party at the time of the alleged violation.[80]

(c) The alleged violation must be of rights in the Covenant. In this regard, however, note may be taken of the extremely wide scope of the equality provision in article 26.[81]

(d) The Covenant is not retroactive and thus the alleged violation must have occurred after the State acceded both to it and to the Optional Protocol.[82] However, a violation preceding that date with effects which persist may be actionable.

(e) In determining whether a violation has occurred care must be taken to ensure that the State has not "contracted out" of the specific provisions by means of a reservation (or by a declaration under article 4). It has also been determined that an individual cannot advance a complaint regarding self-determination (article 1 of the Covenant).[83]

---

[77] Rules of Procedure of the Human Rights Committee, Rule 92 para. 2. United Nations Doc. HRI/GEN/3 at page 56.

[78] Rules of Procedure of the Human Rights Committee, Rules 87–92 United Nations Doc. HRI/GEN/3 at pp. 55–57.

[79] Rules of Procedure of the Human Rights Committee, Rule 90 (b) United Nations Doc. HRI/GEN/3 at page 56.

[80] Rules of Procedure of the Human Rights Committee, Rule 90 (a) United Nations Doc. HRI/GEN/3 at page 56.

[81] Rules of Procedure of the Human Rights Committee, Rule 90 (b) United Nations Doc. HRI/GEN/3 at page 56. See also Article 3 of the Optional Protocol of ICCPR and *G. v Canada* Comm No. 934/2000.

[82] The Committee has established that the operative moment in respect of jurisdiction is the time at which the alleged violation of the Covenant took place rather than the time of submission of the communication. See P. R. Ghandi, "The Human Rights Committee and the Rights of Individual Communication", (1986) 57 BYIL 201, pp. 220–225. See, also, Article 1 of the Optional Protocol of ICCPR and *Koutny v Czech Republic*, Comm No. 807/1998.

[83] *A. D. v Canada*, Comm. No. 78/1980.

(f) Cases may only be taken against the State. Accordingly it is necessary to indicate culpability on the part of the State. Committee practice indicates that such culpability can be established where the State can be shown to have failed to take adequate action to restrain or channel the actions of non-governmental entities or delegated autonomous organs.[84]

(g) Cases may not be taken which are subject to consideration by another international redress mechanism.[85]

(h) As with other international redress procedures, the alleged victim must show that all relevant domestic (local) redress procedures have been exhausted.[86] The requirement is waived if it can be shown that the pursuit of the local remedy would be ineffective[87] or is unreasonably prolonged.[88]

(i) There is no time limit following exhaustion of local remedies for submission of a communication. However, an extreme delay might possibly be deemed by the Committee as "an abuse of the right of petition" and therefore inadmissible.[89]

(j) The claim must be substantiated.[90] In other words, it is necessary to indicate the right of the Covenant that is allegedly violated and the act or omission of the State that caused this violation.

Ultimately, a case is sent by the Working Group for consideration and decision by the Committee regarding admissibility (in all cases where the Working Group was unable to decide unanimously in favour of admissibility) and for adoption of Views on the merits.

The Views of the Committee take the form of a single consensus report, though individual or dissenting opinions may be and occasionally are attached thereto.

The Committee has reported its approach regarding the status of its Views as follows, "Bearing in mind that, by becoming a party to the Optional Protocol, the State party has recognised the competence of the Committee to determine whether there has been a violation of the Covenant or not and that, pursuant to article 2 of the Covenant, the State party has undertaken to ensure to all individuals within its territory and subject to its jurisdiction the rights recognised in the Covenant and to provide an effective and enforceable remedy in case a violation has been established, the Committee wishes to receive from the State party, within 90 days,

---

[84] Comm. No. 178/1984.

[85] Rules of Procedure of the Human Rights Committee, Rule 90 (e), United Nations Doc. HRI/GEN/3 at page 56. The Committee has determined that the resolution 1503 procedure of the Commission on Human Rights does not constitute an international procedure of investigation or settlement: *Estrella v Uruguay*, Comm. No. 74/1980.

[86] Rules of Procedure of the Human Rights Committee, Rule 90 (f), United Nations Doc. HRI/GEN/3 at page 56.

[87] *Santullo (Valcado) v Uruguay*, Comm. No. 9/1977.

[88] Article 5 (2b) of the Optional Protocol of ICCPR; *G. v Canada* Comm No. 934/2000; *Mansur v Netherlands* Comm No. 883/1999.

[89] Article 3 of the Optional Protocol of ICCPR. In its summer session of 2001 the Committee agreed that normally a communication should be submitted within five years after the last domestic decision.

[90] Article 2 of the Optional Protocol of ICCPR. See *G. v Canada* Comm No. 934/2000.

information about the measures taken to give effect to the Committee's Views".[91]

Where the Committee is of the view that there has been a violation it will indicate how the matter should be rectified. Such indications may include the stipulation that compensation be paid.[92] On a number of occasions, States have indicated problems with regard to the payment of compensation due to an absence of enabling legislation. The Committee has recommended that such States take the necessary legislative action and, in the meantime, make payments *ex gratia*.[93]

A member of the Committee, "the Special Rapporteur for the Follow-up of Views",[94] is charged with maintaining contact with the parties to observe the manner in which effect is given to the action of the Committee. The Rules of Procedure accord considerable scope to the Special Rapporteur for the development of flexible working methods. The Special Rapporteur currently, (a) recommends to the Committee to conduct meetings with State parties in light of the information received, if any, following the ninety-day period given to States to provide a remedy in cases of a violation; (b) holds meetings with selected States parties in the cases of a failure to provide a remedy; (c) reports to the Committee on these meetings; and, (d) recommends to the Committee any further activities after the follow-up meetings. To effectively carry out his functions it is important that the Special Rapporteur have access to a wide range of information sources. In this regard the Committee has indicated that it "welcomes any information which non-governmental organisations might wish to submit as to what measures States Parties have taken, in respect of the implementation of the Committee's Views."[95]

In 1995, the Special Rapporteur conducted a mission to investigate compliance with views of the Committee by a State Party, Jamaica. In the course of his mission, the Rapporteur met not only with Government officials but also with independent lawyers and NGOs.[96] The Committee has unsuccessfully requested that the United Nations allocate funds to allow the Rapporteur to carry out at least one such mission each year.[97]

The Committee, in its Annual Reports, draws particular attention to follow-up activities and names recalcitrant States. In 2000 the Committee reported that some thirty per cent of the replies received from States Parties regarding implementation of Views of the Committee could be considered as satisfactory.[98]

---

[91] United Nations Doc., A/55/40 (Vol. I), para 593. This formulation has been used in Views since the 1994 Views in *Kone v Senegal*, Comm No. 386/1989.

[92] See for instance, *Laptsevich v. Belarus*, Comm No. 780/1997.

[93] United Nations Doc., A/50/40, para. 551.

[94] Rules of Procedure of the Human Rights Committee, Rule 95, United Nations Doc., HRI/GEN/3 page 58. See M. Schmidt, "Follow-up Mechanisms Before UN Human Rights Treaty Bodies and the UN Mechanisms Beyond", in *The UN Human Rights Treaty System in the 21st Century*, (A.F. Bayefsky Ed. 2000), pp. 233–249.

[95] United Nations Doc., A/48/40, para. 466.

[96] See United Nations Doc., A/50/40, paras. 557–562.

[97] United Nations Doc., A/55/40, (Vol. I), para 617.

[98] United Nations Doc., A/55/40, (Vol. I) para. 599.

CHAPTER 3

THE COMMITTEE ON ECONOMIC, SOCIAL AND CULTURAL RIGHTS

1. THE SUBSTANTIVE PROVISIONS OF THE INTERNATIONAL COVENANT ON ECONOMIC, SOCIAL AND CULTURAL RIGHTS[1]

Article 1

1. *All peoples have the right of self-determination. By virtue of that right they freely determine their political status and freely pursue their economic, social and cultural development.*
2. *All peoples may, for their own ends, freely dispose of their natural wealth and resources without prejudice to any obligations arising out of international economic co-operation, based upon the principle of mutual benefit, and international law. In no case may a people be deprived of its own means of subsistence.*
3. *The States Parties to the present Covenant, including those having responsibility for the administration of Non-Self-Governing and Trust Territories, shall promote the realization of the right of self-determination, and shall respect that right, in conformity with the provisions of the Charter of the United Nations.*

---

[1] For a recent extensive bibliography see United Nations Doc. E/C.12/1989/L.3/Rev.3; M. Craven, *The International Covenant on Economic, Social and Cultural Rights*, (1995 and 1998); A. Eide, C. Krause and A. Rosas, Eds., *Economic, Social and Cultural Rights*, (1995); K. Arambulo, *Strenghtening the Supervision of the International Covenant on Economic, Social and Cultural Rights*, (1999); P. Alston, "The International Covenant on Economic, Social and Cultural Rights", in *Manual on Human Rights Reporting*, (United Nations, 1997) at pp. 65–170; R. Burchill, D. Harris, A. Owers, Eds., *Economic, Social and Cultural Rights: Their implementation in United Kingdom Law*, (1999); A. Chapman, "A violation Aproach for Monitoring the International Covenant on Economic, Social and Cultural Rights", Hum. Rts. Q. 18 (1996), pp. 23–66; V. Dankwa, C. Flintermann, S. Leckie, "Commentary to the Masstricht Guidelines on Violations of Economic, Social and Cultural Rights", Hum. Rts. Q 20 (1998), pp. 705–730 (the Guidelines themselves are in the same volume at pp. 691–704); S. Leckie, "Another Step Towards Indivisibility; Identifying the Key Features of Violations of Economic, Social and Cultural Rights", Hum. Rts. Q 20 (1998), pp. 81–124; L. B. Sohn, *Guide to Interpretation of the International Covenant on Economic, Social and Cultural Rights*, (forthcoming);); S. Leckie, "The United Nations Committee on Economic, Social and Cultural Rights and the Rights to Adequate Housing: Towards an Appropriate Approach", 11 Hum. Rts. Q., (1989), pp. 522–560; *Fact Sheet 16 (Rev.1)*, *The Committee on Economic, Social and Cultural Rights, (*United Nations), P. Hunt, *Reclaiming Social Rights*, 1998; *Circle of Rights*, (International Human Rights Internship Programme, 2000).

Article 2

1. *Each State Party to the present Covenant undertakes to take steps, individually and through international assistance and co-operation, especially economic and technical, to the maximum of its available resources, with a view to achieving progressively the full realization of the rights recognized in the present Covenant by all appropriate means, including particularly the adoption of legislative measures.*
   [Image]General comment on its implementation
2. *The States Parties to the present Covenant undertake to guarantee that the rights enunciated in the present Covenant will be exercised without discrimination of any kind as to race, colour, sex, language, religion, political or other opinion, national or social origin, property, birth or other status.*
3. *Developing countries, with due regard to human rights and their national economy, may determine to what extent they would guarantee the economic rights recognized in the present Covenant to non-nationals.*

Note

In General Comment 3[2] the Committee notes that the article imposes obligations of conduct and obligations of result, some of which are of immediate effect. Of these, two are of particular importance: the "undertaking to guarantee" that relevant rights "will be exercised without discrimination..." and "to take steps...with a view to achieving progressively the full realization of the rights recognized" in the Covenant. The Committee further observes in both General Comment 3[3] and General Comment 9[4] that the phrase "by all appropriate means" includes, in addition to legislation, the provision of judicial remedies and other administrative, financial, educational and social measures. Where specific policies have been adopted in legislative form, General Comment 3[5] invites States parties to inform the Committee as to whether such laws create any right of action on behalf of individuals or groups who feel that their rights are not being fully realised. The Committee also underlines[6] that in order for a State Party to be able to attribute its failure to meet at least its minimum core obligation to a lack of available resources it must demonstrate that every effort has been made to use all resources that are at its disposition in an effort to satisfy, as a matter of priority, those minimum obligations.

Article 3

The States Parties to the present Covenant undertake to ensure the equal right of men and women to the enjoyment of all economic, social and cultural rights set forth in the present Covenant.

---

[2] United Nations Doc. HRI/GEN/1/Rev. 5, p. 18.
[3] *Ibid.*
[4] United Nations Doc. HRI/GEN/1/Rev. 5, p. 58.
[5] United Nations Doc. HRI/GEN/1/Rev. 5, p. 18.
[6] *Ibid.*

Note

General Comment 5[7] notes that "the double discrimination suffered by women with disabilities is often neglected." The Committee therefore urges States Parties to address the situation of women with disabilities, with high priority being given in future to the implementation of programmes related to this group's realisation of their rights under this article. General Comment 6[8] draws particular attention to the rights of older women who, because they have spent all or part of their lives caring for families without engaging in a remunerated activity entitling them to an old-age pension and who are also not entitled to a widow's pension, are often in critical situations. Accordingly, the Committee holds that "States Parties should institute non-contributory old-age benefits or other assistance for all persons, regardless of sex, who find themselves without resources on attaining an age specified in national legislation."

Article 4

The States Parties to the present Covenant recognize that, in the enjoyment of those rights provided by the State in conformity with the present Covenant, the State may subject such rights only to such limitations as are determined by law only in so far as this may be compatible with the nature of these rights and solely for the purpose of promoting the general welfare in a democratic society.

Article 5

1. *Nothing in the present Covenant may be interpreted as implying for any State, group or person any right to engage in any activity or to perform any act aimed at the destruction of any of the rights or freedoms recognized herein, or at their limitation to a greater extent than is provided for in the present Covenant.*
2. *No restriction upon or derogation from any of the fundamental human rights recognized or existing in any country in virtue of law, conventions, regulations or custom shall be admitted on the pretext that the present Covenant does not recognize such rights or that it recognizes them to a lesser extent.*

Article 6

1. *The States Parties to the present Covenant recognize the right to work, which includes the right of everyone to the opportunity to gain his living by work which he freely chooses or accepts, and will take appropriate steps to safeguard this right.*
2. *The steps to be taken by a State Party to the present Covenant to achieve the full*

---

[7] United Nations Doc. HRI/GEN/1/Rev. 5, p. 33, with reference to E/CN.4/Sub.2/1991/31. Cf. also General Comment 9 of 1998, United Nations Doc. E/1999/22/Annex IV, in United Nations Doc. HRI/GEN/1/Rev. 5, p. 58.
[8] United Nations Doc. HRI/GEN/1/Rev. 5, p. 38.

realization of this right shall include technical and vocational guidance and training programmes, policies and techniques to achieve steady economic, social and cultural development and full and productive employment under conditions safeguarding fundamental political and economic freedoms to the individual.

Note

In its General Comment 5[9] the Committee states that the integration of persons with disabilities into the regular workforce should be actively supported. The Committee likewise stresses that "therapeutical treatment" in institutions "which amounts to forced labour", is incompatible with the Covenant. General Comment 5 calls for States Parties to support the removal of physical barriers from within the workplace which inhibit disabled persons from being integrated into the workforce. Also, the Committee notes that access to specially tailored forms of transportation, is "crucial to the realization by persons with disabilities of virtually all rights recognized in the Convention".[10]

Other workers frequently have difficulty finding and retaining employment. Thus, General Comment 6[11] stresses the need for measures to prevent discrimination on the grounds of age in employment and occupation. Also the Committee recommends that programmes be implemented for older workers, prior to retirement, to help prepare them to cope with retired life.

Article 7

The States Parties to the present Covenant recognize the right of everyone to the enjoyment of just and favourable conditions of work which ensure, in particular:

(a) Remuneration which provides all workers, as a minimum, with:
  (i) Fair wages and equal remuneration for work of equal value without distinction of any kind, in particular women being guaranteed conditions of work not inferior to those enjoyed by men, with equal pay for equal work;
  (ii) A decent living for themselves and their families in accordance with the provisions of the present Covenant;
(b) Safe and healthy working conditions;
(c) Equal opportunity for everyone to be promoted in his employment to an appropriate higher level, subject to no considerations other than those of seniority and competence;
(d) Rest, leisure and reasonable limitation of working hours and periodic holidays with pay, as well as remuneration for public holidays.

---

[9]   United Nations Doc. HRI/GEN/1/Rev. 5, p. 33.
[10] *Ibid.*
[11] United Nations Doc. HRI/GEN/1/Rev. 5, p. 43.

Note

In General Comment 5[12] the Committee observes that "States Parties have a responsibility to ensure that disability is not used as an excuse for creating low standards of labour protection or for paying below minimum wages." Moreover, in General Comment 9[13] the Committed notes that also in relation to rights such as the one enshrined in art. 7, paragraph (a)(i), there should be immediate implementation into domestic law with judicial remedies for its violation.

Article 8

1. *The States Parties to the present Covenant undertake to ensure:*
    (a) *The right of everyone to form trade unions and join the trade union of his choice, subject only to the rules of the organization concerned, for the promotion and protection of his economic and social interests. No restrictions may be placed on the exercise of this right other than those prescribed by law and which are necessary in a democratic society in the interests of national security or public order or for the protection of the rights and freedoms of others;*
    (b) *The right of trade unions to establish national federations or confederations and the right of the latter to form or join international trade-union organizations;*
    (c) *The right of trade unions to function freely subject to no limitations other than those prescribed by law and which are necessary in a democratic society in the interests of national security or public order or for the protection of the rights and freedoms of others;*
    (d) *The right to strike, provided that it is exercised in conformity with the laws of the particular country.*
2. *This article shall not prevent the imposition of lawful restrictions on the exercise of these rights by members of the armed forces or of the police or of the administration of the State.*
3. *Nothing in this article shall authorize States Parties to the International Labour Organisation Convention of 1948 concerning Freedom of Association and Protection of the Right to Organize to take legislative measures which would prejudice, or apply the law in such a manner as would prejudice, the guarantees provided for in that Convention.*

Article 9

The States Parties to the present Covenant recognize the right of everyone to social security, including social insurance.

---

[12] United Nations Doc. HRI/GEN/1/Rev. 5, p. 33.
[13] United Nations Doc. HRI/GEN/1/Rev. 5, p. 60.

Note

General Comment 5[14] states that the "institutionalisation of persons with disabilities, unless necessary for other reasons, cannot be regarded as an adequate substitute for social security and income-support rights of such persons".

In General Comment 6[15], the Committee notes that, "States Parties must take appropriate measures to establish general regimes of compulsory old-age insurance, starting at a particular age, to be prescribed by national law". States Parties must likewise "guarantee the provision of survivors" and orphan's benefits on the death of the breadwinner who was covered by social security or receiving a pension."

Article 10

The States Parties to the present Covenant recognize that:

1. *The widest possible protection and assistance should be accorded to the family, which is the natural and fundamental group unit of society, particularly for its establishment and while it is responsible for the care and education of dependent children. Marriage must be entered into with the free consent of the intending spouses.*
2. *Special protection should be accorded to mothers during a reasonable period before and after childbirth. During such period working mothers should be accorded paid leave or leave with adequate social security benefits.*
3. *Special measures of protection and assistance should be taken on behalf of all children and young persons without any discrimination for reasons of parentage or other conditions. Children and young persons should be protected from economic and social exploitation. Their employment in work harmful to their morals or health or dangerous to life or likely to hamper their normal development should be punishable by law. States should also set age limits below which the paid employment of child labour should be prohibited and punishable by law.*

Note

In General Comment 5[16] the Committee calls on States Parties to protect the right of persons with disabilities to be able to continue living with their own families, if they so wish. General Comment 6[17] states that the Government must "support, protect and strengthen" the family and help it cope with needs of its dependent ageing members. Reference to art. 10 is further made in General Comment 9,[18] listing paragraph 3 as a provision "immediately capable of implementation" and which should lead to a judicial remedy in case of breach.

---

[14] United Nations Doc. HRI/GEN/1/Rev. 5, p. 34.
[15] United Nations Doc. HRI/GEN/1/Rev. 5, p. 43.
[16] United Nations Doc. HRI/GEN/1/Rev. 5, p. 34.
[17] United Nations Doc. HRI/GEN/1/Rev. 5, p. 44.
[18] United Nations Doc. HRI/GEN/1/Rev. 5, p. 60.

Article 11

1. *The States Parties to the present Covenant recognize the right of everyone to an adequate standard of living for himself and his family, including adequate food, clothing and housing, and to the continuous improvement of living conditions. The States Parties will take appropriate steps to ensure the realization of this right, recognizing to this effect the essential importance of international co-operation based on free consent. General comment on its implementation*
2. *The States Parties to the present Covenant, recognizing the fundamental right of everyone to be free from hunger, shall take, individually and through international co-operation, the measures, including specific programmes, which are needed:*
   (a) To improve methods of production, conservation and distribution of food by making full use of technical and scientific knowledge, by disseminating knowledge of the principles of nutrition and by developing or reforming agrarian systems in such a way as to achieve the most efficient development and utilization of natural resources;
   (b) Taking into account the problems of both food-importing and food-exporting countries, to ensure an equitable distribution of world food supplies in relation to need.

Note

In General Comment 4[19] the Committee observes that article 11 is the most comprehensive and perhaps the most important of the provisions enshrined in the Covenant. It notes[20] that there is a disturbingly large gap between the standards set in paragraph 1 and the situation prevailing in many parts of the world. General Comment 4 further clarifies[21] that the reference to "himself and his family" reflects assumptions as to gender roles and economic activity-patterns commonly accepted in 1966 when the Covenant was adopted, and that the concept of "family" must be understood in a wide sense and, in particular, in accordance with article 2(2). Moreover, in the Committee's view,[22] the right to housing should not be interpreted in a narrow or restrictive sense, but rather it should be seen as the right to live somewhere in security, peace and dignity. Also the Committee believes that the right to housing should encompass certain key aspects including: legal security of tenure, availability of services, materials, facilities and infrastructure, affordability, habitability, health principles of housing, accessibility, location and cultural adequacy. However, many of the measures required to promote the right to housing only require the abstention by the Government from certain practices and a commitment to facilitating "self-help" by affected groups.[23] Among these, for example, there is the practice of forced eviction, which was considered in General Comment 7.[24]

---

[19] United Nations Doc. HRI/GEN/1/Rev. 5, p. 22.
[20] United Nations Doc. HRI/GEN/1/Rev. 5, p. 22.
[21] *Ibid.*
[22] *Ibid.*
[23] General Comment 4, United Nations Doc. HRI/GEN/1/Rev. 5, p. 25.
[24] United Nations Doc. HRI/GEN/1/Rev. 5, p. 49.

General Comment 6[25] further emphasises the need for States Parties to take the "functional capacity of the elderly" into account "in order to better provide them with a better living environment" and to facilitate mobility and communication.

As regards the right to adequate food, instead, in General Comment 12[26], the Committee states that this right is of crucial importance for the enjoyment of all rights and that therefore the reference in article 11.1 to "himself and his family" does not imply any limitation upon the applicability of this right to individuals or to female-headed households. Moreover, triggered by the request of States during the 1996 World Food Summit for a better definition of the rights relating to food in article 11, the Committee concluded that this right is realized "when every man, woman and child, alone or in community with others, have physical and economic access at all times to adequate food or means for its procurement. The *right to adequate food* shall therefore not be interpreted in a narrow or restrictive sense which equates it with a minimum package of calories, proteins and other specific nutrients. The *right to adequate food* will have to be realized progressively. However, States have a core obligation to take the necessary action to mitigate and alleviate hunger as provided for in paragraph 2 of article 11, even in times of natural or other disasters."[27]

Article 12

1. The States Parties to the present Covenant recognize the right of everyone to the enjoyment of the highest attainable standard of physical and mental health.
2. The steps to be taken by the States Parties to the present Covenant to achieve the full realization of this right shall include those necessary for:
    (a) The provision for the reduction of the stillbirth-rate and of infant mortality and for the healthy development of the child;
    (b) The improvement of all aspects of environmental and industrial hygiene;
    (c) The prevention, treatment and control of epidemic, endemic, occupational and other diseases;
    (d) The creation of conditions which would assure to all medical service and medical attention in the event of sickness.

Note
The Committee notes the growing incidents of chronic degenerative diseases and the high cost of hospitalisation. Accordingly, General Comment 6[28] recommends that States Parties encourage "healthier lifestyles (food, exercise, elimination of tobacco and alcohol, etc.) amongst older persons, rather than relying solely upon "curative treatment". It also recalls that "the realization of the right to health may be pursued

---

[25] United Nations Doc. HRI/GEN/1/Rev. 5, p. 44.
[26] United Nations Doc. HRI/GEN/1/Rev. 5, p. 66.
[27] General Comment 12, United Nations Doc. HRI/GEN/1/Rev.5, p. 68.
[28] General Comment 6, United Nations Doc. HRI/GEN/1/Rev.5, p. 45.

through numerous complementary approaches, such as the formulation of health policies, the implementation of health programmes developed by the World Health Organization (WHO), the adoption of specific legal instruments" and that moreover, "the right to health includes certain components which are legally enforceable.[29] The right to health, like all human rights, imposes three types or levels of obligations on States parties: the obligations to *respect*, *protect* and *fulfil*. In turn, the obligation to fulfil contains obligations to facilitate, provide and promote."[30] This right is not confined to the right to health care but extends to the underlying determinants of health, such as food and nutrition, housing, access to safe and potable water and adequate sanitation, safe and healthy working conditions, and a healthy environment.[31] It is not to be understood as a right to be healthy. It contains both freedoms and entitlements. The freedoms include the right to control one's health and body, including sexual and reproductive freedom, and the right to be free from interference, such as the right to be free from torture, non-consensual medical treatment and experimentation. By contrast, the entitlements include the right to a system of health protection which provides equality of opportunity for people to enjoy the highest attainable level of health.[32] Additionally, this right imposes an obligation on State Parties to respect this right also in third countries and therefore the Committee notes that States parties should refrain at all times from imposing embargoes or similar measures restricting the supply of another State with adequate medicines and medical equipment and that restrictions on such goods should never be used as an instrument of political and economic pressure.[33]

Article 13

1. *The States Parties to the present Covenant recognize the right of everyone to education. They agree that education shall be directed to the full development of the human personality and the sense of its dignity, and shall strengthen the respect for human rights and fundamental freedoms. They further agree that education shall enable all persons to participate effectively in a free society, promote understanding, tolerance and friendship among all nations and all racial, ethnic or religious groups, and further the activities of the United Nations for the maintenance of peace.*
2. *The States Parties to the present Covenant recognize that, with a view to achieving the full realization of this right:*
   (a) Primary education shall be compulsory and available free to all;
   (b) Secondary education in its different forms, including technical and vocational secondary education, shall be made generally available and accessible to all by every appropriate means, and in particular by the progressive introduction of free education;

---

[29] General Comment 14, United Nations Doc. HRI/GEN/1/Rev.5, p. 90.
[30] General Comment 14, United Nations Doc. HRI/GEN/1/Rev.5, p. 98.
[31] General Comment 14, United Nations Doc. HRI/GEN/1/Rev.5, p. 91.
[32] General Comment 14, United Nations Doc. HRI/GEN/1/Rev.5, p. 91.
[33] General Comment 14, United Nations Doc. HRI/GEN/1/Rev.5, p. 100.

(c) Higher education shall be made equally accessible to all, on the basis of capacity, by every appropriate means, and in particular by the progressive introduction of free education;
(d) Fundamental education shall be encouraged or intensified as far as possible for those persons who have not received or completed the whole period of their primary education;
(e) The development of a system of schools at all levels shall be actively pursued, an adequate fellowship system shall be established, and the material conditions of teaching staff shall be continuously improved.
3. The States Parties to the present Covenant undertake to have respect for the liberty of parents and, when applicable, legal guardians to choose for their children schools, other than those established by the public authorities, which conform to such minimum educational standards as may be laid down or approved by the State and to ensure the religious and moral education of their children in conformity with their own convictions.
4. No part of this article shall be construed so as to interfere with the liberty of individuals and bodies to establish and direct educational institutions, subject always to the observance of the principles set forth in paragraph 1 of this article and to the requirement that the education given in such institutions shall conform to such minimum standards as may be laid down by the State.

Note

The Committee notes in General Comment 13[34] that education is both a human right in itself and an indispensable means of realising other human rights. The Committee takes the view that the right to education requires to be interpreted in light of the World Declaration on Education for All, the Convention on the Rights of the Child, the Vienna Declaration and Programme of Action and the Plan of Action for the United Nations Decade for Human Rights Education. While the Covenant provides for progressive realisation and acknowledges the constraints due to the limits of available resources, it also imposes on States parties various obligations which are of immediate effect, such as regarding the guarantee that the rights will be excercised without discrimination of any kind and the obligation to take steps towards the full realisation of article 13. With regard to "progressive realisation", States parties have specific obligations to move as expeditiously and effectively as possible towards the full realisation of article 13.

Article 14

Each State Party to the present Covenant which, at the time of becoming a Party, has not been able to secure in its metropolitan territory or other territories under its jurisdiction compulsory primary education, free of charge, undertakes, within two years, to work out and adopt a detailed plan of action for the progressive

---

[34] United Nations Doc.HRI/GEN/1/Rev.5, p. 74.

implementation, within a reasonable number of years, to be fixed in the plan, of the principle of compulsory education free of charge for all.

Note

The Committee notes in General Comment 11[35] that each State Party which has not been able to secure compulsory primary education, free of charge, shall undertake, within two years, to work out and adopt a detailed plan of action for the progressive implementation, within a reasonable number of years, to be fixed in the plan, of the principle of compulsory primary education free of charge for all. This must be interpreted as meaning within two years of the Covenant's entry into force of the State concerned, or within two years of a subsequent change in circumstances which has led to the non-observance of the relevant obligation.[36] The Committee also observes that "where a state party is clearly lacking the financial resources and/or expertise to "work out and adopt" a detailed plan, the international community has the obligation to assist."[37]

Article 15

1. *The States Parties to the present Covenant recognize the right of everyone:*
   (a) To take part in cultural life;
   (b) To enjoy the benefits of scientific progress and its applications;
   (c) To benefit from the protection of the moral and material interests resulting from any scientific, literary or artistic production of which he is the author.
2. *The steps to be taken by the States Parties to the present Covenant to achieve the full realization of this right shall include those necessary for the conservation, the development and the diffusion of science and culture.*
3. *The States Parties to the present Covenant undertake to respect the freedom indispensable for scientific research and creative activity.*
4. *The States Parties to the present Covenant recognize the benefits to be derived from the encouragement and development of international contacts and co-operation in the scientific and cultural fields.*

Note

In General Comment 9[38] the Committee observes that art. 15 (3) is capable of being implemented into domestic law and thus to be justiciable.

---

[35] United Nations Doc.HRI/GEN/1/Rev. 5, p. 63.
[36] United Nations Doc.HRI/GEN/1/Rev.5, p. 65.
[37] United Nations Doc.HRI/GEN/1/Rev.5, p. 65.
[38] United Nations Doc.HRI/GEN/1/Rev.5, p. 60.

2. THE COMMITTEE ON ECONOMIC, SOCIAL AND CULTURAL RIGHTS[39]

The Covenant does not make provision for the establishment of a treaty body. Instead, various responsibilities for the supervision of its implementation are entrusted to the United Nations Economic and Social Council (ECOSOC).[40] That body, in 1985, created the Committee on Economic, Social and Cultural Rights and entrusted to it the task of "assisting it" in the monitoring of implementation of the Covenant, primarily by means of the examination of periodic reports submitted by States Parties.[41] There are 18 members[42] elected by ECOSOC from a list of

---

[39] For a recent extensive bibliography see United Nations Doc. E/C.12/1989/L.3/Rev.3: M. Craven, *The International Covenant on Economic, Social and Cultural Rights*, (1995); S. Guillet, *Nous, peuples des Nations Unies – L'action des ONG au sein du système de protection international des droits de l'homme* (1995), pp. 62–65; P. Alston, "The Committee on Economic, Social and Cultural Rights", in *The United Nations and Human Rights – A Critical Appraisal*, (P. Alston Ed. 1992), pp. 473–508; C. Dommen and M. Craven, "Making Way for Substance: The Fifth Session of the Committee on Economic, Social and Cultural Rights", 9, *Netherlands Quarterly of Human Rights* (1991), pp. 83–95; S. Leckie, "An Overview and Appraisal of the Fifth Session of the United Nations Committee on Economic, Social and Cultural Rights", 13 Hum. Rts. Q., (1991); P. Alston and B. Simma, "Second Session of the United Nations Committee on Economic, Social and Cultural Rights", 82 Am. J. Int'l L., (1988), pp. 747–756; M. Mohr, "Procedural Problems Pertaining to the Work of the Committee on Economic, Social and Cultural Rights", 14 GDR Committee Hum. Rts. Bull., 1988, pp. 112–129; P. Alston, "Out of the Abyss: The Challenges Confronting the New United Nations Committee on Economic, Social and Cultural Rights", 9 Hum. Rts. Q., (1987), pp. 332–381; L. B. Sohn, *Guide to Interpretation of the International Covenant on Economic, Social and Cultural Rights*, (forthcoming); *Fact Sheet 16, The Committee on Economic, Social and Cultural Rights,* (United Nations); A. Chapman, "A 'Violations Approach' for Monitoring the International Covenant on Economic, Social and Cultural Rights", 18 Hum. Rts. QL. (1996) 23–66); K. Arambulo, *Strenghtening the Supervision of the International Covenant on Economic, Social and Cultural Rights; Theoretical and Procedural Aspects,* (1999); M. Craven, *The International Covenant on Economic, Social and Cultural Rights: A Perspective on its Development,* (1998); S. Leckie, "The Committee on Economic, Social and Cultural Rights: Catalyst for Change in a System Needing Reform", in *The Future of UN Human Rights Treaty Monitoring,* (P. Alston and J. Crawford, Eds., 2000); United Nations Doc. E/1996/101. See, generally, the following studies by P. Alston, *Long Term Approaches to Enhancing the Effectiveness of the United Nations Human Rights Treaty Bodies,* United Nations Doc. A/44/668; *Interim Report on Updated Study,* United Nations Doc. A/CONF.157/PC/62/Add.11/Rev.1; *Final Report on Enhancing the Long Term Effectiveness of the United Nations Human Rights Treaty System,* United Nations Doc. E/CN.4/1997/74; and, also, A. Bayefsky, *Report: The UN Human Rights Treaty System: Universality at the Crossroads,* (2001); P. Alston and J. Crawford Eds., *The Future of UN Human Rights Treaty Monitoring,* (2000); A. Bayefsky, Ed., *The UN Human Rights System in the 21st Century,* (2000).

[40] Articles 16–25 of the Covenant.

[41] ECOSOC resolution 1985/17 United Nations Doc. E/1995/85. See also resolution 1988 (LX) of 1976, United Nations Doc. E/C.12/1989/4. See also General Comment 1 of 1989, in United Nations Doc., HRI/GEN/1/Rev.4, p. 3 and Articles 16 and 17 of the Covenant.

[42] Membership as of December 2000: Mahmoud Samir Ahmed (Egypt), Ivan Antanovich (Belarus), Clement Atangana (Cameroon), Virginia Bonoan Dandan (Philippines), Dumitru Ceasu (Romania), Oscar Ceville (Panama), Abdessatar Grissa (Tunisia), Paul Hunt (New Zealand), Maria de los Angeles Jimenez Butragueno (Spain), Veleri Koutznetsov (Russian Federation), Jaime Marchan Romero (Ecuador), Ariranga Govindasamy Pillay (Mauritius), Kenneth Osborne Rattray (Jamaica), Eibe Riedel (Germany), Waleed M. Sadi (Jordan), Philippe Texier (France), Nutan Thapalia (Nepal), Javier Wimer Zambrano (Mexico).

candidates submitted by the States Parties for terms of four years. Members serve in their private capacities and make a solemn declaration of impartiality upon taking up office. The Committee presently meets twice each year, in May and in November/ December for sessions of three working weeks each. The Committee has also been authorised by ECOSOC to convene in each of 2000 and 2001 one further extraordinary session of three weeks duration (the 2000 extraordinary session took place in August/September). Each session is followed by a meeting of one week's duration of a pre-sessional Working Group. All sessions presently take place in Geneva. Secretariat services are provided by the United Nations Office of the High Commissioner for Human Rights.[43]

The Committee places considerable importance in developing its working relationship with NGOs and has developed innovative working practices to facilitate the effective flow of information.[44] NGOs in consultative status with ECOSOC have a particularly strong position in that they benefit from their official status before that body and subsidiary organs such as the Committee.

Four of the activities of the Committee are of particular interest for NGOs: the reporting procedure, days of general discussion, the occasional missions undertaken by Committee members and the drafting of General Comments. NGOs may also be able to elicit exceptional action by the Committee when the situation so warrants.

3. THE REPORTING PROCEDURE[45]

(a) The obligation on the State

Under article 16 of the Covenant, States are obliged to submit reports to ECOSOC on the measures they have adopted to give effect to the rights in the Covenant and on the progress made in achieving the observance of those rights. It is stipulated in article 17 that reports may indicate factors and difficulties affecting the degree of fulfilment of the obligations. The Covenant itself does not indicate the periodicity for

---

[43] Secretariat of the Committee on Economic, Social and Cultural Rights, Support Services Branch, Office of the High Commissioner for Human Rights, UNOG, 1211 Geneva 10, Switzerland (Tel.: 41 22 917 1234; Fax 41 22 917 0099).

[44] "Non-governmental organisation participation in the activities of the Committee on Economic, Social and Cultural Rights", United Nations Doc., E/C.12/2000/21, at Annex V. See also V. Dandan, "The Committee on Economic, Social and Cultural Rights and Non-Governmental Organisations", in *The UN Human Rights Treaty System in the 21st Century*, (A. Bayefsky Ed., 2000), 227–230; S. Leckie, "The Committee on Economic, Social and Cultural Rights: Catalyst for Change in a System Needing Reform", in *The Future of UN Human Rights Treaty Monitoring*, (P.Alston and J. Crawford, Eds., 2000).

[45] See M. Craven, *The International Covenant on Economic, Social and Cultural Rights* (1995), Chap. 2; P. Alston, "The Committee on Economic, Social and Cultural Rights", *The United Nations and Human Rights* (P. Alston Ed. 1992), Chap. 12; P. Alston, "The International Covenant on Economic, Social and Cultural Rights, in *Manual on Human Rights Reporting* (United Nations, 1997), pp. 65–170; D. Harris, "Commentary by the Rapporteur on the Consideration of States Parties' Reports and International Co-operation", 9 Hum. Rts. Q., (1987).

reports. Instead, the requirement, established in 1988, is that initial reports must be submitted within two years of the Covenant coming into force for a State and thereafter every five years.[46] However, at its 24th session, in 2000, the Committee decided that, as a general rule, a State Party's next periodic report should be submitted five year's after the Committee's consideration of the State's preceding report, but that the Committee may reduce this five-year period on the basis of the following criteria and taking into account all relevant circumstances: (a) the timeliness of the State Party's submission of its periodic reports: (b) the quality of all information submitted by the State; (c) the quality of the dialogue between the Committee and the State; (d) the adequacy of the State response to the Committee's concluding observations; and, (e) the State's actual record regarding implementation of the Covenant[47]

General Comment 1[48] states seven objectives of the reporting process:

i.   facilitation of a comprehensive review by a State of its rules, procedure and practice in implementing the Covenant;
ii. ensuring the ongoing monitoring by a State of the actual implementation to all beneficiaries of the rights in the Covenant;
iii. allowing a State to demonstrate the extent to which it has developed policies and programmes to progressively implement the Covenant;
iv. facilitation of public scrutiny of relevant government policies;
v.   provision of a basis on which a State, together with the Committee, can effectively evaluate the extent to which progress has been made towards realisation of the obligations in the Covenant;
vi. identification of factors and difficulties inhibiting implementation of the Covenant;
vii. enabling the Committee and States Parties to facilitate the exchange of information among States thus encouraging a better understanding of the common problems faced by States ad appropriate responses thereto.

The General Guidelines[49] for the content of both initial and subsequent reports provide detailed directions for States Parties.[50] The lengthy Guidelines eschew generalised observations and instead proceed, article by article, to indicate information to be provided and precise questions to be answered. States must describe the actual situation, draw attention to the range of problems, opine as to causes of problems and show both a commitment to change and a planned

---

[46] ECOSOC resolution 1988/4, United Nations Doc. E/C.12/1989/4.
[47] United Nations Doc. E/C.12/2000/21 para. 637.
[48] United Nations Doc. HRI/GEN/1/Rev.4 page 3.
[49] United Nations Doc. E/C.12/1991/1. For an explication of the report requirements under each of the substantive articles, see also, P. Alston, "The International Covenant on Economic, Social and Cultural Rights", in *Manual on Human Rights Reporting*, (United Nations, 1997), pp. 65–170.
[50] The first part of reports should also comply with the consolidated guidelines relating to the preparation of the initial part of reports under the various international human rights instruments. See United Nations Doc. HRI/CORE/1.

programme to effect that commitment. The high level of detail in the Guidelines is such that States can be left in no doubt as to the precise reporting requirements under each article. Consonant with article 17 of the Covenant, the Guidelines indicate that where States have already reported comprehensively and relevantly to other international review mechanisms[51] they may refer to such reporting rather than to restate matters for the Committee.

A notable feature of the Guidelines is the consistent insistence on provision of information with regard to the non-discriminatory implementation of rights.

(b) The procedure

i. The scheduling process

At present, reports, once submitted, can be expected to be taken up by the Committee within some two to two and a half years. The Committee decides the reports which it will consider two sessions in advance and this information is published both in the reports of the Committee and on the OHCHR website. Precise timetabling of the consideration of reports by the Committee should be available some three months before a session and this information also is posted to the website. State party reports, once published as United Nations documents, can be ordered from the United Nations Documents Distribution and Sales Section. The symbol number can be obtained from the Secretariat. Reports are usually available in all of the working languages of the Committee (English, French, Spanish and Russian). Reports are also posted on the OHCHR website.

ii. The Working Group

Periodic reports first receive the attention of a five-member Working Group of the Committee.[52] The Working Group meets in unreported and closed meetings at the end of each session and, *inter alia,* considers reports scheduled for consideration at the next session. The purpose of the consideration is, "to identify in advance the questions which will constitute the principal focus of the dialogue with the representatives of the reporting States. The aim is to improve the efficiency of the system and to ease the task of States' representatives by facilitating more focussed preparations for the discussion."[53] The Working Group prepares a list of issues[54] for transmission to the State Parties with a request for written replies to be submitted sufficiently in advance of the session to enable the replies to be translated and made available to all members of the Committee. Lists of Issues are published on the OHCHR website (occasionally but not consistently together with whatever replies will have been received from the State party concerned) approximately one month before the session at which the Committee considers the State Party report.

---

[51] Such as the ILO, WHO, UNESCO and human rights treaty bodies.
[52] United Nations Doc. E/C.12/2000/21, paras 29–37.
[53] *Ibid* at para. 30.
[54] A sample list of Issues (for France) is reproduced in Appendix I.

To aid in its task, the Working Group has before it, regarding each State report, a draft list of issues drawn up by a member serving as a "Country Rapporteur", together with a "country profile" prepared by the Secretariat. Country profiles may contain reference to material provided by a wide range of information sources, including intergovernmental organisations, such as ILO and WHO, as well as by NGOs. The Committee has also instructed the Secretariat to put before the Working Group, all pertinent documents containing information relevant to each of the reports to be examined and, for this purpose, "invites all concerned individuals, bodies and non-governmental organisations to submit relevant and appropriate documentation to the Secretariat".[55] States are not present at meetings of the Working Group. NGOs may be invited to provide information orally (see further below).[56]

iii. Consideration by the Committee

Reports are considered by the Committee in public session and in dialogue with representatives of the State,[57] usually over the course of three meetings, each of three hours' duration. Reports are introduced by representatives of the State Party. The scrutiny which follows pays close attention to the List of Issues and generally follows an article by article basis. The Chairperson invites questions or comments from Committee members in relation to each issue and then invites the representatives of the State party to reply. Representatives of relevant specialised UN agencies and other international bodies (but not NGOs) may also be invited to contribute at any stage of the dialogue.

Following the consideration in public meetings, the Committee meets in private to identify central concerns to be included in the Concluding Observations.[58] Following this meeting, the Country Rapporteur, assisted by the Secretariat, prepares a draft. The draft is then considered and adopted by the Committee in private session. The observations comprise a critique of the State report and of the response of the State representative to the scrutiny of the Committee, noting positive aspects, identifying factors and difficulties impeding implementation of the Covenant, drawing attention to principal subjects of concern and making suggestions and recommendations. Concluding Observations are issued as public documents at the end of each session of the Committee, posted on the OHCHR website (initially solely in the language of adoption) and included in the Committee's annual report.

At its twenty-first session, in 1999, the Committee decided that, (a) all Concluding Observations will request the State to inform the Committee in its next report of steps taken to implement the recommendations in the Concluding Observations; (b) if it so chooses, the Committee may, in Concluding Observations, request a State to

---

[55] United Nations Doc. E/C.12/2000/21 para 33.
[56] Rules of Procedure of the Committee on Economic, Social and Cultural Rights, Rule 69, United Nations Doc. HRI/GEN/3 page 25.
[57] Rules of Procedure of the Committee on Economic, Social and Cultural Rights, Rules 28 and 62, United Nations Doc. HRI/GEN/3 pages 14 and 23.
[58] A sample of Concluding Observations (on Belgium) is reproduced in Appendix II.

provide specific information within a stipulated timeframe whereby the Committee, advised by its Working Group, can determine whether to take such further action as to schedule a new dialogue with the State or to issue additional Concluding Observations. In the case of failure of a State to comply in whole or in part with requests for information, the Committee Chairperson, in consultation with the Committee's bureau, may be authorised to follow the matter up with it.[59]

On occasion, the Committee may reject a report on the basis that it fails to comply with the reporting guidelines to an unacceptable degree.[60] In such situations the State may be asked to draw up a proper report within a given deadline. The United Nations Office of the High Commissioner for Human Rights, through its technical co-operation programmes, may be asked to assist the State in this task.

With regard to States which are very much overdue in submitting reports, including initial reports, the Committee has developed a procedure whereby it proceeds with a review of implementation of the Covenant in that country.[61] States which are selected for the application of the process are notified that the consideration will proceed at a future session. If a report is not subsequently submitted or promised, the review proceeds. In situations where no report has ever been received from the State the review is based on as wide a range of information sources as the Committee considers to be appropriate. Reviews take place in public meetings and State representatives, as in the case of consideration of reports, are invited to participate. Reviews conclude with the preparation and publication of Concluding Observations. These Concluding Observations may include a request that the State concerned avail itself of the technical co-operation programmes of the Office of the High Commissioner for Human Rights to assist in its drawing-up of a report for submission to the Committee.

(b) The role of non-governmental organisations[62]

The Secretariat has been asked by the Committee to compile lists of relevant NGOs active within States Parties with a view toward their submissions being solicited when the State's reports are to be considered. It is, accordingly, useful for NGOs to "register" their interest with the Secretariat. In any case, once NGOs become aware that a State's report has been received by the United Nations they should indicate their interest. At this early stage submissions, and, indeed, any other information,[63]

---

[59] United Nations Doc. E/C.12/2000/21 para. 43. For applications in practice of the procedure see *ibid* at paras 572–577.

[60] See, for example, United Nations Doc. E/1995/22, paras. 159–164.

[61] United Nations Doc. E/C.12/2000/21 paras. 47–49. For a discussion of the procedure see M. Craven, *Covenant on Economic, Social and Cultural Rights*, (1995), pp. 57–61.

[62] See further at Chapter 1. See also, V. Dandan, "The Committee on Economic, Social and Cultural Rights and Non-Governmental Organisations", *in The UN Human Rights Treaty System in the 21st Century*, (A.F. Bayefsky, Ed., 2000), pp. 227–230.

[63] Such as press clippings, NGO newsletters, videotapes, reports, academic publications, studies, joint statements, etc. See United Nations Doc. E/C.12/2000/21 Annex V.

may also be forwarded. These submissions and other forms of information will be put to use by the Secretariat in preparing country files and, eventually, country profiles, and by the Country Rapporteur in writing draft lists of issues for eventual consideration by the Working Group. Regarding submissions which are intended for distribution to the Working Group or the Committee it is advisable to submit sufficient copies to the Secretariat and to specifically request that they be distributed to the members. NGOs which are in consultative status with ECOSOC may submit documentation to the Secretariat for translation and publication in the working languages of the Committee.[64] All written submissions received by the Secretariat, at all stages of the reporting process, are made available to the State concerned.[65]

The Committee has also indicated that it encourages NGO to seek the assistance of the Secretariat in order to establish direct contact with Country Rapporteurs[66]

It is very important that NGOs which wish to be invited to make oral submissions to the Working Group so indicate. In so doing, they should indicate their areas of expertise. No financial assistance is provided by the United Nations to assist NGOs in attending the Working Group or, indeed, the Committee. To gain access to the United Nations building in Geneva, contact should first be made with the Secretary of the Committee. On arrival at the meeting room, NGOs should indicate their presence to the Secretariat in order to ensure that they are allowed to enter the private meeting and that they are called on to speak. The length of speaking time given to each NGO usually turns on the amount of pressure on the Working Group's time. In general, however, oral contributions should be kept short and to the point (focusing on the report and on the terms of the Covenant) and provide suggestions for specific questions that the Working Group may consider incorporating in the list of issues with respect to the State concerned. Oral submissions may be made in any of the working languages of the Committee: English, French, Russian or Spanish. If an NGO wishes to employ audio-visual aids it should make the appropriate request to the Secretariat in good time. At the conclusion of the NGO presentations Committee members make comments and may put questions.

Following the meeting of the Working Group, final submissions can be prepared. The submissions should be sent to the Secretariat in good time for their distribution to the members prior to the scheduled dates for consideration by the Committee of the report. At least 24 copies should be provided. The Committee has advised that national NGOs should, to the extent possible, collaborate, co-ordinate and consult when preparing submissions, "to produce a single consolidated submission representing a broad consensus by a number of NGOs. That could be accompanied by shorter, more targeted and detailed submissions by individual NGOs on their own priority areas"[67]

---

[64] Rules of Procedure of the Committee on Economic, Social and Cultural Rights, Rule 69., United Nations Doc. E/C.12/1990/4/Rev.1.

[65] Following a decision of the Committee at its eleventh session. See United Nations Doc. E/1995/22, para. 28.

[66] United Nations Doc. E/C.12/2000/21 Annex V.

[67] United Nations Doc. E/C.12/2000/21 Annex V.

NGOs in consultative status with or on the roster of ECOSOC, may, of course, formally submit documentation for translation into the working languages of the Committee and issuance as a UN document. Such statements should be no more than 2000 words long for NGOs in consultative status or 1500 words long for those in special status or on the roster, and must be submitted to the Secretariat at least three months in advance of the session at which distribution is intended.

At the beginning of each session, in open meetings but without summary records, the Committee hears oral submissions from NGOs concerning States the reports of which are to be considered. Those NGOs which wish to make such submissions should liaise closely with the Secretariat to ensure that they are called on. The Rules of Procedure of the Committee stipulate that such submissions should: (a) focus specifically on the provisions of the Covenant; (b) be of direct relevance to matters under consideration by the Committee; (c) be reliable, and (d) not be abusive.[68] Submissions may be made in the working languages of the Committee.

The Committee has further indicated[69] that NGOs, in oral submissions, may, (a) state their opinion about the State party report: (b) indicate whether or not there was any domestic Government/NGO consultation or co-operation through the reporting process; (c) discuss the main critical points of the NGO submissions; (d) identify prevailing trends relevant to economic, social and cultural rights in the country; (e) present any new information that has become available since the NGO submission was prepared; (f) propose solutions to problems encountered in the implementation of the Covenant; (g) report any positive examples of problem-solving by the Government in implementing the Covenant. States concerned are informed of the presentations by NGOs and are invited to attend as observers.

In circumstances where too many NGOs wish to speak, the Committee Chairperson, in consultation with the Committee Bureau, may choose those organisations which may make a contribution.[70]

NGOs have no right of audience at the Committee meetings at which the report itself is reviewed. However, presence at the meetings permits informal contact with members, provision of updated submissions and other documentation, the channelling of information back to the country and the making of a comprehensive record of the proceedings. Opportunities may also arise for useful meetings with the Government representatives, with international media in Geneva, with OHCHR staff and with the international human rights NGOs.

The role of NGOs in promoting awareness and implementation of Concluding Observations is discussed in general terms in Chapter 1. The Committee on Economic, Social and Cultural Rights has also addressed the issue specifically, as follows, "NGOs can give publicity to the concluding observations locally and nationally, and monitor the Government's performance in implementing the Committee's recommendations. NGOs reporting back to the Committee on the

---

[68] Rule 69 United Nations Doc. HRI/GEN/3 page 25.
[69] United Nations Doc. E/C.12/2000/21 Annex V.
[70] United Nations Doc. E/C.12/1993/WP.14.

basis of their local monitoring and awareness-raising activities would contribute to more effective follow-up on the part of the Committee by keeping it informed of developments in the country after the consideration of the State party report. It would also be useful for local and national NGOs actively involved in the monitoring activities of the Committee to prepare a document on their experiences and on the working methods of the Committee, with comments, advice for other NGOs and suggestions for improvement of the system. Such a document, if distributed widely within the country and sent to the Secretariat of the Committee, would serve as a tool for awareness-raising, and would assist the Committee and the Secretariat in improving their performance"[71]

4. TABLE OF STATES PARTIES INDICATING WHEN A REPORT WAS LAST CONSIDERED AND IS NEXT DUE[72]

State Party	Entry into force	Last report considered	Next report due	Date due or overdue since
Afghanistan	24.04.83	Initial (1991)	2nd–3rd periodic	30.06.95 3
Albania	04.01.92		Initial–2nd periodic	30.06.94
Algeria	12.12.89	2nd periodic* (2001)		
Angola	10.04.92		Initial–2nd periodic	30.06.94
Argentina	08.11.86	2nd periodic (1999)	3rd periodic	30.06.01
Armenia	13.09.93	Initial (1999)	2nd periodic	30.06.00
Australia	10.03.76	3rd periodic (2000)	4th periodic	30.06.05
Austria	10.12.78	2nd periodic (1994)	3rd periodic	30.06.97
Azerbaijan	13.11.92	Initial (1997)	2nd periodic	30.06.99
Bangladesh	05.06.99		Initial	30.06.00
Barbados	03.01.76	Initial (1983)	2nd–3rd periodic	30.06.91
Belarus	03.01.76	3rd periodic (1996)	4th periodic	30.06.99
Belgium	21.07.83	2nd periodic (2000)	3rd periodic	30.06.05
Benin	12.06.92	Initial (2002)*		
Bolivia	12.11.82	Initial (2001)*	2nd periodic	30.06.05
Bosnia and Herzegovina	06.03.92		Initial–2nd periodic	30.06.95
Brazil	24.04.92		Initial–2nd periodic	30.06.94
Bulgaria	03.01.76	3rd periodic (1999)	4th periodic	30.06.99
Burkina Faso	04.04.99		Initial	30.06.00
Burundi	09.08.90		Initial–2nd periodic	30.06.92
Cambodia	26.08.92		Initial–2nd periodic	30.06.94
Cameroon	27.09.84	Initial (1999)	2nd periodic	30.06.01
Canada	19.08.76	3rd periodic (1998)	4th periodic	30.06.00
Cape Verde	06.11.93		Initial–2nd periodic	30.06.95

---

[71] United Nations Doc. E/C.12/2000/21 Annex V.
[72] As of July 2001.

State Party	Entry into force	Last report considered	Next report due	Date due or overdue since
Central African Republic	08.08.81		Initial–3rd periodic	30.06.90
Chad	09.09.95		Initial	08.09.96
Chile	03.01.76	2nd periodic (1988)	3rd–4th periodic	30.06.94
China	27.06.01	Initial (on Hong Kong) (2001)	Initial	30.06.02
Colombia	03.01.76	4th periodic (2001)*		
Congo	05.01.84		Initial–3rd periodic	30.06.90
Costa Rica	03.01.76	Initial (1990)	2nd periodic	30.06.93
			3rd periodic	30.06.98
Croatia	08.10.91	Initial (2001)*		
Cyprus	03.01.76	3rd periodic (1998)	4th periodic	30.06.99
Czech Republic	01.01.93	Initial (2002)*		
Cote d'Ivoire	26.06.92		Initial–2nd periodic	30.06.94
Democratic People's Republic of Korea	14.12.81	Initial (1989)	2nd–3rd periodic	30.06.92
Democratic Republic of the Congo	01.02.77	Initial (1988)	2nd–3rd periodic	30.06.92
Denmark	03.01.76	3rd periodic (1999)	4th periodic	30.06.99
Dominica	17.09.93		Initial–2nd periodic	30.06.95
Dominican Republic	04.04.78	2nd periodic (1997)	3rd periodic	30.06.99
Ecuador	03.01.76	Initial (1990)	2nd–3rd periodic	30.06.92
Egypt	14.04.82	Initial (2000)	2nd–3rd periodic	30.06.95
El Salvador	29.02.80	Initial (1996)	2nd–3rd periodic	30.06.95
Equatorial Guinea	25.12.87		Initial–3rd periodic	30.06.90
Eritrea	17.07.01		Initial	30.06.03
Estonia	21.01.92		Initial–2nd periodic	30.06.94
Ethiopia	11.09.93		Initial–2nd periodic	30.06.95
Finland	03.01.76	4th periodic (2000)	5th periodic	30.06.05
France	04.02.81	2nd periodic (2001)*		
Gabon	21.04.83		Initial–3rd periodic	30.06.90
Gambia	29.03.79		Initial–3rd periodic	30.06.90
Georgia	03.08.94	Initial (2000)	2nd periodic	30.06.01
Germany	03.01.76	4th periodic (2001)*		
Ghana	07.12.00		Initial	30.06.03
Greece	16.08.85		Initial–3rd periodic	30.06.90
Grenada	06.12.91		Initial–2nd periodic	30.06.93
Guatemala	19.08.88	Initial (1996)	2nd–3rd periodic	30.06.95
Guinea	24.04.78		Initial–3rd periodic	30.06.90
Guinea Bissau	02.10.92		Initial–2nd periodic	30.06.94
Guyana	15.05.77	Initial (1995)*	2nd periodic	30.06.00
Honduras	17.05.81	2nd periodic (2001)*		
Hungary	03.01.76	2nd periodic (1992)	3rd–4th periodic	30.06.94
Iceland	22.11.79	2nd periodic (1999)	3rd periodic	30.06.01
India	10.07.79	Initial (1990)	2nd–3rd periodic	30.06.91

State Party	Entry into force	Last report considered	Next report due	Date due or overdue since
Islamic Republic of Iran	03.01.76	Initial (1993) Initial (arts. 6-9) (1977)*	2nd–3rd periodic	30.06.95
Iraq	03.01.76	3rd periodic (1997)	4th periodic	30.06.00
Ireland	08.03.90	2nd periodic (2000)*		
Israel	03.01.92	Initial (1998)	2nd periodic	30.06.99
Italy	15.12.78	3rd periodic (2000)	4th periodic	30.06.01
Jamaica	03.01.76	2nd periodic (2002)*		
Japan	21.09.79	2nd periodic (2001)*		
Jordan	03.01.76	2nd periodic (2000)	3rd periodic	22.01.97
Kenya	03.01.76	Initial (1994)	2nd periodic	30.06.00
Kuwait	21.08.96		Initial	30.06.98
Kyrgyzstan	07.10.94	Initial (2000)	2nd periodic	30.06.05
Latvia	14.07.92		Initial	30.06.94
			2nd periodic	30.06.99
Lebanon	03.01.76	Initial (1993)	2nd–3rd periodic	30.06.95
Lesotho	09.12.92		Initial–2nd periodic	30.06.94
Libyan Arab Jamahiriya	03.01.76	Initial (1997)	2nd–3rd periodic	30.06.95
Liechtenstein	10.03.99		Initial	30.06.01
Lithuania	20.02.92		Initial–2nd periodic	30.06.94
Luxembourg	18.11.83	2nd periodic (1997)	3rd periodic	30.06.98
Madagascar	03.01.76	Initial (1986)	2nd–4th periodic	30.06.90
Malawi	22.03.94		Initial	30.06.96
Mali	03.01.76		Initial–3rd periodic	30.06.90
Malta	13.12.90		Initial–2nd periodic	30.06.92
Mauritius	03.01.76	Initial (1995)	2nd–3rd periodic	30.06.95
Mexico	23.06.81	3rd periodic (1999)	4th periodic	30.06.02
Monaco	28.11.97		Initial	30.06.99
Mongolia	03.01.76	3rd periodic (2000)	4th periodic	30.06.03
Morocco	03.08.79	2nd periodic (2000)	3rd periodic	30.06.04
Namibia	28.02.95		Initial	30.06.97
Nepal	14.08.91	Initial (2000)*		
Netherlands	11.03.79	2nd periodic on Aruba (1998)	3rd periodic	30.06.97
New Zealand	28.03.79	Initial (1993)	2nd–3rd periodic	30.06.95
Nicaragua	12.06.80	Initial (1993)	2nd–3rd periodic	30.06.95
Niger	07.06.86		Initial–3rd periodic	30.06.90
Nigeria	29.10.93	Initial (1998)	2nd periodic	30.06.00
Norway	03.01.76	3rd periodic (1995)	4th periodic	30.06.99
Panama	08.06.77	2nd periodic (2001)*		
Paraguay	10.09.92	Initial (1996)	2nd periodic	30.06.99
Peru	28.07.78	Initial (1997)	2nd periodic	30.06.95
Philippines	03.01.76	Initial (1995)	2nd–3rd periodic	30.06.95
Poland	18.06.77	3rd periodic (1998)		
Portugal	31.10.78	3rd periodic (2000)	4th periodic	30.06.05

State Party	Entry into force	Last report considered	Next report due	Date due or overdue since
Republic of Korea	10.07.90	2nd periodic (2001)*		
Republic of Moldova	26.03.93		Initial–2nd periodic	30.06.95
Romania	03.01.76	2nd periodic (1994)	3rd–4th periodic	30.06.94
Russian Federation	03.01.76	3rd periodic (1997)	4th periodic	30.06.99
Rwanda	03.01.76	Initial (1987)	2nd–4th periodic	30.06.90
Saint Vincent and the Grenadines	09.02.82		Initial–3rd periodic	30.06.90
San Marino	18.01.86		Initial–3rd periodic	30.06.90
Senegal	13.05.78	2nd periodic (2001)*		
Seychelles	05.08.92		Initial–2nd periodic	04.08.93
Sierra Leone	23.11.96		Initial	30.06.98
Slovakia	28.05.93	Initial (2002)*		
Slovenia	06.07.92		Initial–2nd periodic	30.06.94
Solomon Islands	17.03.82		Initial–3rd periodic	30.06.90
Somalia	24.04.90		Initial–2nd periodic	30.06.92
Spain	27.07.77	3rd periodic (1996)	4th periodic	30.06.99
Sri Lanka	11.09.80	Initial (1998)	3rd periodic	30.06.00
Sudan	18.06.86	2nd periodic (1997)	3rd periodic	07.11.01
Suriname	28.03.77	Initial (1995)	2nd–3rd periodic	30.06.95
Sweden	03.01.76	4th periodic (2001)*		
Switzerland	18.09.92	Initial (1998)	2nd periodic	30.06.99
Syrian Arab Republic	03.01.76	3rd periodic (2001)*		
Tajikistan	04.04.99		Initial	30.06.01
Thailand	05.12.99		Initial	30.06.01
Togo	24.08.84		Initial -3rd periodic	30.06.90
Trinidad and Tobago	08.03.79	2nd periodic (2002)*		
Tunisia	03.01.76	2nd periodic (1999)	3rd periodic	30.06.00
Turkmenistan	1.08.97		Initial	30.06.99
Uganda	21.04.87		Initial–3rd periodic	30.06.90
Ukraine	03.01.76	4th periodic (2001)*		
United Kingdom of Great Britain and Northern Ireland	20.08.76	• 3rd periodic on dependent territories • 4th periodic on overseas territories • 4th periodic (2002)*		
United Republic of Tanzania	11.09.76		Initial–3rd periodic	30.06.90
Uruguay	03.01.76	2nd periodic (1997)	3rd periodic	30.06.00
Uzbekistan	28.09.95		Initial	30.06.97
Venezuela	10.08.78	2nd periodic (2001)*		
Vietnam	24.12.82	Initial (1993)	2nd–3rd periodic	30.06.95
Yemen	09.05.87		Initial–3rd periodic	30.06.90
Yugoslavia	03.01.76	2nd periodic (1998)	3rd periodic	30.06.02
Zambia	10.07.84	Initial, art. 10-12 (1986)	Initial–3rd periodic	30.06.90
Zimbabwe	13.08.91	Initial (1997)	2nd periodic	30.06.98

(An asterisk indicates that a report has been submitted but has not yet been considered by the Committee)

5. Days of General Discussion

The Committee usually devotes one day in each session, usually the Monday of its third week, to a general discussion of a particular right or aspect of the Covenant. The Committee has stated that the purpose is "two-fold: the day assists the Committee in developing in greater depth its understanding of the relevant issues; and it enables the Committee to encourage inputs into its work from all interested parties".[73] The discussions have proved useful in deepening the Committee's understanding of its task, in providing an international forum for the exchange of views and, occasionally, in helping formulate general comments. Topics in the past have included the right to adequate food, the right to housing, economic and social indicators, the right to take part in cultural life, the rights of the ageing and elderly, the rights to health, the role of social safety nets, human rights education and public information activities relating to the Covenant, the interpretation and practical application of the obligations incumbent on States parties, a draft optional protocol to the Covenant, revision of the general guidelines for reporting, the normative content of the rights to food, globalisation and its impact on the enjoyment of economic, social and cultural rights, the right to education, and the right of everyone to benefit from the protection of the moral and material interests resulting from any scientific, literary or artistic production of which he is the author.

As well as Committee members, recognised experts and representatives of relevant international and non-governmental organisations are invited to make written and oral interventions. Written submissions, of no more than 15 double-spaced pages in length, which are received by the Secretariat at least three months in advance, will be translated into the working languages of the Committee and issued as UN documents. Days of General Discussion are normally announced a year in advance and the relevant decisions of the Committee can be found in its annual report and on the OHCHR website. NGOs which wish to be invited to make an input to the discussion should contact the Secretariat, indicating their particular competence regarding the chosen theme.

6. Missions[74]

In situations where the Committee considers that its regular procedure of consideration of State party reports or the follow up procedure adopted in 1999 (described above), are not successful in eliciting information from a State Party about implementation of the Covenant, it may, on an exceptional basis, indicate a

---

[73] United Nations Doc. E/C.12/2000/21 para 50.
[74] United Nations Doc. E/C.12/2000/21 paras 44-46.

desire to have its representatives invited to visit a State. Such a decision is made in circumstances where it is considered necessary in order to, (a) collect information necessary for the Committee to continue its dialogue with the State Party and to enable it to carry out its functions in relation to the Covenant, and (b) assist the Committee in exercising its functions under articles 22 and 23 of the Covenant concerning technical assistance and advisory services. Missions may also serve to assess whether a State might benefit from the technical assistance programmes of the United Nations Office of the High Commissioner for Human Rights. The confidential reports of missions are put before the Committee in closed meetings and recommendations are adopted. Both the mission reports and the recommendations are subsequently made public and published.

Once States have agreed to accept a mission of the Committee, NGOs have a role in conveying relevant information to the Secretariat in order to assist it and the relevant Committee members in putting together an appropriate mission programme. NGOs also can greatly enhance the impact of missions by promoting appropriate publicity in the State concerned and encouraging the submission of information to the Committee. To date, there have been two missions of the Committee, both dealing with issues of the right to housing. On one of these occasions the Committee representatives were accompanied at all times by a senior official of an international NGO in the field of housing rights.

7. EXCEPTIONAL ACTION

Outside the regular reporting procedure, NGOs may choose to communicate information of an urgent nature to the Committee, requesting its rapid response thereto. This occurred, for instance, in 1995, when a well-organised coalition of NGOs from one State Party drew to the Committee's attention imminent changes to the social welfare laws which might be construed as detrimental to implementation of the Covenant in that country. Written materials were submitted and the NGOs also sought and obtained the consent of the Committee to address it during the day of the session set aside for NGO submissions. The Committee agreed that its Chairperson would communicate the allegations to the Government and solicit its views on the matter.[75]

8. GENERAL COMMENTS

The Committee continues to elaborate General Comments based on the various articles and provisions of the Covenant with a view to assisting States Parties in fulfilling their reporting obligation, and elucidating the full significance for law and practice of the Covenant. The Committee has acknowledged that the General

---

[75] See United Nations Doc. E/C.12/1995/SRs.4 and 5.

Comments are intended as "authoritative interpretation of the Covenant".[76] By 2001 the Committee had adopted fourteen General Comments. The Committee has indicated that, "(d)uring the stages of the drafting and discussion of a general comment, specialised NGOs can address the Committee in writing. During discussions, NGOs can make short oral statements on specific points of the draft general comment. It is preferred that nay recommendations as to the text of a general comment be presented also in written form (and on electronic diskette) for ease of eventual incorporation in the document"[77]

---

[76] United Nations Doc. E/C.12/2000/21 para 58.
[77] United Nations Doc. E/C.12/2000/21 Annex V.

CHAPTER 4

THE COMMITTEE ON THE ELIMINATION OF RACIAL DISCRIMINATION

1. THE SUBSTANTIVE PROVISIONS OF THE INTERNATIONAL CONVENTION ON THE ELIMINATION OF ALL FORMS OF RACIAL DISCRIMINATION[1]

Article 1

1. *In this Convention, the term "racial discrimination" shall mean any distinction, exclusion, restriction or preference based on race, colour, descent, or national or ethnic origin which has the purpose or effect of nullifying or impairing the recognition, enjoyment or exercise, on an equal footing, of human rights and fundamental freedoms in the political, economic, social, cultural or any other field of public life.*
2. *This Convention shall not apply to distinctions, exclusions, restrictions or preferences made by a State Party to this Convention between citizens and non-citizens.*

---

[1] M. Banton, *International Action Against Racial Discrimination*, (1996); M. O'Flaherty, "Substantive Provisions of the International Convention on the Elimination of All Forms of Racial Discrimination", in *Indigenous Peoples, The United Nations and Human Rights*, (S. Pritchard Ed., 1998) 162–183; N. Lerner, *The U.N. Convention on the Elimination of All Forms of Racial Discrimination*, (1980); N. Lerner, "Curbing Racial Discrimination – Fifteen Years CERD", 13 *Israel Yearbook on Human Rights* (1983), pp. 170–182; J. Symonides, "The United Nations System Standard-Setting Instruments and Programmes to Combat Racism and Racial Discrimination", in *United To Combat Racism*, (UNESCO, 2001); R. Wolfrum, "The Elimination of Racial Discrimination: Achievements and Challenges", in *United To Combat Racism*, (UNESCO, 2001); L. Valencia Rodriguez, "Racial Discrimination in Economic, Social and Cultural Life", in *United To Combat Racism*, (UNESCO, 2001); E. R. Richardson, "Will the Rapidly Accumulating Body of the United Nations Law on Racial Discrimination Truly be Effective?", 64 Am. Soc. Int,'l L. Proc., (1970), pp. 110–114; *Fact Sheet 12, The Committee on the Elimination of Racial Discrimination* (United Nations); L. Valencia Rodriguez, "The International Convention on the Elimination of All Forms of Racial Discrimination", in *Manual on Human Rights Reporting*, (United Nations, 1997) pp. 267–304; T. Meron, *Human Rights Law-making in the United Nations – A Critique of Instruments and Process*, (1986); K. Das, "The International Convention on the Elimination of All Forms of Racial Discrimination", in *The International Dimension of Human Rights*, (K. Vasak and P. Alston, Eds., 1982), pp. 307–330; E. Schwelb, "The International Convention on the Elimination of All Forms of Racial Discrimination", 15 I.C.L.Q., (1966), pp. 996–1068.

3. *Nothing in this Convention may be interpreted as affecting in any way the legal provisions of States Parties concerning nationality, citizenship or naturalization, provided that such provisions do not discriminate against any particular nationality.*

4. *Special measures taken for the sole purpose of securing adequate advancement of certain racial or ethnic groups or individuals requiring such protection as may be necessary in order to ensure such groups or individuals equal enjoyment or exercise of human rights and fundamental freedoms shall not be deemed racial discrimination, provided, however, that such measures do not, as a consequence, lead to the maintenance of separate rights for different racial groups and that they shall not be continued after the objectives for which they were taken have been achieved.*

Note

Three General Recommendations of the Committee address article 1. General Recommendation 8[2] states that membership of a group "shall, if no justification exists to the contrary, be based upon self-identification by the individual concerned." General Recommendation 14[3] indicates that not all forms of discrimination are automatically invidious and that the measure of acceptability is their actual effect. In General Recommendation 24[4] the Committee notes that although States Parties should provide the Committee as far as possible with information on the presence within their territory of such groups, a number of them seem to recognize the presence on their territory of *some* national or ethnic groups or indigenous peoples, while disregarding others. The Committee therefore recommends to adopt criteria which should be uniformly applied to all groups, in particular the number of persons concerned and their being of a race, colour, descent or national or ethnic origin different from the majority or from other groups within the population.

Article 2

1. *States Parties condemn racial discrimination and undertake to pursue by all appropriate means and without delay a policy of eliminating racial discrimination in all its forms and promoting understanding among all races, and, to this end:*

    (a) Each State Party undertakes to engage in no act or practice of racial discrimination against persons, groups of persons or institutions and to en sure that all public authorities and public institutions, national and local, shall act in conformity with this obligation;

    (b) Each State Party undertakes not to sponsor, defend or support racial discrimination by any persons or organizations;

    (c) Each State Party shall take effective measures to review governmental, national and local policies, and to amend, rescind or nullify any laws and regulations which have the effect of creating or perpetuating racial discrimination wherever it exists;

---

[2] United Nations Doc. HRI/GEN/1/Rev.5, p. 180.
[3] United Nations Doc. HRI/GEN/1/Rev.5, p. 183.
[4] United Nations Doc. HRI/GEN/1/Rev.5, p. 193.

(d) Each State Party shall prohibit and bring to an end, by all appropriate means, including legislation as required by circumstances, racial discrimination by any persons, group or organization;

(e) Each State Party undertakes to encourage, where appropriate, integrationist multiracial organizations and movements and other means of eliminating barrier between races, and to discourage anything which tends to strengthen racial division.

2. *States Parties shall, when the circumstances so warrant, take, in the social, economic, cultural and other fields, special and concrete measures to ensure the adequate development and protection of certain racial groups or individuals belonging to them, for the purpose of guaranteeing them the full and equal enjoyment of human rights and fundamental freedoms. These measures shall in no case en tail as a con sequence the maintenance of unequal or separate rights for different racial groups after the objectives for which they were taken have been achieved.*

Note

In General Recommendation 13,[5] the Committee recalls that, in order to guarantee the non-engagement in any practice of racial discrimination by all public authorities and institutions, law enforcement officials should receive intensive training "to ensure that in the performance of their duties they respect as well as protect human dignity and maintain and uphold the human rights of all persons without distinction as to race, colour or national or ethnic origin." In this regard, the standards of the Convention, as well as the Code of Conduct for Law Enforcement Officials (1979), should be fully implemented and information thereupon should be included in the periodic reports to the Committee.

Article 3

States Parties particularly condemn racial segregation and apartheid and undertake to prevent, prohibit and eradicate all practices of this nature in territories under their jurisdiction.

Note

General Recommendation 19[6] invites States Parties to control all tendencies likely to provoke racial segregation, address all the negative consequences which arise therefrom, and report fully on these matters in their periodic reports to the Committee.

---

[5] United Nations Doc. HRI/GEN/1/Rev.5, p. 183.
[6] United Nations Doc. HRI/GEN/1/Rev.5, p. 188.

Article 4

States Parties condemn all propaganda and all organizations which are based on ideas or theories of superiority of one race or group of persons of one colour or ethnic origin, or which attempt to justify or promote racial hatred and discrimination in any form, and undertake to adopt immediate and positive measures designed to eradicate all incitement to, or acts of, such discrimination and, to this end, with due regard to the principles embodied in the Universal Declaration of Human Rights and the rights expressly set forth in article 5 of this Convention, inter alia:

(a) Shall declare an offence punishable by law all dissemination of ideas based on racial superiority or hatred, incitement to racial discrimination, as well as all acts of violence or incitement to such acts against any race or group of persons of another colour or ethnic origin, and also the provision of any assistance to racist activities, including the financing thereof;

(b) Shall declare illegal and prohibit organizations and also organized and all other propaganda activities, which promote and incite racial discrimination, and shall recognize participation in such organizations or activities as an offence punishable by law;

(c) Shall not permit public authorities or public institutions, national or local, to promote or incite racial discrimination.

Note

In its General Recommendation 15[7] the Committee reminds States both of the mandatory nature of the article and of the obligation not only to establish certain criminal laws but also to ensure that the laws are effectively enforced. The General Recommendation also states that the prohibition of the dissemination of all ideas based upon racial superiority or hatred is compatible with the right to freedom of opinion and expression.

Article 5

In compliance with the fundamental obligations laid down in article 2 of this Convention, States Parties undertake to prohibit and to eliminate racial discrimination in all its forms and to guarantee the right of everyone, without distinction as to race, colour, or national or ethnic origin, to equality before the law, notably in the enjoyment of the following rights

(a) The right to equal treatment before the tribunals and all other organs administering justice;

(b) The right to security of person and protection by the State against violence or bodily harm, whether inflicted by government officials or by any individual group or institution;

(c) Political rights, in particular the right to participate in elections-to vote and to

---

[7]   United Nations Doc. HRI/GEN/1/Rev.5, p. 184.

> stand for election-on the basis of universal and equal suffrage, to take part in the
> Government as well as in the conduct of public affairs at any level and to have
> equal access to public service;
>
> *(d) Other civil rights, in particular:*
>> *(i)* The right to freedom of movement and residence within the border of the
>> State;
>> *(ii)* The right to leave any country, including one's own, and to return to one's
>> country;
>> *(iii)* The right to nationality;
>> *(iv)* The right to marriage and choice of spouse;
>> *(v)* The right to own property alone as well as in association with others;
>> *(vi)* The right to inherit;
>> *(vii)* The right to freedom of thought, conscience and religion;
>> *(viii)* The right to freedom of opinion and expression;
>> *(ix)* The right to freedom of peaceful assembly and association;
>
> *(e) Economic, social and cultural rights, in particular:*
>> *(i)* The rights to work, to free choice of employment, to just and favourable
>> conditions of work, to protection against unemployment, to equal pay for
>> equal work, to just and favourable remuneration;
>> *(ii)* The right to form and join trade unions;
>> *(iii)* The right to housing;
>> *(iv)* The right to public health, medical care, social security and social services;
>> *(v)* The right to education and training;
>> *(vi)* The right to equal participation in cultural activities;
>
> *(f)* The right of access to any place or service intended for use by the general public,
> such as transport hotels, restaurants, cafes, theatres and parks.

Note

General Recommendation 13[8] restates that the obligation in article 5 is to ensure rights "to everyone". However, in General Recommendation 20,[9] the Committee notes that whereas many of the rights and freedoms mentioned in article 5, such as the right to equal treatment before tribunals, are to be enjoyed by *all* persons living in a given State; others such as the right to participate in elections, to vote and to stand for election are the rights of *citizens*. The Committee also observes that article 5, apart from requiring a guarantee that the exercise of human rights shall be free from racial discrimination, does not of itself create civil, political, economic, social or cultural rights, but assumes the existence and recognition of these rights. The Convention obliges States to prohibit and eliminate racial discrimination in the enjoyment of such human rights.[10]

In 1996, following the occurrence of numerous ethnic conflicts resulting in

---

[8] United Nations Doc. HRI/GEN/1/Rev.5, p. 183.
[9] United Nations Doc. HRI/GEN/1/Rev.5, p. 189.
[10] United Nations Doc. HRI/GEN/1/Rev.5, p. 188.

massive flows of refugees, the Committee passed General Recommendation 22,[11] emphasizing that all refugees and displaced persons have the right freely to return to their homes of origin under conditions of safety and that their return must be voluntary and subject to the principle of *non-refoulement*. Moreover, after their return they have the right to have restored to them their property of which they were deprived during the conflict, as well as to be compensated for any such property that cannot be restored. Their return must also correspond to a full reintegration into public life, equating to the right to participate in public affairs and to receive rehabilitation services.

Article 6

States Parties shall assure to everyone within their jurisdiction effective protection and remedies, through the competent national tribunals and other State institutions, against any acts of racial discrimination which violate his human rights and fundamental freedoms contrary to this Convention, as well as the right to seek from such tribunals just and adequate reparation or satisfaction for any damage suffered as a result of such discrimination.

Note

In relation to gender related discrimination, the Committee notes[12] that since there are circumstances in which racial discrimination only or primarily affects women, or affects women in a different way, or to a different degree than men, it is necessary that States Parties describe factors affecting and difficulties experienced in ensuring the equal enjoyment by women, free from racial discrimination, of rights under the Convention.

In General Recommendation 26[13] the Committee notes that the degree to which acts of racial discrimination and racial insults damage the injured party's perception of his/her own worth and reputation should not be underestimated. It further notifies States Parties that the right to seek reparation for any damage suffered is not necessarily secured solely by the punishment of the perpetrator of the discrimination, but may be also secured by awarding financial compensation.

Article 7

States Parties undertake to adopt immediate and effective measures, particularly in the fields of teaching, education, culture and information, with a view to combating prejudices which lead to racial discrimination and to promoting understanding, tolerance and friendship among nations and racial or ethnical groups, as well as to propagating the purposes and principles of the Charter of the United Nations, the

---

[11] United Nations Doc. HRI/GEN/1/Rev.5, p. 191.
[12] General Recommendation 25, in United Nations Doc. HRI/GEN/1/Rev.5, p. 194.
[13] United Nations Doc. HRI/GEN/1/Rev.5, p. 195.

Universal Declaration of Human Rights, the United Nations Declaration on the Elimination of All Forms of Racial Discrimination, and this Convention.

Note

General Recommendation 5[14] reminds States of the mandatory nature of the article even in States which hold that they experience no problems of racial discrimination. In General Recommendation 13,[15] States are called upon to "review and improve the training of law enforcement officials so that the standards of the Convention, as well as the Code of Conduct for Law Enforcement Officials (1979) are fully implemented". The Reporting Guidelines draw attention, *inter alia*, to the crucial role played by the media in achieving the objectives of the article.[16]

2. THE COMMITTEE ON THE ELIMINATION OF RACIAL DISCRIMINATION[17]

The Committee is established pursuant to the provisions of article 8 of the Convention. There are 18 members, elected by the States Parties for terms of four

---

[14] United Nations Doc. HRI/GEN/1/Rev.5, p. 177.

[15] United Nations Doc. HRI/GEN/1/Rev.5, p. 183.

[16] United Nations Doc. CERD/C/70/Rev. 4. See also General Comment 27, United Nations Doc. HRI/GEN/1/Rev.5, p.199.

[17] M. Banton, *International Action Against Racial Discrimination*, (1996); M. Banton, "Effective Implementation of the United Nations Racial Convention", *New Community*, 20 (3), 475–487; R. Wolfrum, "The Elimination of Racial Discrimination: Achievements and Challenges", in *United To Combat Racism*, (UNESCO, 2001); M. O'Flaherty, "The Committee on the Elimination of Racial Discrimination as an Implementation Agency", in *Anti-Discrimination Law Enforcement – A Comparative Perspective*, (MacEwen Ed. 1997) 209–233; M. Banton, "Decision-making in the Committee on the Elimination of Racial Discrimination", in *The Future of UN Human Rights Treaty Monitoring*, (P. Alston and J. Crawford Eds., 2000) 55–78; S. Guillet, *Nous, Peuples des Nations Unies – L'action des ONG au sein système de protection international des droits de l'homme*, (1995), pp. 70–71; K. Partsch, "The Racial Discrimination Committee", in *The United Nations and Human Rights*, (P. Alston Ed. 1992), pp. 339–368; N. Benard-Maugiron, "Twenty Years After: Thirty-eighth session of the Committee on the Elimination of Racial Discrimination), *Netherlands Quarterly of Human Rights*, Vol.8, (1990), pp. 395–415; J. Gomez del Prado, "United Nations Conventions on Human Rights: The Practice of the Human Rights Committee and the Committee on the Elimination of Racial Discrimination in Dealing with Reporting Obligations of States Parties", 7 Hum. Rts. Q., (1986), pp. 492–513; N. Lerner, "Curbing Racial Discrimination – Fifteen Years CERD", 13 *Israel Yearbook on Human Rights* (1983), pp. 170–182; E. R. Richardson, "Will the Rapidly Accumulating Body of the United Nations Law on Racial Discrimination Truly be Effective?", 64 Am. Soc. Int,'l L. Proc., (1970), pp. 110–114; A. F. Bayefsky, "Making the Human Rights Treaties Work" in *Human Rights: An Agenda for the Next Century*, (L. Henkin and J. L. Hargrove, Eds., 1994), pp. 229–296; *Fact Sheet 12, The Committee on the Elimination of Racial Discrimination* (United Nations). See, generally, the following studies by P. Alston, *Long Term Approaches to Enhancing the Effectiveness of the United Nations Human Rights Treaty Bodies*, United Nations Doc. A/44/668; *Interim Report on Updated Study*, United Nations Doc. A/CONF.157/PC/62/Add.11/Rev.1; *Final Report on Enhancing the Long Term Effectiveness of the United Nations Human Rights Treaty System*, United Nations Doc. E/CN.4/1997/74; and, also, A. Bayefsky, *Report: The UN Human Rights Treaty System: Universality at the Crossroads*, (2001); P. Alston and J. Crawford Eds., *The Future of UN Human Rights Treaty Monitoring*, (2000); A. Bayefsky, Ed., *The UN Human Rights System in the 21st Century*, (2000).

years.[18] Members, though all nominated by States Parties, serve in their private capacities and make a solemn declaration of impartiality upon taking up office. The Committee presently meets twice each year, in March and August, for sessions of three to four working weeks each. All sessions now take place in Geneva. Secretariat services are provided by the United Nations Office of the High Commissioner for Human Rights.[19]

Four of the activities of the Committee are of particular interest for NGOs and individuals: the reporting procedure, the "early warning and urgent procedure", the consideration of communications from individuals or groups of individuals under article 14, and the recently inaugurated "thematic discussions".

3. THE REPORTING PROCEDURE[20]

(a) The obligation on the State

Under article 9 of the Convention, States are obliged to submit reports to CERD one year after the Convention comes into effect for the State and thereafter every two years, on the legislative, judicial, administrative or other measures which they have adopted and which give effect to the provisions of the Convention.[21]

States which are overdue in submitting a number of reports may consolidate these in one document for submission to the Committee.[22] Also, the Committee has attempted to ameliorate the two-year periodicity rule by occasionally stipulating, on

---

[18] Membership as of 2001 (one vacancy): Mahmoud Aboul-Nasr (Egypt), Patrick Thornberry (United Kingdom of Great Britain and Northern Ireland), Marc Bossuyt (Belgium), Gabrielle Britz (Germany), Ion Diaconu (Romania), Régis de Gouttes (France), Francois Lonseny Fall (Guinea), Patricia Nozipho January-Bardill (South Africa), Carlos Lechuga Hevia (Cuba), Gay McDougall (United States of America), Raghavan Vasudevan Pillai (India),Yuri A. Rechetov (Russian Federation), Agha Shahi (Pakistan), Michael E. Sherifis (Cyprus), Luis Valencia Rodriguez (Ecuador), Tang Chengyuan (China). Mario Jorge Yutzis (Argentina).

[19] Secretariat of CERD, Support Services Branch, Office of the High Commissioner for Human Rights, UNOG, 1211 Geneva 10, Switzerland (Tel.: 41 22 917 1234; Fax 41 22 917 0099).

[20] Article 9, ICERD; Rules of Procedure of the Committee on the Elimination of Racial Discrimination, Rules 63–68, United Nations Doc. HRI/GEN/3; S. Guillet, *Nous, Peuples des Nations Unies – L'action des ONG au sein su système de protection international des droits de l'homme*, (1995), pp. 70–71; K. English and A. Stapleton, *The Human Rights Handbook – A Practical Guide to Monitoring Human Rights*, (1995), pp. 179–180; M. R. Burrowes, "Implementing the United Nations Racial Convention: Some Procedural Aspects", 7 Australian YB Int'l L., (1981), pp. 236–278; I. Dore, "United Nations Measures to Combat Racial Discrimination: Progress and Problems in Retrospect", 10 Den. J. Int'l L. & Pol., (1981) pp. 299–330; T. Buergenthal, "Implementing the United Nations Racial Convention", 12 Tex. Int'l L. J., (1977), pp. 187–221; K. Das, "Measures of Implementation of the International Convention on the Elimination of All Forms of Racial Discrimination with Special Reference to the Provisions Concerning Reports from States Parties to the Convention", 4 Rev. des droits de l'homme, (1971), pp. 313–362.

[21] See, L. Valencia Rodriguez, "The International Convention on the Elimination of All Forms of Racial Discrimination", in *Manual on Human Rights Reporting*, (United Nations, 1997) pp. 267–304;.

[22] See, e.g., Report of the Committee on the Elimination of Racial Discrimination, United Nations Doc. A/55/18, para. 24.

the occasion of the examination of a report, that the next report be of an updating rather than a comprehensive nature.[23] Furthermore, in its most recent sessions, the Committee has adopted a revised procedure, as follows, "(I)n a case where the period between the date of the examination of the last periodic report and the scheduled date for submission of the next periodic report is less than two years, the Committee may suggest in its concluding observations that the State party concerned, if it so wishes, submits the latter report jointly with the periodic report to be submitted at the following date fixed in accordance with article 9 of ICERD".[24] This revision is not reflected in the Rules of Procedure.

Consonant with the State's implementation obligation as stated in the Convention, the Committee, in its Reporting Guidelines,[25] has indicated that the reporting requirement is a substantial one requiring that the report provide exhaustive information on implementation of the Convention (taking account of both its provisions and the General Recommendations and Decisions adopted by the Committee[26]) and that it comprehensively indicate the actual situation within the State even with regard to issues and circumstances which may appear to be beyond the appropriate or normal purview of governmental interference. The Committee requests that copies be provided of all relevant legislation, judicial decisions and regulations.[27] Reports must also contain detailed information concerning the racial and ethnic configuration of society. Following additions to the Reporting Guidelines, adopted in 1999 and 2000, it is stipulated that, "(T)he inclusion of information on the situation of women is important for the Committee to consider whether racial discrimination has an impact upon women different from that upon men, in conformity with General Recommendation XXV on gender-related dimensions of racial discrimination (2000). Reporting officers are asked to describe, as far as possible in quantitative and qualitative terms, factors affecting and difficulties experienced in ensuring for women the equal enjoyment, free from racial discrimination, of rights under the Convention. It is also difficult to protect against

---

[23] At its thirty-eighth session in 1988, the Committee decided to accept the proposal of the States Parties that States Parties submit a comprehensive report every four years and a brief updating report in the two-year interim (see L. Valencia Rodriguez,"The International Convention on the Elimination of All Forms of Racial Discrimination", in *Manual on Human Rights Reporting*, (United Nations, 1997) pp. 267–304; and United Nations Doc A/51/18 at para 591. However, this practice has not been followed in all cases.

[24] United Nations Docs. CERD/C/SR.1446 and CERD/C/SR.1454 (Proposal of Mr. Bossuyt).

[25] United Nations Doc. HRI/GEN/2/Rev.1 pp. 32–40. See K. Partsch "The Racial Discrimination Committee", in *The United Nations and Human Rights* (P. Alston Ed. 1992) pp. 350–351). For an elucidation of the reporting obligations with regard to each article of the Convention see L. Valencia Rodriguez, ,"The International Convention on the Elimination of All Forms of Racial Discrimination", in *Manual on Human Rights Reporting*, (United Nations, 1997) pp. 267–304 . The first part of reports should also comply with the consolidated guidelines relating to the preparation of the initial part of reports under the various international human rights instruments. See United Nations Doc. HRI/CORE/1.

[26] These are contained in United Nations Doc. HRI/GEN/1/Rev.5.

[27] L. Valencia Rodriguez, "The International Convention on the Elimination of All Forms of Racial Discrimination", in *Manual on Human Rights Reporting*, (United Nations, 1997) pp. 267–304.

racial discrimination the rights of persons, both women and men, who belong to vulnerable groups, such as indigenous persons, migrants, and those in the lowest socio-economic categories. Members of such groups often experience complex forms of disadvantage which persist over generations and in which racial discrimination is mixed with other causes of social inequality. Reporting officers are asked to bear in mind the circumstances of such persons, and to cite any available social indicators of forms of disadvantage that may be linked with racial discrimination".[28]

In reporting regarding implementation of article 5 of the Convention, the Reporting Guidelines state that, for situations where quantitative data relevant to the enjoyment of the rights is unobtainable, "it may be appropriate to report the opinions of representatives of disadvantaged groups"[29]

(b) The procedure

i. The scheduling process

Reports once submitted can be expected to be taken up by the Committee within one year. Some three months before each session the list of reports to be considered is settled and posted on the OHCHR website. It is unusual, though not unknown, for the scheduling to be changed after this point. More common, however, are adjustments in the timetabling within sessions. Such changes sometimes occur during sessions and with very little advance notice. State party reports, once published as United Nations documents, can be ordered from the United Nations Documents Distribution and Sales Section. The symbol number can be obtained from the Secretariat. Reports are usually available in all of the working languages of the Committee (English, French, Spanish and Russian). Reports are also posted on the OHCHR website.

ii. Before the session

Each report receives the attention of a member designated as Country Rapporteur.[30] The Country Rapporteur is expected to undertake a detailed analysis of the report in preparation for the consideration by the Committee and to both identify key issues and prepare questions and comments to be put to the representatives of the Government. Country Rapporteurs base their analysis on the report itself, previous reports of the State, the records of the Committee's consideration of previous reports, and any other information, regardless of source, which the Country Rapporteur considers to be of use.

Occasionally, Country Rapporteurs make their lists of issues and questions available to the States concerned and to interested NGOs prior to the Committee's consideration. There is, however, no standard practice in this regard.

---

[28] United Nations Doc. HRI/GEN/2/Rev.1 pp. 33–34.
[29] United Nations Doc. HRI/GEN/2/Rev.1 p. 36.
[30] See M. O'Flaherty, "The Committee on the Elimination of Racial Discrimination as an Implementation Agency", in *Anti-Discrimination Law Enforcement – A Comparative Perspective* (MacEwen Ed. 1997) 209–233.

iii. Consideration by the Committee

Reports are considered by the Committee in public sessions and in dialogue with representatives of the State,[31] usually over two consecutive three-hour meetings. Reports are introduced by representatives of the Government who will often use the occasion to provide further information or elaborate on aspects of the report. The Country Rapporteur then takes the floor and typically presents an exhaustive analysis regarding the entire report and all relevant provisions of the Convention. Whichever of the members who wish then pose their questions or make comments. Once the members have spoken the representative has the opportunity to reply. Usually, representatives will reply to a number of the questions posed and undertake to provide outstanding answers either in the form of additional information or in the next report. The exchange between Committee and representatives ends with the concluding remarks of the Country Rapporteur and the members.

Later in the session of the Committee at which a State Party report has been considered, the Committee adopts its "Concluding Observations". The Concluding Observations, the first draft of which is prepared by the Country Rapporteur with the assistance of the Secretariat, comprises a critique of the State report and of the response of the State representative to the scrutiny of the Committee, noting positive factors, drawing attention to matters of concern and making recommendations.[32] Uniquely among treaty bodies, CERD has decided (at its forty-seventh session in 1995) to consider and adopt Concluding Observations in meetings open to the public. Concluding Observations are presently issued as public documents twenty-four hours after adoption (they can be adopted at any time during a Committee session), are included in the annual report to the General Assembly of the United Nations, and are posted on the OHCHR website (initially solely in the language of adoption).

(c) The role of non-governmental organisations[33]

NGOs do not have formal standing under the reporting procedure. Thus, they may not have their documents received and processed as "United Nations documents" and they may not formally address the proceedings. NGOs do however have a wide range of opportunities to convey information informally to Committee members and thus to influence proceedings.[34]

Once a State's report has been scheduled for consideration NGOs should indicate

---

[31] Rules of Procedure of the Committee on the Elimination of Racial Discrimination, Rules 63–68, United Nations Doc. HRI/GEN/3 pp. 84–85.

[32] A sample of Concluding Observations (for The Netherlands) is reproduced in Appendix II.

[33] See further at Chapter 1. See, also, M. O'Flaherty, "The Committee on the Elimination of Racial Discrimination: Non-governmental Input and the Early Warning and Urgent Procedure", in *Indigenous Peoples, The United Nations and Human Rights*, (S. Pritchard Ed., 1998) 151–160.

[34] The Committee, in Decision 1 (XI) of 1991 stated that, "members of the Committee must have access, as independent experts, to all (other) available sources of information, governmental and non-governmental". See United Nations Doc. A/51/18 para 594.

their interest to the Secretariat and send as much preliminary material as possible for transmission to the Country Rapporteur and other members. Rather than rely on the Secretariat to copy these, multiple copies should be sent. Certain Country Rapporteurs and members may also be happy to establish direct contact with NGOs.

Some weeks before the session NGOs should send to the Secretariat a final version of their written submission with the request that it be distributed to members. At least 20 copies should be provided.

NGOs may also choose to send copies of their submissions to a specialised NGO in Geneva, the Anti-Racism Information Service (ARIS),[35] which exists to facilitate transmission of information to and from the Committee. ARIS summarises information made available to it and furnishes the summaries to members together with a clear citation of the source of the information. The existence of ARIS, however, in no way precludes NGOs from directly approaching Committee members.

If at all possible, NGOs should send representatives to attend the Committee meetings. Presence at the meetings permits informal contact with members, provision of updated submissions and other documentation, the channelling of information back to the country and the making of a comprehensive record of the proceedings. Opportunities may also arise for useful meetings with the Government representatives, with international media in Geneva, with OHCHR staff and with the international human rights NGOs.

Meetings with members can either take place on an individual basis or in the form of an informal group meeting with those members willing to attend. The Secretariat has, in the past, been willing to facilitate such meetings through the booking of a room, etc., and ARIS can also be of great assistance in this regard. If NGOs anticipate holding such meetings they should first endeavour to co-ordinate their activities to ensure that a range of matters can be put to the members at the same time. It should be borne in mind that at such informal meetings no interpretation facilities will be provided and no records will be kept.

Access to the United Nations buildings in Geneva can be arranged in advance with the Secretary of the Committee.

The role of NGOs following the conclusion of the Committee proceedings is described in chapter one.

4. THE PROCEDURE FOR EXAMINING STATES THE REPORTS OF WHICH ARE SERIOUSLY OVERDUE

CERD has developed a procedure[36] whereby it will proceed with consideration of the situation in a State which is seriously overdue in its reporting obligation. In order to comply with article 9 of the Convention, the Committee states that the basis for the consideration is the last report submitted. In the case of States which have not

---

[35] ARIS (Anti-Racist Information Service), 14 avenue Trembley, 1209 Geneva, Switzerland.
[36] See United Nations Doc. A/51/18, paras 601–608.

submitted an initial report the Committee considers as an initial report all information submitted by the State party to other organs of the United Nations or, in the absence of such material, reports and information prepared by organs of the United Nations. The procedure was devised by CERD to indicate to recalcitrant States that they could not totally avoid the Committee's scrutiny and it has been surprisingly successful in drawing States back into the reporting cycle. Thus, during 1999-2000, three of the fours States which the Committee announced would be subject to the procedure actually submitted their overdue reports. The fourth State indicated its intention to submit its overdue reports shortly.[37]

The practice of CERD further allows for what is called a "second-round review" of States parties in situations where no report has been received from the State party five years after the initial consideration under the above procedure.[38]

The role of NGOs in this procedure is no different to that under the regular reporting process. Indeed, information provided by them may have even greater impact in that the State will not have made its contribution and the members will, in general, have access to a rather small range of information sources.

A number of considerations are scheduled in each session and the identity of the countries and the assigned dates usually becomes available at the same time as the list of States to be considered under the regular report procedure. Timetabling is, however, uncertain in that deferrals may occur on short notice either because a State promises to speedily send a report or due to pressure of the Committee's other business.

Each State is assigned a Country Rapporteur who fulfils a similar role to that under the regular reporting procedure both in closely examining the situation of the country and in leading the discussion in the Committee. The discussion itself is usually confined to less than one meeting. Brief Concluding Observations are subsequently issued.[39]

---

[37] United Nations Doc. A/55/18 para 474. See M. O'Flaherty, "The Committee on the Elimination of Racial Discrimination as an Implementation Agency", in *Anti-Discriminatory Law Enforcement – A Comparative Perspective* (MacEwen Ed. 1997) 209–233.

[38] United Nations Doc. A/55/18 para 606.

[39] A vigorous and enhanced application of the procedure, in the case of Liberia in 2001, occurred too late for consideration. See CERD Decision 2 (59) of 14 August 2001, in United Nations Doc. CERD/C/59/CRP.1/Add.17.

5. TABLE OF STATES PARTIES INDICATING WHEN A REPORT WAS LAST CONSIDERED AND IS NEXT DUE[40]

State Party	Entry into force	Last report considered	Next report due	Date due or overdue since
Afghanistan	05.08.83	Initial (1984)	2nd–9th periodic.	05.08.86
Albania	10.06.94		Initial–3rd periodic	10.06.95
Algeria	15.03.72	13th–14th periodic (2001)	15th periodic	15.03.01
Antigua and Bermuda	25.10.88		Initial–6th periodic	24.11.89
Argentina	04.01.69	15th periodic (2001)	16th periodic	04.01.00
Armenia	23.07.93	Initial–2nd periodic (1998)	3rd–4th periodic	23.07.98
Australia	30.10.75	10th - 12th periodic (2000)	13th periodic	30.10.00
Austria	08.06.72	14th periodic (2000)*	15th periodic	08.06.01
Azerbaijan	15.09.96	Initial, 2nd periodic (1999)	3rd periodic	15.09.01
Bahamas	05.08.75	3rd–4th periodic (1983)	5th–13th periodic	04.09.84
Bahrain	26.04.90	Initial–5th periodic (2000)	6th periodic	26.04.01
Bangladesh	11.07.79	7th–11th periodic (2001)	12th periodic	11.07.02
Barbados	08.12.72	7th periodic (1991)	8th–12th periodic	08.12.87
Belarus	08.05.69	14th periodic (1997)	15th–16th periodic	05.05.98
Belgium	06.09.75	11th–13th periodic (2002)*	14th periodic	06.09.02
Bolivia	22.10.70	8th–13th periodic (1996)	14th–15th periodic	21.10.97
Bosnia and Herzegovina	16.07.93		Initial–4th periodic	16.07.94
Botswana	22.03.74	3rd–5th periodic (1984)	6th–14th periodic	22.03.85
Brazil	04.01.69	10th–13th periodic (1996)	14th–16th periodic	04.01.96
Bulgaria	04.01.69	12th–14th periodic (1997)	15th–16th periodic	04.01.98
Burkina Faso	17.08.74	6th–11th periodic (1997)	12th periodic	17.08.99
Burundi	26.11.77	7th–10th periodic (1997)	11th–12th periodic	26.11.98
Cambodia	28.12.83	2nd–7th periodic (1998)	8th–9th periodic	28.12.00
Cameroon	24.07.71	10th–14th periodic (1998)	14th periodic	24.07.00
Canada	15.11.70	11th–12th periodic (1994)	13th–15th periodic	13.11.99
Cape Verde	02.11.79	2nd periodic (1984)	3rd- 9th periodic	02.11.84
Central African Republic	15.04.71	7th periodic (1986)	8th–15th periodic	15.04.86
Chad	16.09.77	5th–9th periodic (1995)	10th–12th periodic	16.09.96
Chile	19.11.71	11th–14th periodic (1999)	15th periodic	19.11.00
China	28.01.82	8th–9th periodic (2001)*	10th periodic	28.01.01
Colombia	02.10.81	8th–9th periodic (1999)	10th periodic	02.10.00
Congo	10.08.89		Initial–6th periodic	10.08.89
Costa Rica	04.01.69	16th periodic (2002)*	17th periodic	04.01.02
Cote d'Ivoire	03.02.73	2nd–4th periodic (1981)	5th–14th periodic	03.02.82
Croatia	08.10.91	4th periodic (2000)*	5th periodic	08.10.02
Cuba	16.03.72	10th–13th periodic (1998)	14th–15th periodic	16.03.99

---

[40] As of July 2001.

State Party	Entry into force	Last report considered	Next report due	Date due or overdue since
Cyprus	04.01.69	15th–16th periodic (2001)*	17th periodic	04.01.2002
Czech Republic	01.01.93	3rd–4th periodic (2000)	4th periodic	01.01.00
Democratic Republic of the Congo	21.05.76	10th periodic (1996)	11th–12th periodic	21.05.97
Denmark	08.01.72	15th periodic (2001)*	16th periodic	08.01.03
Dominican Republic	24.06.83	4th–8th periodic (1999)	9th periodic	24.06.00
Ecuador	04.01.69	13th–15th periodic (2000)*	16th periodic	04.01.00
Egypt	04.01.69	13th –16th periodic (2000)*	17th periodic	04.01.02
El Salvador	30.12.79	3rd–8th periodic (1995)	9th- 11th periodic	30.12.96
Estonia	20.11.91	Initial–4th periodic (2000)	5th periodic	20.11.00
Ethiopia	23.07.76	6th periodic (1990)	7th–12th periodic	23.07.89
Fiji	11.01.73	5th periodic (1983)	6th–14th periodic	11.01.84
Finland	13.08.70	15th periodic (2000)	16th periodic	13.08.01
France	27.08.71	12th–14th periodic (2000)	15th periodic	27.08.00
Gabon	30.03.80	2nd–9th periodic (1998)	10th–11th periodic	30.03.99
Gambia	28.01.79	Initial (1982)	2nd–11th periodic	28.01.82
Georgia	02.07.99	Initial (2001)	2nd periodic	02.07.02
Germany	15.06.69	15th periodic (2001)	17th periodic	15.06.00
Ghana	04.01.69	12th–15th periodic (2000)	16th periodic	04.01.00
Greece	18.07.70	12th–15th periodic (2001)	16th periodic	18.07.01
Guatemala	17.02.83	7th periodic (1997)	8th–9th periodic	17.02.00
Guinea	13.04.77	2nd–11th periodic (1999)	12th periodic	13.04.00
Guyana	17.03.77		Initial–12th periodic	17.03.78
Haiti	18.01.73	10th–13th periodic (1999)	14th periodic	18.01.00
Holy See	31.05.69	13th–15th periodic (2000)	16th periodic	31.05.00
Hungary	04.01.69	11th–13th periodic (1996)	14th–16th periodic	04.01.96
Iceland	04.01.69	15th periodic (1999)*	17th periodic	04.01.02
India	04.01.69	10th–14th periodic	15th–16th periodic	04.01.98
Indonesia	25.07.99		Initial	25.07.00
Islamic Republic of Iran	04.01.69	9th–12th periodic (1993)	16th periodic	04.01.00
Iraq	13.02.70	14th periodic (1999)	15th–16th periodic	13.02.99
Israel	02.02.79	7th–9th periodic (1998)	10th–11th periodic	02.02.98
Italy	04.02.76	12th- 13th periodic (2001) *	14th periodic	04.02.03
Jamaica	04.07.71	5th–7th periodic (1985)	8th- 15th periodic	04.07.86
Japan	14.01.96	Initial–2nd periodic (2001)	3rd periodic	14.01.01
Jordan	29.06.74	9th–12th periodic (1998)	13th periodic	29.06.99
Kazakhstan	26.09.98		Initial	26.09.00
Kuwait	04.01.69	13th–14th periodic (1999)	15th–16th periodic	04.01.98
Kyrgyzstan	05.10.97	Initial (1999)	2nd periodic	05.10.00
Lao People's Democratic Republic	24.03.74	3rd–5th periodic (1985)	6th–14th periodic	24.03.85
Latvia	14.05.92	Initial–3rd periodic (1999)	4th periodic	14.05.99

State Party	Entry into force	Last report considered	Next report due	Date due or overdue since
Lebanon	12.12.71	6th–13th periodic (1998)	14th–15th periodic	12.12.00
Lesotho	04.12.71	7th–14th periodic (2000)	15th periodic	04.12.00
Liberia	05.12.76		Initial–12th periodic	05.12.77
Libyan Arab Jamahiriya	04.01.69	11th–14th periodic (1998)	14th–16th periodic	04.01.98
Liechtenstein	31.03.00	Initial (2002)*	2nd periodic	01.03.03
Lithuania	09.01.99	Initial (2001)*	2nd periodic	09.01.02
Luxembourg	31.05.78	9th periodic (1997)	10th–11th periodic	31.05.99
Madagascar	09.03.69	9th periodic (1989)	10th–15th periodic	09.03.90
Malawi	11.07.96		Initial–2nd periodic	11.07.97
Maldives	24.05.84	3rd–4th periodic (1992)	5th–8th periodic	24.05.93
Mali	15.08.74	5th–6th periodic (1986)	7th–13th periodic	15.08.87
Malta	26.06.71	13th–14th periodic (2000)	15th periodic	26.06.00
Mauritania	12.01.89	Initial–5th periodic (1999)	6th periodic	12.01.00
Mauritius	29.06.72	13th –14th periodic (2000)	15th periodic	29.06.99
Mexico	22.03.75	11th periodic (1997)	12th–13th periodic	22.03.00
Monaco	27.09.95		Initial–3rd periodic	27.10.96
Mongolia	05.09.69	11th–15th periodic (1999)	16th–17th periodic	05.09.00
Morocco	17.01.71	12th–13th periodic (1998)	13th periodic	17.01.96
Mozambique	18.05.83	Initial (1984)	2nd–9th periodic	18.05.00
Namibia	11.12.82	4th–7th periodic (1996)	8th - 9th periodic	11.12.97
Nepal	01.03.71	14th periodic (2000)	15th periodic	01.03.00
Netherlands	09.01.72	13th–14th periodic (2000)	15th periodic	09.01.01
New Zealand	22.12.72	10th –11th periodic (1995)	12th –14th periodic	22.12.95
Nicaragua	17.03.78	5th–9th periodic (1995)	10th–12th periodic	17.03.97
Niger	04.04.69	11th –14th periodic (1998)	15th–16th periodic	04.01.98
Nigeria	04.01.69	13th periodic (1995)	14th–16th periodic	04.06.96
Norway	05.09.70	15th periodic (2000)	16th periodic	05.09.01
Pakistan	04.01.69	10th–14th periodic (1997)	15th–16th periodic	04.01.98
Panama	04.01.69	15th periodic (1998)*	16th periodic	04.01.00
Papua New Guinea	26.02.82	Initial (1984)	2nd–10th periodic	26.02.85
Peru	29.10.71	12th–13th periodic (1999)	14th 15th periodic	29.10.98
Philippines	04.01.69	11th–14th periodic (1997)	15th–16th periodic	04.01.98
Poland	04.01.69	13th–14th periodic (1997)	15th–16th periodic	04.01.98
Portugal	23.09.82	9th periodic (2001)	10th periodic	23.09.01
Qatar	21.08.76	9th–12th periodic (2001)	13th periodic	21.08.01
Republic of Korea	04.01.79	9th–10th periodic (1999)	11th periodic	04.01.00
Republic of Moldova	25.02.93		Initial–4th periodic	25.02.94
Romania	15.10.70	12th–15th periodic (1999)	16th periodic	15.10.01
Russian Federation	06.03.69	14th periodic (1998)	15th–16th periodic	06.03.98
Rwanda	16.05.75	8th–12th periodic (2000)	13th periodic	16.05.00
Saint Lucia	14.02.90		Initial–6th periodic	16.03.91

State Party	Entry into force	Last report considered	Next report due	Date due or overdue since
Saint Vincent and the Grenadines	09.12.81	Initial (1984)	2nd–10th periodic	09.12.84
Saudi Arabia	23.10.97		Initial–2nd periodic	23.10.98
Senegal	19.05.72	9th–10th periodic (1994)	11th–14th periodic	19.05.93
Seychelles	06.04.78	4th–5th periodic (1988)	6th–12th periodic	06.04.89
Sierra Leone	04.01.69	2nd–3rd periodic (1974)	4th–16th periodic	04.01.76
Slovakia	28.05.93	Initial–3rd periodic (2000)	4th periodic	28.05.00
Slovenia	06.07.92	Initial (1994)	2nd periodic	24.06.97
Solomon Islands	17.03.82	Initial (1983)	2nd–10th periodic	16.04.85
Somalia	25.09.75	2nd–4th periodic (1985)	5th–13th periodic	25.09.84
South Africa	09.01.99		Initial–2nd periodic	09.01.99
Spain	04.01.69	14th–15th periodic (2000)	16th periodic	04.01.00
Sri Lanka	20.03.82	7th–9th periodic (2001)*	10th periodic	20.03.01
Sudan	20.04.77	9th–11th periodic (2001)	12th periodic	20.04.00
Suriname	15.03.84		Initial–8th periodic	14.04.85
Swaziland	07.05.69	4th–14th periodic (1997)	15th–16th periodic	06.05.98
Sweden	05.01.72	13th–14th periodic (2000)	15th periodic	04.01.01
Switzerland	29.12.94	2nd and 3rd periodic (2002)*	4th periodic	29.12.01
Syrian Arab Republic	21.05.69	12th–15th periodic (1999)	16th periodic	21.05.00
Tajikistan	10.02.95		Initial–3rd periodic	10.02.96
Togo	01.10.72	Initial–5th periodic (1983)	6th–14th periodic	01.10.83
Tonga	17.03.72	14th periodic (2000)	15th periodic	17.03.01
Trinidad and Tobago	03.11.73	11th–14th periodic (2001)*	15th periodic	03.11.02
Tunisia	04.01.69	2nd periodic (1999)	3rd periodic	30.06.00
Turkmenistan	29.10.94		Initial–3rd periodic	29.10.99
Uganda	21.12.80	Initial (1984)	2nd–10th periodic	21.12.83
Ukraine	06.04.69	15th–16th periodic (2001)	17th periodic	06.01.02
United Arab Emirates	20.07.74	7th–11th periodic (1995)	12th 13th periodic	20.07.99
United Kingdom of Great Britain and Northern Ireland	06.04.69	15th periodic (2000)	16th periodic	06.04.00
United Republic of Tanzania	26.11.72	6th–7th periodic (1988)	8th–14th periodic	26.11.87
United States of America	20.11.94	Initial–3rd periodic (2001)*	4th periodic	20.11.01
Uruguay	04.01.69	12th –15th periodic (1999)	16th periodic	04.01.00
Uzbekistan	28.09.95	Initial (2000)	3rd periodic	28.10.00
Venezuela	04.01.69	10th–13th periodic (1996)	14th–16th periodic	04.01.96
Vietnam	09.07.82	6th–9th periodic (2001)*	10th periodic	09.06.01
Yemen	17.11.72	9th–10th periodic (1992)	11th- 14th periodic	17.11.93

State Party	Entry into force	Last report considered	Next report due	Date due or overdue since
Yugoslavia	04.01.69	11th–14th periodic (1998)	15th–16th periodic	04.01.98
Zambia	05.03.72	7th–11th periodic (1993)	12th–14th periodic	05.03.95
Zimbabwe	12.06.91	2nd–4th periodic (2000)	5th periodic	12.06.00t

(An asterisk indicates that a report has been submitted but has not yet been considered by the Committee)

6. THE EARLY WARNING AND URGENT PROCEDURE[41]

Commencing in 1993, the Committee has developed an "early warning and urgent" procedure whereby it examines the situation in States Parties in circumstances where it considers that there is particular cause for concern on the basis of the actual situation or potential circumstances.[42] The Committee indicates that its, "early warning measures are to be directed at preventing existing problems from escalating into conflicts and can also include confidence-building measures to identify and support whatever strengthens and reinforces racial tolerance, particularly to prevent a resumption of conflict where it has previously occurred. Urgent procedures are to respond to problems requiring immediate attention to prevent or limit the scale or number of serious violations of the Convention".[43]

The procedure has two defining elements: (a) it is not dependent on the State having submitted a report for consideration, and (b) there are as yet no relevant rules of procedure and matters are dealt with on an *ad hoc* case-by-case basis.

By the end of 2000, the procedure had been invoked concerning 16 States Parties.[44] In each case members named the States in public session of the Committee and then or later in the session the situation was considered. Consideration has taken place in both public and private sessions and, on occasion, the Committee has invited participation in the discussion of State representatives and experts such as Rapporteurs of the Commission on Human Rights. Sometimes the consideration by

---

[41] Michael O'Flaherty, "The Committee on the Elimination of Racial Discrimination as an Implementation Agency", in *Anti-Discriminator Law Enforcement – A Comparative Perspective* (MacEwen Ed. 1997) 209–233; M. O'Flaherty, "The Committee on the Elimination of Racial Discrimination: Non-governmental Input and the Early Warning and Urgent Procedure", in *Indigenous Peoples, The United Nations and Human Rights*, (S. Pritchard Ed., 1998) 151–160; T. van Boven, "Prevention, Early Warning and Urgent Procedures: A new Approach by the Committee on the Elimination of Racial Discrimination", in, *Reflections on International Law from the Low Countries in Honour of Paul de Waart*, (1998) 165–182; M. O'Flaherty, "Treaty Bodies Responding to States of Emergency: The Case of Bosnia and Herzegovina", in, *The Future of UN Human Rights Treaty Monitoring*, (P. Alston and J. Crawford Eds., 2000) 439–460.

[42] See, United Nations Doc. A/51/18, paras. 609–613.

[43] United Nations Doc. A/51/18 para 611.

[44] Algeria, Australia, Bosnia and Herzegovina, Burundi, Croatia, Cyprus, Democratic Republic of the Congo, Israel, Liberia, Mexico, Papua New Guinea, Russian Federation, Rwanda, Sudan, Former Yugoslav Republic of Macedonia, Yugoslavia.

the Committee has included examination of the question of whether a particular situation actually raises issues under the Convention or not, and requests for further information have been made to States with a view to clarifying the matter.

Among the outcomes of the consideration by the Committee have been formal Decisions expressing the views of the Committee and usually requesting the immediate submission by the State of a report, the bringing of particular situations to the attention of the High Commissioner for Human Rights and, or, the U.N. Secretary-General, and to the General Assembly and the Security Council, and the undertaking, with the consent of the Governments concerned, of Good-Offices or technical co-operation missions to the territory concerned.

Once a State is placed under the procedure it remains indefinitely on the agenda of the Committee and may receive attention at forthcoming sessions. Accordingly, there have been a series of Committee initiatives concerning a number of the named States. The Committee, may, however, remove names from the list of States being considered under the procedure.

NGOs have not played a large part in the development of the procedure. However, they have a potentially important role in bringing actual or potentially egregious situations of racial discrimination to the attention of Committee members and suggesting that the States concerned be considered under the procedure. NGOs can also play a useful role in providing information concerning States already under consideration and in suggesting the appropriate form of action or Decision for the Committee to take. Finally, NGOs can draw public attention to whatever actions have been taken by the Committee and use this information in their own activities.

7. THE COMMUNICATIONS PROCEDURE

The procedure permits individuals and groups of individuals to complain directly or through representatives to the Committee about a State Party in circumstances where they are the alleged victims of violations of the Convention and the State Party has made the necessary declaration under article 14.[45]

The function of the Committee is to gather all necessary information, primarily by means of written exchanges with the parties (the State and the complainant), to consider the admissibility and merits of complaints and to issue its "Opinion" accordingly. It should be noted that the Committee is not a court, does not issue "judgements" and has no means to enforce any views which it might adopt.

---

[45] Rules of Procedure of the Committee on the Elimination of Racial Discrimination, Rules 80–97, United Nations Doc. CERD/C/65/Rev.3, as amended in 1993. See, M. O'Flaherty, "Individual Communications: The Convention Against Torture and the Convention on the Elimination of All Forms of Racial Discrimination", in *Indigenous Peoples, the United Nations and Human Rights*, (S. Pritchard Ed., 1998); T. van Boven, "The Petition System under the International Convention on the Elimination of All Forms of Racial Discrimination: A Sobering Balance-Sheet", in, Max Planck Yearbook of United Nations Law 4 (2000), 271–287; R. de Gouttes, "Reinforcement of International and Regional Mechanism for Individual Complaints of Racial Discrimination", in *United To Combat Racism*, (UNESCO, 2001); L. Zwaak, *International Human Rights Procedures: Petitioning to ECHR, CCPR and CERD* (1991).

Furthermore, all exchanges with the Committee currently take only written form. There is no provision for the awarding of any financial assistance to needy applicants to assist them in taking a case to the Committee.

All steps of the procedure under article 14 are confidential until the point where the Committee adopts its Opinion or otherwise concludes a case. As a matter of practice, Opinions are reported in the Committee's annual report together with a summary of the information made available to the Committee. Decisions on non-admissibility are also reported.

By March 2001, 30 States had made the declaration accepting the article 14 procedure.[46] By that date the Committee had adopted Opinions concerning only ten communications and declared four others to be inadmissible[47] In 60% of the cases considered the Committee has found there to be a violation of the Convention.

A case must negotiate two stages, those of consideration for admissibility and on the merits. A case can take from one to three years to negotiate its way through all stages of the process.

The first step in bringing a case to the attention of the Committee is to communicate with the Secretariat.[48] At this or any other stage complainants are free to maintain contact with members of the Secretariat to obtain advice and guidance.

Once all the key details have been supplied in writing the case may be assigned to a Working Group or Special Rapporteur with the task of preparing the case for consideration on admissibility (as provided for in the Rules of Procedure, but not yet actually implemented).[49] A Rapporteur or Working Group may seek further information or clarifications and indicate a time limit for replies.

Once a Working Group or the Committee itself is satisfied that the communication is not anonymous, an abuse of the right of petition or incompatible with the Covenant, it is sent to the State party for comment on the issue of admissibility. The State party has a time limit (usually two months) in which to reply and this reply is made available to the applicant for comment. If the State party argues that local remedies have not been exhausted (see below) the onus falls on it to indicate remedies which could have been pursued.[50]

Decisions on admissibility are made by the Committee in plenary session. Decisions of inadmissibility may be reconsidered on application and in the light of

---

[46] Algeria, Australia, Belgium, Bulgaria, Chile, Costa Rica, Cyprus, Czech Republic, Denmark, Ecuador, Finland, France, Hungary, Iceland, Italy, Luxembourg, Malta, Netherlands, Norway, Peru, Poland, Portugal, Republic of Korea, Russian Federation, Senegal, Slovakia, South Africa, Spain, Ukraine and Uruguay. Current information on the status of ratification of human rights instruments can be found at the OHCHR website: www.unhchr.ch.

[47] See United Nations Doc. A/55/18 paras 454–461..

[48] Where the matter will be dealt with by a dedicated "petitions team" which handles all communications under the Optional Protocol to the International Covenant on Civil and Political Rights, the Convention Against Torture and the Convention on the Elimination of All Forms of Racial Discrimination.

[49] United Nations Doc. HRI/GEN/3 pp. 89–96.

[50] United Nations Doc. HRI/GEN/3 pp. 89–96.

changed circumstances.[51] The Committee may choose to consider both the admissibility and merits issues together.[52]

The conditions for admissibility are as follows:

(a) A communication may only be made regarding a State and never an individual.

(b) For a communication to be admissible the alleged victim must have been subject to the jurisdiction of the State Party at the time of the alleged violation.

(c) The alleged violation must be of rights in the Convention.

(d) The Convention is not retroactive and thus the alleged violation must have occurred after the State Party acceded to it and made the declaration under article 14. However, a violation preceding that date with effects which persist may be actionable.

(e) In determining whether a violation has occurred care must be taken to ensure that the State Party has not "contracted out" of the specific provisions by means of a reservation.

(f) Anonymous communications will not be accepted. However, the wish of the complainant to have his name withheld will be respect.[53]

(g) Communications may be submitted by or on behalf of alleged victims and persons acting as representatives must display their authority to act given them by the alleged victim.[54]

(h) Communications will be considered inadmissible if they are deemed to be an abuse of the rights of petition or incompatible with the provisions of the Convention. These provisions are sufficiently unclear to allow for an overlapping of concern with other admissibility requirements. It is clear that they may cover a wide range of factual situations and would certainly preclude communications designed to subvert the work of the Committee, containing allegations of a frivolous nature or abusive of the Committee or the Convention. Cases will also be deemed inadmissible if the complainant fails to provide a minimum amount of information indicating a possible violation of the Convention.

(i) Before a communication can be taken to the Committee all domestic remedies should have been exhausted. However, this rule does not apply where the application of domestic remedies is unreasonable prolonged or is unlikely to bring effective relief to the victim.[55] Article 14 makes provision for the establishment of national bodies to consider petitions concerning allegations of racial discrimination and for the subsequent submission of such petitions to the Committee in given circumstances. This provision, which has not been

---

51 United Nations Doc. HRI/GEN/3 pp. 89–96.
52 United Nations Doc. HRI/GEN/3 pp. 89–96.
53 Article 14 (6) a, of the Convention.
54 See N. Lerner, "Curbing Racial Discrimination – Fifteen Years of CERD", 13 *Israel Yearbook of Human Rights*, (1983), PP. 180–182.
55 See A. Byrnes, "The Committee against Torture", in *The United Nations and Human Rights*, (P. Alston Ed. 1992).

implemented by States Parties, is probably not an obligatory one and the absence of such bodies may not be seen as an impediment to the exercise of the right of petition to the Committee. Certainly the Committee in its jurisprudence and its Rules of Procedure[56] has not understood the provision in an obstructive manner.

(j) The Rules of Procedure indicate that communications must be submitted within six months after available domestic remedies have been exhausted, "except in the case of duly verified exceptional circumstances".[57] It would appear from an examination of article 14 that this time restriction is not stipulated therein. The rule instead has its origins[58] in the Committee's desire to adequately acknowledge the provisions of article 14 concerning the role in the complaints procedure of national bodies while at the same time not allowing them to obstruct the right of petition. Perhaps a reformulation of the Rules of Procedure could continue to achieve this purpose while at the same time removing the six-month time limit for those petitions emanating from the jurisdiction of States Parties which have not established such bodies.

Decisions on admissibility are communicated immediately to the State Party and the complainant. If the matter has been found admissible and the merits have not been considered, the State Party is forwarded all relevant information and is requested to offer its views within three months.[59] The identify of the alleged victim may only be revealed to the State Party with his or her consent.[60]

In the case of communications which have been found admissible or where admissibility and the merits of the case are dealt with jointly, the Committee may request that the State take interim measures to safeguard the alleged victim. Such a request has no binding force.[61]

In its consideration of the merits the Committee may defer decision pending receipt of further information. In all cases where further information is requested the State Party and the complainant are kept fully informed.

The rules of procedure of the Committee allow for the conducting of confidential oral hearings by the Committee in cases where they are of the view that these would be of assistance to them in gathering necessary information concerning the merits of

---

[56] Rule United Nations Doc. HRI/GEN/3 pp. 89–96.

[57] Rules of Procedure of the Committee on the Elimination of Racial Discrimination, Rule 91 (f), United Nations Doc. HRI/GEN/3 p. 93.

[58] E. Schwelb, "The International Convention on the Elimination of All Forms of Racial Discrimination" 15 ICLQ, (1966), p. 1043.

[59] Rules of Procedure of the Committee on the Elimination of Racial Discrimination, Rule 94, para. 2, United Nations Doc. United Nations Doc. HRI/GEN/3 p. 95.

[60] Rules of Procedure of the Committee on the Elimination of Racial Discrimination, Rule 94, para. 1, United Nations Doc. United Nations Doc. HRI/GEN/3 p. 94.

[61] Rules of Procedure of the Committee on the Elimination of Racial Discrimination, Rule 94, para. 3, United Nations Doc. United Nations Doc. HRI/GEN/3 p. 95.

case.[62] There is no such provision with regard to cases which are only at the admissibility stage. No hearings have as yet occurred.

When the Committee is of the view that it has gathered sufficient information it proceeds to a consideration of the merits and the adoption of its Opinion and of any suggestions and recommendations which it might wish to make.

The practice of the Committee is to adopt Opinions by consensus. Members are free however to append individual views to those of the Committee. Though the Committee has no power to make awards, pecuniary or otherwise, it is free to make recommendations to the State Party regarding such matters. The Opinion of the Committee, together with any suggestions and recommendations it may wish to make are communicated to the State Party and the complainant.[63] Further to the rules of procedure the State Party is invited to inform the Committee in due course of the action it takes in conformity with the Committee's Opinion.[64]

The Committee has not as yet developed a procedure for the follow-up of cases subsequent to the adoption of its views, though it does question relevant States on the matter in the course of consideration of periodic reports.

8. THEMATIC DISCUSSIONS

In 2000 the Committee, on the basis of its authority under article 9 of the Convention, inaugurated the practice of convening thematic discussions on issues of racial discrimination common to several States and worthy of examination from a general perspective. The theme adopted for the first thematic discussion was, "Discrimination Against Roma".[65] The discussion was conducted over two meetings, each of three hours duration, and was preceded by an informal meeting with concerned NGOs. In advance of the meeting written submissions were solicited from States parties, as well as from NGOs, UN agencies and relevant expert bodies and intergovernmental organisations. Based on the information submitted and collected for the thematic discussion and the outcome of the general debate, the Committee adopted a General Recommendation on discrimination against Roma.[66]

The thematic discussions afford opportunities to NGOs to engage in debate with the Committee, place information before it and, perhaps most importantly, influence the drafting process of general recommendations. NGOs may also wish to informally propose to members of the Committee themes for future discussions. One theme currently being considered for discussion by the Committee is that of the issue of "descent" under article 1 of the Convention.

---

[62] Rules of Procedure of the Committee on the Elimination of Racial Discrimination, Rule 94 (2), United Nations Doc. United Nations Doc. HRI/GEN/3 p. 95.

[63] Rules of Procedure of the Committee on the Elimination of Racial Discrimination, Rule 95, para. 3, United Nations Doc. United Nations Doc. HRI/GEN/3 p. 96.

[64] Rules of Procedure of the Committee on the Elimination of Racial Discrimination, Rule 95, para. 5, United Nations Doc. United Nations Doc. HRI/GEN/3 p. 96.

[65] Reported in United Nations Doc. A/55/18 paras 442–453.

[66] General Recommendation XXVII, reported in United Nations Doc A/55/18 Annex V.

CHAPTER 5

THE COMMITTEE ON THE ELIMINATION OF DISCRIMINATION AGAINST WOMEN

1. THE SUBSTANTIVE PROVISIONS OF THE CONVENTION ON THE ELIMINATION OF ALL FORMS OF DISCRIMINATION AGAINST WOMEN[1]

Article I

For the purposes of the present Convention, the term "discrimination against women" shall mean any distinction, exclusion or restriction made on the basis of sex which has the effect or purpose of impairing or nullifying the recognition, enjoyment or exercise by women, irrespective of their marital status, on a basis of equality of men and women, of human rights and fundamental freedoms in the political, economic, social, cultural, civil or any other field.

Note

General Recommendation 19[2] reminds States Parties that the definition of discrimination includes gender-based violence, that is, violence that is directed against a woman because she is a woman or that affects women disproportionately, and that discrimination under the Convention is not restricted to action by or on behalf of governments.

---

[1] M. A. Freeman and A. S. Fraser, "Women's Human Rights: Making the Theory a Reality", in *Human Rights: An Agenda for the Next Century*, (L. Henkin and J. Hargrove Eds. 1994), pp. 112–124; J. A. Minor, "An Analysis of Structural Weaknesses in the Convention on the Elimination of All Forms of Discrimination Against Women", Georgia Journal of International and Comparative Law, (1994), pp. 137–153; S. C. Zearfoss, "Convention on the Elimination of All Forms of Discrimination Against Women: Radical, Reasonable or Reactionary", Michigan Journal of International Law, 12(4), 1991; N. Burrows, "The 1979 Convention on the Elimination of All Forms of Discrimination Against Women", Netherlands International Law Review, (1985), pp. 419–460; Japanese Association of International Women's Rights, *Commentary on the Convention on the Elimination of All Forms of Discrimination Against Women*, (1995); R. Cooke Ed., *Human Rights of Women: National and International Perspectives*, (1995); Z. Ilic and I. Corti, "The Convention on the Elimination of All Forms of Discrimination Against Women", in *Manual on Human Rights Reporting*, (United Nations 1997), at pp. 305–366; *Fact Sheet 22, Discrimination Against Women: The Convention and the Committee*, (United Nations); A. Fraser, "The Convention on the Elimination of All Forms of Discrimination Against Women", in *Women, Politics and the United Nations*, (1995).
[2] United Nations Doc. HRI/GEN/1/Rev.5, p. 216.

Article 2

States Parties condemn discrimination against women in all its forms, agree to pursue by all appropriate means and without delay a policy of eliminating discrimination against women and, to this end, undertake:

(a) *To embody the principle of the equality of men and women in their national constitutions or other appropriate legislation if not yet incorporated therein and to ensure, through law and other appropriate means, the practical realization of this principle;*

(b) *To adopt appropriate legislative and other measures, including sanctions where appropriate, prohibiting all discrimination against women;*

(c) *To establish legal protection of the rights of women on an equal basis with men and to ensure through competent national tribunals and other public institutions the effective protection of women against any act of discrimination;*

(d) *To refrain from engaging in any act or practice of discrimination against women and to ensure that public authorities and institutions shall act in conformity with this obligation;*

(e) *To take all appropriate measures to eliminate discrimination against women by any person, organization or enterprise;*

(f) *To take all appropriate measures, including legislation, to modify or abolish existing laws, regulations, customs and practices which constitute discrimination against women;*

(g) *To repeal all national penal provisions which constitute discrimination against women.*

Note

In General Recommendations 12 and 16 respectively, the Committee suggests that States Parties include in their periodic reports information, (a) about the legislative and other measures adopted to protect women against the incidence of all kinds of violence in everyday life, including sexual violence, abuses in the family, sexual harassment at the workplace, etc.,[3] and (b) about the legal and social situation of unpaid women working in family enterprises.[4] General Recommendation 19[5] stipulates that gender-based violence, which impairs or nullifies the enjoyment by women of human rights and fundamental freedoms under general international law or under human rights conventions, is discrimination within the meaning of article 1 of the Convention. Furthermore, discrimination under the Convention is not restricted to action by or on behalf of Governments.

---

[3] General Recommendation 12, United Nations Doc. HRI/GEN/1/Rev.5, p. 210.
[4] General Recommendation 16, United Nations Doc. HRI/GEN/1/Rev.5, p. 214.
[5] General Recommendation 19, United Nations Doc. HRI/GEN/1/Rev.5, p. 216.

Article 3

States Parties shall take in all fields, in particular in the political, social, economic and cultural fields, all appropriate measures, including legislation, to ensure the full development and advancement of women , for the purpose of guaranteeing them the exercise and enjoyment of human rights and fundamental freedoms on a basis of equality with men.

Note

In General Recommendation 18, the Committee encourages States Parties to provide information on disabled women in their periodic reports, including special measures taken to deal with their situation.[6]

Article 4

1. *Adoption by States Parties of temporary special measures aimed at accelerating de facto equality between men and women shall not be considered discrimination as defined in the present Convention, but shall in no way entail as a consequence the maintenance of unequal or separate standards; these measures shall be discontinued when the objectives of equality of opportunity and treatment have been achieved.*
2. *Adoption by States Parties of special measures, including those measures contained in the present Convention, aimed at protecting maternity shall not be considered discriminatory.*

Note

In General Recommendation 5[7] the Committee recommends that States Parties make more use of temporary special measures such as positive action, preferential treatment or quota systems to advance women's integration into education, the economy, politics and employment.

Article 5

States Parties shall take all appropriate measures:

(a) *To modify the social and cultural patterns of conduct of men and women, with a view to achieving the elimination of prejudices and customary and all other practices which are based on the idea of the inferiority or the superiority of either of the sexes or on stereotyped roles for men and women;*
(b) *To ensure that family education includes a proper understanding of maternity as a social function and the recognition of the common responsibility of men and women in the upbringing and development of their children, it being understood that the interest of the children is the primordial consideration in all cases.*

---

[6] United Nations Doc. HRI/GEN/1/Rev.5, p. 215.
[7] United Nations Doc. HRI/GEN/1/Rev.5, p. 204.

Note

The Committee notes in General Recommendation 19[8] that traditional attitudes, by which women are regarded as subordinate to men or as having stereotypical roles, perpetuate widespread practices involving violence or coercion, such as family violence and abuse, forced marriage, dowry deaths, acid attacks and female circumcision. The Committee further observes[9] that these attitudes also contribute to the propagation of pornography and the depiction and other commercial exploitation of women as sexual objects, rather than as individuals, and that this, in turn, encourages gender-based violence.

Article 6

States Parties shall take all appropriate measures, including legislation, to suppress all forms of traffic in women and exploitation of prostitution of women.

Note

The Committee observes in General Recommendation 19[10] that poverty and unemployment, on the one hand, and wars, armed conflicts and the occupation of territories on the other hand, increase opportunities for trafficking in women, forcing them, including young girls, into prostitution. The Committee further remarks[11] that in addition to established forms of trafficking there are new forms of sexual exploitation, such as sex tourism, the recruitment of domestic labour from developing countries to work in developed countries, and marriages between women from developing countries and foreign nationals, practices which are incompatible with the equal enjoyment of rights by women and with respect for their rights and dignity.

Article 7

States Parties shall take all appropriate measures to eliminate discrimination against women in the political and public life of the country and, in particular, shall ensure to women, on equal terms with men, the right:

(a) To vote in all elections and public referenda and to be eligible for election to all publicly elected bodies;
(b) To participate in the formulation of government policy and the implementation thereof and to hold public office and perform all public functions at all levels of government;
(c) To participate in non-governmental organizations and associations concerned with the public and political life of the country.

---

[8]   United Nations Doc. HRI/GEN/1/Rev.5, p. 216.
[9]   United Nations Doc. HRI/GEN/1/Rev.5, p. 218.
[10] United Nations Doc.HRI/GEN/1/Rev.5, p. 216.
[11] *Ibid.*

Note

In General Recommendation 23[12] the Committee observes that the obligation specified in article 7 extends to all areas of public and political life and that it is not limited to those areas specified in subparagraphs (a), (b) and (c). The expression "political and public life" is a broad concept that covers *all* aspects of public administration as well as the formulation and implementation of policies at all levels (international, national, regional and local). The Committee, recalling that cultural traditions and religious beliefs have played a part in confining women to the private spheres of activity and in excluding them from active participation in public life, further suggests that beside the removal of *de jure* barriers, temporary special measures under art. 4 should also be taken when necessary.[13]

Article 8

States Parties shall take all appropriate measures to ensure to women, on equal terms with men and without any discrimination, the opportunity to represent their Governments at the international level and to participate in the work of international organizations.

Article 9

1. *States Parties shall grant women equal rights with men to acquire, change or retain their nationality. They shall ensure in particular that neither marriage to an alien nor change of nationality by the husband during marriage shall automatically change the nationality of the wife, render her stateless or force upon her the nationality of the husband.*
2. *States Parties shall grant women equal rights with men with respect to the nationality of their children.*

Note

General Recommendation 21[14] recalls that without status as nationals or citizens, women are deprived of the right to vote or to stand for public office and may be denied access to public benefits and a choice of residence. Therefore the Committee notes[15] that nationality should be capable of change by an adult woman and should not be arbitrarily removed because of marriage or dissolution of marriage or because her husband or father changes his nationality.

---

[12]   United Nations Doc.HRI/GEN/1/Rev.5, p. 234.
[13]   *Ibid*, p. 236.
[14]   United Nations Doc.HRI/GEN/1/Rev.5, p. 222.
[15]   United Nations Doc.HRI/GEN/1/Rev.5, p. 222.

Article 10

States Parties shall take all appropriate measures to eliminate discrimination against women in order to ensure to them equal rights with men in the field of education and in particular to ensure, on a basis of equality of men and women:

(a) The same conditions for career and vocational guidance, for access to studies and for the achievement of diplomas in educational establishments of all categories in rural as well as in urban areas; this equality shall be ensured in pre-school, general, technical, professional and higher technical education, as well as in all types of vocational training;

(b) Access to the same curricula, the same examinations, teaching staff with qualifications of the same standard and school premises and equipment of the same quality;

(c) The elimination of any stereotyped concept of the roles of men and women at all levels and in all forms of education by encouraging coeducation and other types of education which will help to achieve this aim and, in particular, by the revision of textbooks and school programmes and the adaptation of teaching methods;

(d) The same opportunities to benefit from scholarships and other study grants;

(e) The same opportunities for access to programmes of continuing education, including adult and functional literacy programmes, particulary those aimed at reducing, at the earliest possible time, any gap in education existing between men and women;

(f) The reduction of female student drop-out rates and the organization of programmes for girls and women who have left school prematurely;

(g) The same Opportunities to participate actively in sports and physical education;

(h) Access to specific educational information to help to ensure the health and well-being of families, including information and advice on family planning.

Article 11

1. States Parties shall take all appropriate measures to eliminate discrimination against women in the field of employment in order to ensure, on a basis of equality of men and women, the same rights, in particular:

(a) The right to work as an inalienable right of all human beings;

(b) The right to the same employment opportunities, including the application of the same criteria for selection in matters of employment;

(c) The right to free choice of profession and employment, the right to promotion, job security and all benefits and conditions of service and the right to receive vocational training and retraining, including apprenticeships, advanced vocational training and recurrent training;

(d) The right to equal remuneration, including benefits, and to equal treatment in respect of work of equal value, as well as equality of treatment in the evaluation of the quality of work;

(e) The right to social security, particularly in cases of retirement, unemployment, sickness, invalidity and old age and other incapacity to work, as well as the right to paid leave;

(f) The right to protection of health and to safety in working conditions, including the safeguarding of the function of reproduction.

2. In order to prevent discrimination against women on the grounds of marriage or maternity and to ensure their effective right to work, States Parties shall take appropriate measures:

(a) To prohibit, subject to the imposition of sanctions, dismissal on the grounds of pregnancy or of maternity leave and discrimination in dismissals on the basis of marital status;

(b) To introduce maternity leave with pay or with comparable social benefits without loss of former employment, seniority or social allowances;

(c) To encourage the provision of the necessary supporting social services to enable parents to combine family obligations with work responsibilities and participation in public life, in particular through promoting the establishment and development of a network of child-care facilities;

(d) To provide special protection to women during pregnancy in types of work proved to be harmful to them.

3. Protective legislation relating to matters covered in this article shall be reviewed periodically in the light of scientific and technological knowledge and shall be revised, repealed or extended as necessary.

Note

The Committee, in General Recommendation 19,[16] notes that equality in employment can be seriously impaired when women are subjected to gender-specific violence, such as sexual harassment in the workplace, and that it is discriminatory when the woman concerned has reasonable ground to believe that her objection would disadvantage her in connection with her employment, including recruitment or promotion, or when it creates a hostile working environment. General Recommendation 5[17] refers to the value of States Parties making more use of

---

[16] United Nations Doc. HRI/GEN/1/Rev.5, p. 216.
[17] United Nations Doc. HRI/GEN/1/Rev.5, p. 204.

temporary special measures such as positive action, preferential treatment or quota systems to advance women's integration into, *inter-alia*, employment. See also, General Recommendation 24 on women and health.[18]

Article 12

1. *States Parties shall take all appropriate measures to eliminate discrimination against women in the field of health care in order to ensure, on a basis of equality of men and women, access to health care services, including those related to family planning.*
2. *Notwithstanding the provisions of paragraph I of this article, States Parties shall ensure to women appropriate services in connection with pregnancy, confinement and the post-natal period, granting free services where necessary, as well as adequate nutrition during pregnancy and lactation.*

Note

General Recommendation 14[19] and 15[20] invite States Parties to include in their reports to the Committee information about measures taken to eliminate female circumcision, and about the effects of AIDS on the situation of women. According to General Recommendation 24, States Parties compliance with article 12 is central to the heath and well-being of women and requires the elimination of discrimination against women in their access to health-care services throughout the life-cycle, particularly in the areas of family planning, pregnancy and confinement and during the post-natal period. State Parties shall also refrain from obstructing actions taken by women in pursuit of their health goals and should report on how public and private health-care providers meet their duties to respect women's rights to have access to health care. For example, they should not restrict women's access to health services or to the clinics that provide those services on the ground that women do not have the authorization of husbands, partners, parents or health authorities, because they are unmarried or because they are women. Other barriers to women's access to appropriate health care include laws that criminalize medical procedures only needed by women and which punish women who undergo those procedures.[21]

The Committee further expresses its concern about certain traditional practices that are harmful to the health of women and children, such as dietary restrictions for pregnant women and preference for male children.[22]

---

[18] United Nations Doc. HRI/GEN/1/Rev.5, p. 244.
[19] United Nations Doc. HRI/GEN/1/Rev.5, p. 211.
[20] United Nations Doc. HRI/GEN/1/Rev.5, p. 212.
[21] General Recommendation 24, United Nations Doc. HRI/GEN/1/Rev.5, p. 248.
[22] United Nations Doc. HRI/GEN/1/Rev.5, p. 219.

Article 13

States Parties shall take all appropriate measures to eliminate discrimination against women in other areas of economic and social life in order to ensure, on a basis of equality of men and women, the same rights, in particular:

(a) The right to family benefits;

(b) The right to bank loans, mortgages and other forms of financial credit;

(c) The right to participate in recreational activities, sports and all aspects of cultural life.

Article 14

1. *States Parties shall take into account the particular problems faced by rural women and the significant roles which rural women play in the economic survival of their families, including their work in the non-monetized sectors of the economy, and shall take all appropriate measures to ensure the application of the provisions of the present Convention to women in rural areas.*

2. *States Parties shall take all appropriate measures to eliminate discrimination against women in rural areas in order to ensure, on a basis of equality of men and women, that they participate in and benefit from rural development and, in particular, shall ensure to such women the right:*

   (a) To participate in the elaboration and implementation of development planning at all levels;

   (b) To have access to adequate health care facilities, including information, counselling and services in family planning;

   (c) To benefit directly from social security programmes;

   (d) To obtain all types of training and education, formal and non-formal, including that relating to functional literacy, as well as, inter alia, the benefit of all community and extension services, in order to increase their technical proficiency;

   (e) To organize self-help groups and co-operatives in order to obtain equal access to economic opportunities through employment or self employment;

   (f) To participate in all community activities;

   (g) To have access to agricultural credit and loans, marketing facilities, appropriate technology and equal treatment in land and agrarian reform as well as in land resettlement schemes;

   (h) To enjoy adequate living conditions, particularly in relation to housing, sanitation, electricity and water supply, transport and communications.

Note

The Committee, in General Recommendation 19,[23] clarifies that girls from rural

---

[23] United Nations Doc.HRI/GEN/1/Rev.5, p. 216.

communities are at special risk of violence and sexual exploitation when they leave the rural community to seek employment in towns.

Article 15

1. *States Parties shall accord to women equality with men before the law.*
2. *States Parties shall accord to women, in civil matters, a legal capacity identical to that of men and the same opportunities to exercise that capacity. In particular, they shall give women equal rights to conclude contracts and to administer property and shall treat them equally in all stages of procedure in courts and tribunals.*
3. *States Parties agree that all contracts and all other private instruments of any kind with a legal effect which is directed at restricting the legal capacity of women shall be deemed null and void.*
4. *States Parties shall accord to men and women the same rights with regard to the law relating to the movement of persons and the freedom to choose their residence and domicile.*

Note

General Recommendation 19[24] draws attention to various provisions of this article. Firstly, when a woman cannot enter into a contract or have access to financial credit, or can do so only with her husband's or a male relative's concurrence or guarantee, she is denied legal autonomy. Secondly, when countries limit a woman's legal capacity by their laws, or permit individuals or institutions to do the same, they are denying women their rights to be equal with men and are restricting women's ability to provide for themselves and their dependants.[25] Thirdly, as in the case of nationality, examination of State Parties' reports demonstrates that a woman will not always be permitted at law to choose her own domicile, which, instead, should be capable of change at will by an adult woman regardless of her marital status.[26] Finally, with regard to migrant women who live and work temporarily in another country: they should be permitted the same rights as men to have their spouses, partners and children join them.[27]

Article 16

1. *States Parties shall take all appropriate measures to eliminate discrimination against women in all matters relating to marriage and family relations and in particular shall ensure, on a basis of equality of men and women:*

    (a) The same right to enter into marriage;

---

[24] United Nations Doc. HRI/GEN/1/Rev.5, p. 216.
[25] *Ibid.*
[26] *Ibid.*
[27] *Ibid.*

(b) The same right freely to choose a spouse and to enter into marriage only with their free and full consent;

(c) The same rights and responsibilities during marriage and at its dissolution;

(d) The same rights and responsibilities as parents, irrespective of their marital status, in matters relating to their children; in all cases the interests of the children shall be paramount;

(e) The same rights to decide freely and responsibly on the number and spacing of their children and to have access to the information, education and means to enable them to exercise these rights;

(f) The same rights and responsibilities with regard to guardianship, wardship, trusteeship and adoption of children, or similar institutions where these concepts exist in national legislation; in all cases the interests of the children shall be paramount;

(g) The same personal rights as husband and wife, including the right to choose a family name, a profession and an occupation;

(h) The same rights for both spouses in respect of the ownership, acquisition, management, administration, enjoyment and disposition of property, whether free of charge or for a valuable consideration.

2. The betrothal and the marriage of a child shall have no legal effect, and all necessary action, including legislation, shall be taken to specify a minimum age for marriage and to make the registration of marriages in an official registry compulsory.

Note

In General Recommendation 19[28] the Committee notes that family violence is one of the most insidious forms of violence against women and that it is prevalent in all societies. Therefore, the Committee invites States Parties to ensure that laws against family violence give adequate protection to all women, and that appropriate support services are provided for families where incest or sexual abuse has occurred.[29] The Committee also observes, in General Recommendation 21, that an examination of States Parties' reports discloses that there are countries which, on the basis of custom, religious beliefs or the ethnic origin or particular groups of people, permit forced marriage or remarriages.[30] Moreover, the Committee notes that generally a *de facto* union is not given legal protection and that children of such unions do not always enjoy the same status as those born in wedlock.[31] Finally, the Committee notes with alarm the number of States Parties which have entered reservations to the whole or part of this article, especially when a reservation has been entered to article 2, claiming that compliance may conflict with a commonly held vision of the family based, *inter alia*, on cultural or religious beliefs or on the country's economic or political status.[32]

---

[28] United Nations Doc. HRI/GEN/1/Rev.5, p. 219.

[29] United Nations Doc. HRI/GEN/1/Rev.5, p. 219.

[30] United Nations Doc. HRI/GEN/1/Rev.5, p. 226.

[31] United Nations Doc. HRI/GEN/1/Rev.5, p. 227.

[32] United Nations Doc. HRI/GEN/1/Rev.5, p. 230.

2. THE COMMITTEE ON THE ELIMINATION OF DISCRIMINATION AGAINST WOMEN[33]

The Committee on the Elimination of Racial Discrimination against Women is established pursuant to the provisions of article 17 of the Convention with the task of "considering the progress made in the implementation of the Convention". There are 23 members, elected by the States Parties for terms of four years.[34] Members, though all nationals of States Parties, serve in their private capacities and make a solemn declaration of impartiality upon taking up office. The Committee presently meets twice each year, in January and June/July, for sessions of three weeks duration, each preceded by a meeting of one week's duration of a pre-sessional working group.[35] At present the sessions take place in New York.[36] Secretariat

---

[33] M. Bustelo, "The Committee on the Elimination of Discrimination Against Women at the Crossroads", in *The Future of UN Human Rights Treaty Monitoring,* (P. Alston and J. Crawford, Eds., 2000) pp. 79–111; Z. Ilic and I. Corti, "The Convention on the Elimination of All Forms of Discrimination Against Women", in *Manual on Human Rights Reporting,* (United Nations 1997), at pp. 305–366; R. Jacobson, "The Committee on the Elimination of Discrimination against Women", in *The United Nations and Human Rights",* (P. Alston Ed. 1992), pp. 444–472; S. Guillet, *Nous, Peuples des Nations Unies – L'action des ONG au sein du système de protection international des droits de l'homme,* (1995), p. 74; M. A. Freeman and A. S. Fraser, "Women's Human Rights: Making the Theory a Reality" in *Human Rights: an Agenda for the Next Century,* (L. Henking and J. L. Hargrove Eds., 1994), pp. 113–118; A. Byrnes, "The 'Other' Human Rights Treaty Body: The Work of the Committee on the Elimination of Racial Discrimination against Women", 14 Yale J. Int'l L., (1989), pp. 1–67; United Nations Doc., *The Work of CEDAW (1982–1985)* (1989); M. Caron, "Les Travaux du Comité pour l'élimination de la discrimination à l'égard des femmes", 2 Rev. québécoise de droit int'l, (1985), pp. 295–303; *Fact Sheet 22, Discrimination against Women: The Convention and the Committee,* (United Nations). See, generally, the following studies by P. Alston, *Long Term Approaches to Enhancing the Effectiveness of the United Nations Human Rights Treaty Bodies,* United Nations Doc. A/44/668; *Interim Report on Updated Study,* United Nations Doc. A/CONF.157/PC/62/Add.11/Rev.1; *Final Report on Enhancing the Long Term Effectiveness of the United Nations Human Rights Treaty System,* United Nations Doc. E/CN.4/1997/74; and, also, A. Bayefsky, *Report: The UN Human Rights Treaty System: Universality at the Crossroads,* (2001); P. Alston and J. Crawford Eds., *The Future of UN Human Rights Treaty Monitoring,* (2000); A. Bayefsky, Ed., *The UN Human Rights System in the 21st Century,* (2000).

[34] Membership as of January 2001: Charlotte Abaka (Ghana); Ayse Feride Acar (Turkey); Sjamsiah Achmad (Indonesia); Emna Aouij (Tunisia); Ivanka Corti (Italy); Feng Cui (China); Naela Gabr (Egypt); Francoise Gaspard (France); Maria Yolanda Ferrer Gomez (Cuba); Aida Gonzalez Martinez (Mexico); Savitri Gooneskere (Sri Lanka); Rosalynn Hazelle (St. Kitts and Nevis); Fatima Kwaku (Nigeria); Rosario Manalo (Phillipines); Goran Melander (Sweden); Asha Rose Mtengeti-Migiro (United Republic of Tanzania); Mavivi Myakayaka-Manzini (South Africa); Zelmira Regazzoli (Argentina); Hanna Beate Schopp-Schilling (Germany); Livingstone Raday (Israel); Heisoo Shin (Republic of Korea); Maria Regina Tavares da Silva (Portugal); Chikako Taya (Japan).

[35] Article 20 of the Convention stipulates that the Committee shall meet normally for not more that two weeks in each year. The Committee has found this restriction to be a serious impediment to its work (See General Comment 22 of 1995 -United Nations Doc. HRI/GEN/1/Rev.5 at p. 232). Pending the coming into force of an amendment to the Convention to rectify this problem, the Committee is authorised by the General Assembly to extend its meeting time. See General Assembly resolution A/51/68 of 12 December 1996.

[36] Decision of the UN Secretary General, February 1996. Debate continues as to the merits of re-locating the meetings of the Committee to Geneva whereby its work and secretariat could be more closely allied to the activities and secretariat support of the other treaty bodies, all of which have Geneva as their

services are provided by the United Nations Division for the Advancement of Women.[37]

The Committee's Rules of Procedure stipulate that, "Representatives of non-governmental organisations may be invited by the Committee to make oral or written statements and to provide information or documentation relevant to the Committee's activities under the Convention to meetings of the Committee or to the pre-session working group".[38] In practice, six of the activities of the Committee are of particular interest for non-governmental organisations: the periodic reporting procedure, the closely related procedure for the requesting of exceptional reports, the communications and inquiry procedures under the recently adopted[39] Optional Protocol, and the drafting of General Recommendations.

3. THE REPORTING PROCEDURE[40]

(a) The obligation on the State

Article 18 of the Convention obliges States Parties to submit reports to the Committee within one year of the Convention coming into effect for the States concerned and thereafter every four years and whenever the Committee so requests. Article 18 stipulates that reports should indicate the legislative, judicial, administrative or other measures which have been adopted to give effect to the provisions of the Convention and describe progress made in this respect. Reports may also indicate factors and difficulties affecting the degree of fulfilment of the obligations which have been undertaken.

---

principal meeting place. However, a decision of the Secretary-General, in January 2001, that the Committee continue to meet in New York, has stilled the debate for the immediate future.

[37] Secretariat of the Committee on the Elimination of Discrimination against Women (CEDAW), Division for the Advancement of Women, United Nations Plaza, New York, NY, 10017, USA (Tel. 1 212 9631234, Fax 1 212 9633463).

[38] Rules of Procedure of the Committee on the Elimination of Racial Discrimination against Women, Rule 47, United Nations Doc. HRI/GEN/3 at p. 117.

[39] 22 December 2000.

[40] Article 18, ICEDAW; Rules of Procedure of the Committee on the Elimination of Racial Discrimination against Women, Rules 48–54, United Nations Doc. HRI/GEN/3 at pp. 117–120, *The Work of CEDAW, Volume 1 (1982–1985)*, (1989), Annex III; *Assessing the Status of Women, A Guide to Reporting Using the Convention on the Elimination of All Forms of Discrimination against Women*, (International Women's Rights Action Watch, Division for the Advancement of Women and the Commonwealth Secretariat,2000); C. Shalev, "State Reporting and the Convention on the Elimination of All Forms of Discrimination Against Women", in *The UN Human Rights Treaty System in the 21st Century*, (A.F. Bayefsky Ed., 2000) at pp. 23–34; M. Bustelo, "The Committee on the Elimination of Discrimination Against Women at the Crossroads", in *The Future of UN Human Rights Treaty Monitoring*, (P. Alston and J. Crawford, Eds., 2000) pp. 79–111. For an elucidation of the reporting obligations under each of the articles see, Z. Ilic and I. Corti, "The Convention on the Elimination of All Forms of Discrimination Against Women", in *Manual on Human Rights Reporting*, (United Nations 1997), at pp. 305–366.

The Committee has provided detailed guidance to States for the preparation of initial and subsequent periodic reports.[41] Initial reports[42] should provide specific information in relation to each provision of the Convention, in particular:

(a) The constitutional, legislative and administrative provisions or other measures in force;

(b) The developments that have taken place and the programmes and institutions that have been established since the entry into force of the Convention.[43]

(c) Any other information on progress made in the fulfilment of each right;

(d) The *de facto* as distinct from the *de jure* position;

(e) Any restrictions or limitations, even of a temporary nature, imposed by law, practice or tradition, or in any other manner on the enjoyment of each right;

(f) The situation of non-governmental organisations and other womens' associations and their participation in the elaboration and implementation of plans and programmes of the public authorities.

States are requested, as far as possible, to provide all data disaggregated by sex in all areas covered by the Convention and the General Recommendations of the Committee. Reports should also reveal obstacles to the participation of women on an equal basis with men in the political, social, economic and cultural life of their countries and provide information on types and frequencies of cases of non-compliance with the principle of equal rights. States are expected to report on measures taken to implement the twelve critical areas of the Beijing Platform for Action (Fourth World Conference on Women, September 1995).[44]

The Committee asks that States which have made substantive reservations to the Convention report on the reasons for such reservations, their consistency with obligations undertaken under other international instruments and their influence on national laws and policies. It is requested that timetables be indicated for the withdrawal of reservations.[45]

In preparing second and subsequent periodic reports,[46] States are asked to follow the general guidelines and address matters not covered in the initial report. In general, periodic reports should indicate:

(a) Legal and other measures adopted since the previous report to implement the Convention;

---

[41] The first part of reports should also comply with the consolidated guidelines relating to the preparation of the initial part of reports under the various international human rights instruments. See United Nations Doc. HRI/CORE/1.

[42] United Nations Doc. HRI/GEN/2/Rev.1 at pp. 41–43.

[43] Presumably, the Committee is here seeking information concerning the period since the Convention entered into force *for the State concerned.*

[44] See Para 323 of the Beijing Platform for Action, United Nations Doc. A/CONF.177/20.

[45] The Committee also states its view that reservations to articles 2 or 3 which do not specify provisions of the Convention are incompatible with the object and purpose of the Convention.

[46] United Nations Doc. HRI/GEN/2/Rev.1 at p. 43.

(b) Actual progress made to promote and ensure the elimination of discrimination against women;

(c) Any significant changes in the status and equality of women since the previous report;

(d) Any remaining obstacles to the participation of women on an equal basis with men in the political, social, economic and cultural life of the country;

(e) Matters raised by the Committee and which could not be dealt with when the previous report was considered;

(f) Information on measures taken to implement the Beijing Declaration and Platform for Action.

In General Recommendation 6,[47] the Committee recommends that Governments take appropriate steps to ensure the dissemination of the Convention, the reports of the States Parties and the reports of the Committee in the language of the State concerned. The States Parties are invited to include in their initial and periodic reports the action taken in respect of this recommendation.

(b) The procedure

i. The scheduling process

The Committee continues to have a backlog in reports submitted but not yet considered. The delay before consideration can extend to two years. The Committee sessions at which State reports will be considered is, in practice, announced three sessions in advance, included in the Committee's annual report and on the CEDAW website.[48] The Rules of Procedure stipulate that States must confirm in writing their agreement to have their reports examined at the proposed sessions. If they decline, the report of a State listed on a "reserve list" (also published, as above), is taken up by the Committee. States are also invited to attend the meetings at which their reports shall be considered, and, " (I)f a State party fails to respond to this invitation consideration of the report shall be re-scheduled for another session. If at such a subsequent session the State party, after due notification, fails to have a representative present, the Committee may proceed with the examination of the report in the absence of the representative of the State party."[49]

States are permitted to consolidate overdue reports. States may also submit additional information for consideration with their report, such information to reach the Secretariat no later than two and a half months prior to the pre-session working group that would be considering those reports.[50] Reports and additional information, once published as United Nations documents can be ordered from the United Nations Documents Distribution and Sales Section. The symbol number

---

[47] General Recommendation 6, United Nations Doc. HRI/GEN/1/Rev.5 at p. 204.

[48] www.unorg/womenwatch/daw/cedaw.

[49] Rules of Procedure of the Committee on the Elimination of Discrimination Against Women, Rule 51, United Nations Doc. HRI/GEN/3 at p. 119.

[50] United Nations Doc. A/54/38/Rev.1 at para. 412.

can be obtained from the Secretariat. Reports are usually available in all of the working languages of the Committee (English, French, Spanish, Russian, Chinese, Arabic). Reports are also posted on the CEDAW website.

ii. Before the session
Initial reports receive no formal pre-session scrutiny. Subsequent periodic reports, on the other hand, are considered by a pre-sessional Working Group which meets in private session some five months preceding the session of the Committee at which they are to be considered. The Working Group has four members, selected on the basis of geographical distribution. The purpose of preliminary scrutiny by the Working Group is the preparation of lists of issues and questions to be put to the representatives of the reporting State. The list of issues and questions is usually based on draft texts suggested by the Secretariat and a "Country Rapporteur". The Working Group also has access to a wide range of materials including whatever NGO information has been submitted in advance. National and international NGOs may also request the opportunity to orally brief the Working Group.[51] The finalised list of questions should concentrate on major issues and trends and should encourage constructive dialogue with the State Party during the presentation of the report.[52] The list is immediately made available to the State Party concerned in order to allow it to prepare replies, which should be submitted to the Secretariat within one month. The replies are not published prior to the consideration by the Committee of the State's report but they may, when available, be obtained directly from the Secretariat.

iii. Consideration by the Committee
The actual scrutiny of the report by the Committee takes place normally over three (initial reports) and one and a half (periodic reports) meetings held in public.[53] The report is introduced by a Government representative[54] who may take the opportunity to state government policy on a range of issues, to update material in the report and, except in the case of initial reports, to respond to the list of questions prepared by the pre-sessional Working Group. Committee members, led by the Country Rapporteur,[55] then take the floor to put questions relating to implementation of all parts of the Covenant. Once all the questions have been put, the representative has the opportunity to answer as best she may. There follow the

---

[51] United Nations Doc. A/54/38/Rev.1 at para. 411.
[52] United Nations Doc. A/54/38/Rev.1 at para. 410.
[53] In 1995, the Committee expressed the aspiration to accord two and one half meetings to initial reports and two to subsequent reports: United Nations Doc. A/50/38, paras. 640 and 642. Occasionally reports have been dispensed with in one meeting.
[54] Rule 51 stipulates that "Representatives of States Parties shall be invited to attend the meetings of the Committee at which their reports are to be examined", Rules of Procedure of the Committee on the Elimination of Discrimination Against Women, United Nations Doc. HRI/GEN/3 at p. 119.
[55] Who also, in the case of initial reports, briefs the Committee in private prior to the consideration of the report.

concluding comments or observations of individual members. After these, the representative has the opportunity to make concluding remarks.

Following the consideration in public meetings, the Committee proceeds to draft and adopt, in private session, it's "Concluding Comments",[56] comprising the following sections: introduction; positive aspects; factors and difficulties affecting the implementation of the Convention; and, principal areas of concern and recommendations. The first draft of the Concluding Comments is prepared by the Country Rapporteur, assisted by the Secretariat. The Secretariat is directly responsible for drafting the "introduction" section.

Concluding Comments enter the public domain once adopted, are sent immediately to the State party[57] and included in the annual report of the Committee. They are also posted on the Committee website. As well as the Concluding Comments, the annual reports contain summaries of the presentation made by the State party in introducing its report to the Committee.

(c) The role of non-governmental organisations[58]

NGOs and other non-State actors do not have formal standing under the reporting procedure. Thus, they may not have their documents received and processed as "United Nations documents". They may, however, have an opportunity to address the Working Group in closed session. Also, the Committee, sitting as a "Working Group of the Whole", meets with NGOs on the second day of each session. These meetings, which are open and unrecorded, last approximately two hours and deal with all reports upcoming at the session. The speaking time at the meeting is divided equally among those NGOs wishing to speak.

NGOs also have a wide range of opportunities to convey information informally to Committee members and thus to influence proceedings. One NGO, the International Women's Rights Action Watch (IWRAW),[59] has developed exceptional expertise in attracting NGO interest to the Committee's work and in the submission of information. This NGO can furnish advice and guidance and channel information to the Committee. IWRAW also prepares independent country analyses for States about to be considered in which it summarises material provided by local, national and regional NGOs. IWRAW welcomes information from as wide a range of relevant sources as possible. It has produced useful information materials such as, *Assessing the Status of Women, A Guide to Reporting Using the Convention on the*

---

[56] A sample set of Concluding Comments (for The Netherlands) is reproduced in Appendix II.

[57] Decision 14/1, United Nations Doc. A/50/38.

[58] See further at Chapter 1. See, also, A. Miller, "Women's Human Rights NGOs and the Treaty Bodies: Some Case Studies in Using the Treaty Bodies to Protect the Human Rights of Women", in *The UN Human Rights Treaty System in the 21st Century*, (A. F. Bayefsky, Ed., 2000), pp. 195–207; M. Bustelo, "The Committee on the Elimination of Discrimination Against Women at the Crossroads", in *The Future of UN Human Rights Treaty Monitoring*, (P. Alston and J. Crawford, Eds., 2000) pp. 79–111.

[59] IWRAW, Humphrey Institute of Public Affairs, 301, 19th Avenue South, Minneapolis, MN 55455, United States.

Elimination of All Forms of Discrimination against Women.[60] The existence of IWRAW in no way precludes other NGOs from making direct contact with members of the Committee or the Secretariat.

Once it is confirmed by the Secretariat that a State is scheduled to present its report at an upcoming session, NGOs should indicate their interest to both the Secretariat and IWRAW and send as much preliminary material as possible for transmission to members.

As well as providing written pre-sessional material, NGOs may find that certain Committee members are willing to establish direct contact. In both the submission of information and the soliciting of direct contact, it might be prudent to ensure that priority attention is given to members of the pre-sessional Working Group. The membership of the Working Group is identified in the annual report of the previous year.

Some weeks before the session (or meeting of the pre-sessional Working Group), NGOs should send to the Secretariat a final version of their written submission with the request that it be distributed to members. At least 25 copies should be provided. Material for inclusion in the submissions of IWRAW should be provided in the format and within timetables which it may specify.

If at all possible, NGOs should send representatives to meet with the members of the Committee when they assemble for the session as well as to address the Committee's Working Group of the Whole. Many members are happy to meet informally with NGOs and experience confirms that such contacts greatly enhance the impact of written submissions and of earlier meetings with the pre-sessional Working Group. Attendance at the meetings also permits the provision of updated submissions and other documentation, the channelling of information back to the country and the making of a comprehensive record of the proceedings. Opportunities may also arise for useful meetings with the Government representatives, with international media at United Nations headquarters and with international NGOs.

Access to the United Nations building in New York can be arranged in advance with the Secretary of the Committee.

The role of NGOs following the conclusion of the Committee proceedings is described in chapter one.

---

[60] *Assessing the Status of Women, A Guide to Reporting Using the Convention on the Elimination of All Forms of Discrimination against Women,* (International Women's Rights Action Watch, Division for the Advancement of Women and the Commonwealth Secretariat, 2000).

4. TABLE OF STATES PARTIES INDICATING WHEN A REPORT WAS LAST CONSIDERED AND IS NEXT DUE[61]

State Party	Entry into force	Last report considered	Next report due	Date due or overdue since
Albania	10.06.94		Initial–2nd periodic	10.06.95
Algeria	21.06.96	Initial (1999)	2nd periodic	21.06.01
Angola	17.10.86		Initial–4th periodic	17.10.87
Antigua and Bermuda	31.08.89	Initial, 2nd, 3rd periodic (1997)	4th periodic	31.08.02
Argentina	14.08.85	4th periodic (2000)*	5th periodic	14.08.02
Armenia	13.10.93	2nd periodic (1999)*	3rd periodic	12.10.02
Australia	27.08.83	4th periodic (1997)*	5th periodic	27.08.00
Austria	30.04.82	5th periodic (2000)	6th periodic	30.04.03
Azerbaijan	09.08.95	Initial (1998)	2nd periodic	09.08.00
Bahamas	05.11.93		Initial 2nd periodic	05.11.94
Bangladesh	06.12.84	3rd–4th periodic (1997)	5th periodic	06.12.01
Barbados	03.09.81	4th periodic (2000)*	5th periodic	03.09.98
Belarus	03.09.81	3rd periodic (2000)	4th–5th periodic	03.09.94
Belgium	09.08.85	3rd periodic (1998)*	5th periodic	09.08.02
Belize	15.06.90	Initial–2nd periodic (1999)	3rd periodic	15.06.99
Benin	11.04.92		Initial–3rd periodic	11.04.93
Bhutan	30.09.81		Initial–5th periodic	30.09.82
Bolivia	08.07.90	Initial (1995)	2nd–3rd periodic	08.07.95
Bosnia and Herzegovina	01.10.93		Initial–2nd periodic	01.10.94
Botswana	12.09.96		Initial	12.09.97
Brazil	02.03.84		Initial–5th periodic	02.03.85
Bulgaria	10.03.82	2nd- 3rd periodic (1998)	4th–5th periodic	10.03.95
Burkina Faso	13.11.87	2nd- 3rd periodic (2000)	4th periodic	13.11.00
Burundi	07.02.92	Initial (2001)	2nd- 3rd periodic	07.02.97
Cambodia	14.11.92		Initial–2nd periodic	13.11.93
Cameroon	22.09.94	Initial (2000)	2nd periodic	22.09.99
Canada	09.01.82	4th periodic (1997)	5th periodic	09.01.99
Cape Verde	03.09.81		Initial–5th periodic	03.09.82
Central African Republic	21.07.91		Initial–3rd periodic	21.07.92
Chad	09.07.95		Initial–2nd periodic	09.07.96
Chile	06.01.90	2nd–3rd periodic (1999)	4th periodic	06.06.03
China	03.09.81	3rd–4th periodic (1999)	5th periodic	03.09.98
Colombia	18.02.82	4th periodic (1999)	5th periodic	18.02.99
Comoros	30.11.94		Initial–2nd periodic	30.11.95
Congo	25.08.82		Initial–5th periodic	25.08.83
Costa Rica	04.05.86		Initial–4th periodic	04.05.87

---

[61] As of July 2001.

State Party	Entry into force	Last report considered	Next report due	Date due or overdue since
Cote d'Ivoire	17.01.96		Initial–2nd periodic	16.01.01
Croatia	09.10.92	Initial (1998)	2nd periodic	09.10.97
Cuba	03.09.81	4th periodic (2000)	5th periodic	03.09.98
Cyprus	22.08.85	Iinitial–2nd periodic (1996)	3rd–4th periodic	22.08.94
Czech Republic	24.03.93	2nd periodic (2000)*	3rd periodic	24.03.02
Democratic Republic of the Congo	16.11.86	3rd periodic (2000)	4th periodic	16.11.99
Denmark	21.05.83	4th periodic (1997)*	5th–6th periodic	21.05.00
Djibouti	01.01.99		Initial	02.01.00
Dominica	03.09.81		Initial–5th periodic	03.09.82
Dominican Republic	02.10.82	4th periodic (1997)*	5th periodic	02.10.99
Ecuador	09.12.81	3rd periodic (1994)	4th–5th periodic	09.12.94
Egypt	18.10.81	4th–5th periodic (2001)	6th periodic	18.10.02
El Salvador	18.09.81	2nd periodic (1992)	3rd–5th periodic	18.09.90
Equatorial Guinea	22.11.84	2nd–3rd periodic (1994)*	4th periodic	22.11.97
Eritrea	05.10.95		Initial-2nd periodic	05.10.96
Estonia	20.11.91		Initial–3rd periodic	20.11.92
Ethiopia	10.10.81	Initial–3rd periodic	4th–5th periodic	10.10.94
Fiji	27.09.95	Initial (2000)*	2nd periodic	27.09.00
Finland	04.10.86	4th periodic (2001)	5th periodic	04.10.03
France	13.01.84	3rd periodic (1999)*	4rd–5th periodic	13.01.93
Gabon	20.02.83	Initial (1989)	2nd–5th periodic	20.02.88
Gambia	16.05.93		Initial–2nd periodic	16.05.94
Georgia	25.11.94	Initial (1999)	2nd periodic	25.11.99
Germany	09.08.85	2nd–3rd periodic (1996)	5th periodic	09.08.02
Ghana	01.01.86	Initial–2nd periodic (1992)	3rd–4th periodic	01.02.95
Greece	07.07.83	2nd–3rd periodic (1999)	4th–5th periodic	07.07.96
Grenada	29.09.90		Initial–3rd periodic	29.09.91
Guatemala	11.09.82	Initial–2nd periodic (1994)	3rd–5th periodic	11.09.91
Guinea	08.09.82	Initial (2000)*	2nd–5th periodic	08.09.87
Guinea-Bissau	22.09.85		Initial–4th periodic	22.09.86
Guyana	03.09.81	2nd periodic (2001)*	3rd–5th periodic	03.09.90
Haiti	03.09.81		Initial–5th periodic	03.09.82
Honduras	02.04.83	3rd periodic (1992)	4th–5th periodic	02.04.96
Hungary	03.09.81	4th–5th periodic (2000)*	6th periodic	03.09.02
Iceland	18.07.85	3rd–4th periodic (1998)	5th periodic	18.07.02
India	08.08.93	Initial (2000)	2nd periodic	08.08.98
Indonesia	13.10.84	2nd–3rd periodic (1998)	4th periodic	13.10.97
Iraq	12.09.86	2nd–3rd periodic (2000)	4th periodic	12.09.99
Ireland	22.01.86	2nd–3rd periodic (1999)	4th periodic	22.01.03
Israel	02.11.91	Initial–2nd periodic (1997)	3rd periodic	02.11.00
Italy	10.07.85	2nd periodic (1997)	3rd–4th periodic	10.07.94
Jamaica	18.11.84	2nd–4th periodic (2001)	5th periodic	18.11.01

State Party	Entry into force	Last report considered	Next report due	Date due or overdue since
Japan	25.07.85	4th periodic (1998)*	5th periodic	25.07.02
Jordan	31.07.92	2nd periodic (2000)	3rd periodic	31.07.01
Kazakhstan	25.08.98	Initial (2001)	2nd periodic	25.09.03
Kenya	08.04.84	3rd–4th periodic (2000)*	5th periodic	08.04.01
Kuwait	02.10.94		Initial–2nd periodic	02.10.95
Kyrgyzstan	11.03.97	Initial (1999)	2nd periodic	12.03.02
Lao People's Democratic Republic	13.09.81		Initial–5th periodic	13.09.82
Latvia	14.05.92		Initial–2nd periodic	14.05.93
Lebanon	21.05.97		Initial	21.05.97
Lesotho	21.09.95		Initial–2nd periodic	21.09.96
Liberia	16.08.84		Initial–4th periodic	16.08.85
Libyan Arab Jamahiriya	15.06.89	2nd periodic (1999)*	3rd periodic	15.06.98
Liechtenstein	21.01.96	Initial (1999)	2nd periodic	21.01.01
Lithuania	17.02.94	Initial (2000)	2nd periodic	17.02.99
Luxembourg	04.03.89	3rd periodic (2000)	4th periodic	04.03.02
Madagascar	16.04.89	Initial (1994)	2nd–3rd periodic	16.04.94
Malawi	11.04.87	Initial (1990)	2nd–4th periodic	11.04.96
Malaysia	04.08.95		Initial–2nd periodic	04.08.96
Maldives	31.07.93	Initial (2001)	2nd periodic	01.07.98
Mali	10.10.85	Initial (1988)	2nd–4th periodic	10.10.98
Malta	07.04.91		Initial–3rd periodic	07.04.00
Mauritius	08.08.84	Initial–2nd periodic (1995)	3rd–4th periodic	08.08.97
Mexico	03.09.81	3rd–4th periodic (1998)	5th–6th periodic	29.11.00
Mongolia	03.09.81	3rd–4th periodic (2001)	5th periodic	03.09.98
Morocco	21.07.93	Initial (1997)	2nd–3rd periodic	21.07.98
Mozambique	16.05.97		Initial	16.05.98
Myanmar	21.08.97	Initial (2000)	2nd periodic	21.08.02
Namibia	23.12.92	Initial (1997)	2nd periodic	23.12.97
Nepal	22.05.91	Initial (1999)	2nd–3rd periodic	22.05.00
Netherlands	22.08.91	2nd periodic (1998)*	3rd–4th periodic	22.08.04
New Zealand	09.02.85	3rd–4th periodic (1998)	5th periodic	09.02.02
Nicaragua	26.11.81	4th periodic (2001)*	5th–6th periodic	26.11.98
Niger	07.11.99		Initial	08.11.00
Nigeria	13.07.85	2nd –3rd periodic (1998)	4th periodic	13.07.98
Norway	03.09.81	5th periodic (2000)*	6th periodic	03.09.02
Pakistan	11.04.96		Initial–2nd periodic	11.04.97
Panama	28.11.81	2nd–3rd periodic (1998)	4th–5th periodic	28.11.94
Papua New Guinea	11.02.95		Initial–2nd periodic	11.02.96
Paraguay	06.05.87	Initial–2nd periodic (1996)	3rd–4th periodic	06.05.96
Peru	13.10.82	5th periodic (2000)	6th periodic	13.10.03
Philippines	40.09.81	4th periodic (1997)	5th periodic	04.09.98
Poland	03.09.81	3rd periodic (1990)	4th–5th periodic	03.09.94

115

State Party	Entry into force	Last report considered	Next report due	Date due or overdue since
Portugal	03.09.81	4th periodic (1999)	5th periodic	03.09.98
Republic of Korea	26.01.85	4th periodic (1998)	5th periodic	26.01.02
Republic of Moldova	31.07.94	Initial (2000)	2nd periodic	31.07.99
Romania	06.02.82	4th–5th periodic (2000)	6th periodic	06.02.03
Russian Federation	03.09.81	4th periodic (1995)	5th–6th periodic	03.09.98
Rwanda	03.09.81	3rd periodic (1991)	4th–5th periodic	03.09.94
Saint Kitts and Nevis	25.05.85		Initial–4th periodic	25.05.86
Saint Lucia	07.11.82		Initial–5th periodic	07.11.99
Saint Vincent and the Grenadines	03.09.81	Initial–3rd periodic (1997)	4th–5th periodic	03.09.94
Samoa	25.10.92		Initial–2nd periodic	25.10.97
Saudi Arabia	07.10.00		Initial	07.10.01
Senegal	07.03.85	2nd periodic (1994)	3rd–4th periodic	07.03.94
Seychelles	04.06.92		Initial–2nd periodic	04.06.93
Sierra Leone	11.12.88		Initial–3rd periodic	11.12.89
Singapore	05.11.95	Initial (1999)*	2nd periodic	04.11.00
Slovakia	27.06.93	Initial (1998)	2nd periodic	27.06.98
Slovenia	05.08.92	2nd periodic (1999)*	3rd periodic	05.08.01
South Africa	14.01.96	Initial (1998)	2nd periodic	14.01.01
Spain	04.02.84	4th periodic (1999)	5th periodic	04.02.01
Sri Lanka	04.11.81	3rd–4th periodic (1999)*	5th periodic	04.11.98
Suriname	31.03.93		Initial–2nd periodic	31.03.94
Sweden	03.09.81	4th periodic (2001)*	5th periodic	03.09.98
Switzerland	26.04.97		Initial	26.04.98
Tajikistan	25.11.93		Initial–2nd periodic	25.10.94
Thailand	08.09.85	2nd–3rd periodic (1999)	4th periodic	08.09.98
Togo	26.10.83		Initial–5th periodic	26.10.88
Trinidad and Tobago	11.02.90		Initial–3rd periodic	11.02.91
Tunisia	20.10.85	3rd–4th periodic (2000)*	5th periodic	20.10.02
Turkey	19.01.86	2nd–3rd periodic (1997)	4th periodic	19.01.99
Turkmenistan	30.05.97		Initial	25.07.00
Tuvalu	05.11.99		Initial	06.11.00
Uganda	21.08.85	3rd periodic (2000)*	4th periodic	21.08.98
Ukraine	03.09.81	4th–5th periodic (1999)*	6th periodic	03.09.02
United Kingdom of Great Britain and Northern Ireland	07.05.86	4th periodic (1999)	5th periodic	07.05.03
United Republic of Tanzania	19.09.85	2nd–3rd periodic (1998)	4th periodic	19.09.98
Uruguay	08.11.81	2nd–3rd periodic (1998)*	4th–5th periodic	08.11.94

State Party	Entry into force	Last report considered	Next report due	Date due or overdue since
Uzbekistan	18.08.95	Initial (2001)	2nd periodic	18.08.00
Vanuatu	08.10.95		Initial–2nd periodic	08.10.96
Venezuela	01.06.83	3rd periodic (1997)	4th–5th periodic	01.06.96
Vietnam	19.03.82	3rd–4th periodic (2001)*	5th periodic	19.05.99
Yemen	29.06.84	4th periodic (2000)	5th periodic	29.06.01
Yugoslavia	28.03.82	3rd periodic (1998)*	4th–5th periodic	28.03.95
Zambia	21.07.85	3rd–4th periodic (1999)*	5th periodic	21.07.02
Zimbabwe	12.06.91	Initial (1998)	2nd–3rd periodic	12.06.00

(An asterisk indicates that a report has been submitted but not yet been considered by the Committee)

5. THE EXCEPTIONAL REPORTS PROCEDURE

In 1993, the Committee, under article 18 of the Convention, requested reports on an exceptional basis from certain States of the former Yugoslavia.[62] It indicated then that it would adopt such a procedure in order to "look into similar grave violations of human rights being experienced by women in any part of the world."[63] With regard to the reports which have been submitted by States of the former Yugoslavia, the Committee has adopted the procedure of:[64]

(a) Tabling the reports at the upcoming session without sending them for attention of the Working Group;
(b) Permitting the State representative to orally introduce the report at the session;
(c) Inviting questions by members;
(d) Permitting responses by the State representatives;
(e) Adopting and publishing brief comments for inclusion in the annual report.

In 1999, the Committee clarified the purpose of the procedure as being, "in order to obtain and examine the information on an actual or potential violation of women's rights, where there is special cause for concern about such violation".[65] The criteria for requesting an exceptional report are, (a) the existence of reliable and adequate information indicating grave or systematic violations of women's human rights, (b) the violations should be gender-based or directed at women because of their sex. The exceptional reports should focus on whatever particular issues have been identified by the Committee.[66]

---

[62] See M. O'Flaherty, "Treaty Bodies Responding to States of Emergency: The Case of Bosnia and Herzegovina", in *The Future of UN Human Rights Treaty Monitoring*, (P. Alston and J. Crawford, Eds., 2000).
[63] United Nations Doc. A/48/38, Chap. 1, sect. B. Subsequently reports have been requested from Democratic Republic of the Congo (Zaire) and Rwanda.
[64] See United Nations Doc. A/49/38, paras. 729–776 and A/50/38, paras. 553–591.
[65] Decision 21/1, in United Nations Doc. A/54/38/Rev., Chapter I.
[66] *Ibid.*

NGOs may wish to draw to the attention of members of the Committee situations which call for the requesting of exceptional reports. Once such reports have been submitted and are to be considered, NGOs may submit information in the same manner as with regard to regular State reports.

6. THE COMMUNICATIONS PROCEDURE AND THE INQUIRY PROCEDURE[67]

The Optional Protocol to the Convention came into force on 22 December 2000.[68] The Protocol contains two procedures: (a) a communications procedure whereby individuals, or groups of individuals may submit claims of violations of rights protected under the Convention to the Committee, and (b) an inquiry procedure whereby the Committee may undertake inquiries into situations of grave or systematic violation of rights under the Convention.

6.1 The Communications Procedure

The procedure permits individuals or groups of individuals to complain directly or through representatives[69] to the Committee about a State in circumstances where they are the alleged victims of violations of the Convention and the State has ratified or otherwise acceded to the Optional Protocol. The Optional Protocol stipulates that States party must disseminate information in the State concerning the communications procedure.[70] Furthermore, States must take all appropriate steps to ensure that individuals under their jurisdiction are not subjected to ill treatment as a consequence of communicating with the Committee[71]

The function of the Committee is to gather all necessary information, by means of written exchanges with the parties (the State and the complainant), to consider the admissibility and merits of complaints and to issue its "Views" accordingly. It should be noted that the Committee is not a court, does not issue "judgements" and has no

---

[67] *The Optional Protocol, Text and Materials,* (United Nations, 2000); *Claiming Women's Rights: The Optional Protocol to the UN Women's Convention,* (Amnesty International, 2001); A. Byrnes, "Slow and Steady Wins the Race? The Development of an Optional Protocol to the Women's Convention", 91 ASIL Proc. (1997), 383; S. Cartwright, "Rights and Remedies: the Drafting of and Optional Protocol to the Convention on the Elimination of All Forms of Discrimination Against Women", 9 Otago Law Review 239; *Optional Protocol to the Convention on the Elimination of All Forms of Discrimination Against Women: Report of the Secretariat,* United Nations Doc. CEDAW/C/2000/1/5.

[68] As of August 2001 the following are States party to the Optional Protocol: Austria, Azerbaijan, Bangladesh (but opting out of the inquiry procedure), Bolivia, Croatia, Czech Republic, Denmark, Dominican Republic, Finland, France, Hungary, Iceland, Ireland, Italy, Mali, Namibia, New Zealand, Panama, Paraguay, Peru, Senegal, Slovakia, Spain, Thailand, Uruguay. Current information on the status of ratification of human rights instruments can be found at the OHCHR website: www.unhcbr.ch.

[69] Article 2 of the Optional Protocol, "... Where a communication is submitted on behalf of individuals or groups of individuals, this shall be with their consent unless the author can justify acting on their behalf without such consent".

[70] Article 13 of the Optional Protocol.

[71] Article 11 of the Optional Protocol.

means to enforce any Views which it might adopt. Furthermore, all exchanges with the Committee take only written form. There is no provision for the awarding of any financial assistance to needy applicants to assist them in taking a case to the Committee.

All steps of the procedure are confidential until the point where the Committee adopts its Views or otherwise concludes a case.[72] However, unless the Committee (itself or through a rapporteur or working group) requests otherwise, a complainant or the State party may make public any submission or information bearing on the proceedings. Views are reported in the Committee's annual report. Unless the Committee otherwise decides, decisions on admissibility, non-admissibility and discontinuance are also reported as is information furnished by the parties and decisions of the Committee within the framework of follow-up to the Committee's Views.

A communication must negotiate two stages, those of consideration for admissibility and on the merits. However, the Committee may decide on the admissibility and merits of a communication together. At any stage in the process, the Committee, or delegated working groups or rapporteurs, may request that the State take interim measures to safeguard the alleged victim or victims.[73] Such a request does not have binding force.

The first step in bringing a communication to the attention of the Committee is to contact the Secretariat. The Secretariat may then request the complainant(s) to complete a questionnaire concerning the case. At this or any other stage complainants are free to maintain contact with members of the Secretariat to obtain advice and guidance. In any case, the Secretariat is empowered to seek clarification and further information from the complainant(s) and to establish time limits for receipt of responses (but without prejudice to the right of the complainant(s) to have the communication put before the Committee).[74]

Communications are brought to the attention of the Committee at its next regular session. The Committee may be assisted in its consideration of communications at any stage of the proceedings by rapporteurs or working groups.

As soon as possible after being received by the Committee and unless the complainant(s) request anonymity, complaints are brought to the attention of the State Party with a request for a response within six months regarding the complaint's admissibility and merits. Any arguments by the State of inadmissibility must be submitted within two months. Further requests for information may be made of both the complainant(s) and the State, subject to fixed time limits.[75]

---

[72] Rules of Procedure of the Committee on the Elimination of Discrimination Against Women, Rule 74, United Nations Doc. HRI/GEN/3 at p. 128.

[73] Article 5 of the Optional Protocol; Rules of Procedure of the Committee on the Elimination of Discrimination Against Women, Rule 63, United Nations Doc. HRI/GEN/3 at p. 123.

[74] Rules of Procedure of the Committee on the Elimination of Discrimination Against Women, Rules 58 and 59, United Nations Doc. HRI/GEN/3 at p. 125.

[75] Rules of Procedure of the Committee on the Elimination of Discrimination Against Women, Rule 69, United Nations Doc. HRI/GEN/3 at p. 123.

The admissibility requirements are as follows:[76]

(a) The Committee shall not consider a communication unless it has ascertained that all available domestic remedies have been exhausted unless the application of such remedies is unreasonable prolonged or unlikely to bring effective relief.
(b) The alleged violation must have occurred after the State Party acceded to the Optional Protocol. However, facts which occurred before that date with effects which persist may be actionable.
(c) Cases may not be taken which are subject to consideration by another procedure of international investigation or settlement or which have been previously considered by the Committee.
(d) The communication must not be incompatible with the provisions of the Convention, be manifestly ill-founded or insufficiently substantiated or constitute an abuse of the right to submit a communication.

Where the Committee decides that a communication is inadmissible it so advises the complainant(s) and the State Party. The case may be re-opened should further information be submitted indicating that the reasons for inadmissibility no longer apply.[77]

Decisions on admissibility may also be revoked in the light of information provided by the State Party in situations where the issue of admissibility had been considered separate to the merits and where further relevant information is provided by the State Party in the context of commenting on the merits.[78]

Either in cases where the issue of admissibility has been taken separately or where both admissibility and merits are considered together, the Committee formulates its view on the merits of the case in the light of all written information made available to it by the complainant(s) and the State, provided that this information has been transmitted to the other party concerned. The Committee may obtain any document from organisations in the UN system or other bodies that may assist in the disposal of the communication, provided that the complainant(s) and the State have the opportunity to comment on such documentation or information within fixed time limits.[79]

The Views of the Committee, which may include recommendations, are determined by simple majority. Individual opinions of Committee members may be appended.[80]

Within six months of the Committee issuing its Views, the State shall submit to

---

[76] Article 4 of the Optional Protocol.
[77] Rules of Procedure of the Committee on the Elimination of Discrimination Against Women, Rule 70, United Nations Doc. HRI/GEN/3 at p. 126.
[78] Rules of Procedure of the Committee on the Elimination of Discrimination Against Women, Rule 71, United Nations Doc. HRI/GEN/3 at p. 126.
[79] Rules of Procedure of the Committee on the Elimination of Discrimination Against Women, Rule 72, United Nations Doc. HRI/GEN/3 at pp. 126–127.
[80] Rules of Procedure of the Committee on the Elimination of Discrimination Against Women, Rule 72, United Nations Doc. HRI/GEN/3 at p. 126–127.

the Committee a written response, including information on action taken in light of the Views and recommendations of the Committee. Subsequently the Committee may request additional information in this regard and it may request the State to include information on the matter in its periodic reports to the Committee under article 18 of the Convention. All aspects of the follow-up of Views by the Committee are monitored by either a rapporteur or working group. The rapporteur or working group may make such contacts and take such action as appropriate and may recommend further action to be undertaken by the Committee. The Committee includes information on any follow-up activities in its annual report.[81]

6.2. The Inquiry Procedure

This procedure provides for the investigation of reliable indications of grave or systematic violations by a State Party to the Optional Protocol (provided that the State party has not declared at time of accession that it does not recognise the competence in this regard of the Committee) of rights set for the in the Convention. The procedure is confidential but requires to be summarily reported in the Committee's annual report to the General Assembly. The Committee may also invite the State to report on measures taken in response to an inquiry within its reports to the Committee under article 18 of the Convention. The Optional Protocol stipulates that States Parties must disseminate information in the State concerning the procedure.[82] Furthermore, States must take all appropriate steps to ensure that individuals under their jurisdiction are not subjected to ill-treatment as a consequence of communicating with the Committee pursuant to the Optional Protocol.[83]

The Optional Protocol provides that:

Article 8
1. *If the Committee receives reliable information indicating grave or systematic violations by a State party of rights set forth in the Convention, the Committee shall invite that State party to cooperate in the examination of the information and to this end to submit observations with regard to the information concerned.*
2. *Taking into account any observations that may have been submitted by the State party concerned as well as any other reliable information available to it, the Committee may designate one or more of its members to conduct an inquiry and to report urgently to the Committee. Where warranted and with the consent of the State party, the inquiry may include a visit to its territory.*
3. *After examining the findings of such an inquiry, the Committee shall transmit these findings to the State party concerned together with any comments and recommendations.*
4. *The State party concerned shall, within six months of receiving the findings,*

---

[81] Article 12 of the Optional Protocol.
[82] Article 13 of the Optional Protocol.
[83] Article 11 of the Optional Protocol.

comments and recommendations transmitted by the Committee, submit its
observations to the Committee.
5. Such an inquiry shall be conducted confidentially and the co-operation of the State
party shall be sought at all stages of the proceedings.

Article 9
1. *The Committee may invite the State party concerned to include in its report under
   article 18 of the Convention details of any measures taken in response to an inquiry
   conducted under article 8 of the present Protocol.*
2. *The Committee may, if necessary, after the end of the period of six months referred
   to in article 8.4, invite the State party concerned to inform it of the measures taken
   in response to such an inquiry.*

The Committee's Rules of Procedure[84] explain the manner in which the procedure is to
be implemented. It seems that an inquiry can be instigated on the basis of information
received from any source.[85] All such information which appears to be submitted under
the inquiry procedure must be registered and made available to the Committee by the
Secretariat.[86] The Committee may instruct the Secretariat to investigate the reliability
of the information and to seek further or corroborating information.[87]

Once the information is deemed by the Committee to be reliable and indicative of
grave or systematic violations of rights set forth in the Convention, the State Party
concerned is invited to comment within a stated time limit.[88] Other possible sources
of information including NGOs and individuals may also be invited to submit
further information and the Committee shall decide the form and the manner in
which such additional information may be obtained.[89] The Committee may then
decide to conduct an inquiry to be conducted by one or more of its members, assisted
by relevant experts regarding the Convention, in accordance with any modalities
determined by the Committee, and invite the Government to afford its co-operation,
including, if appropriate, the provision of facilities for the conducting of one or more
visiting missions.[90] The visits may involve the conducting of sworn hearings and the

---

[84] Rules of Procedure of the Committee on the Elimination of Discrimination Against Women, Rules 76–
91, United Nations Doc. HRI/GEN/3 at pp. 129–133.
[85] Rules of Procedure of the Committee on the Elimination of Discrimination Against Women, Rule 76,
United Nations Doc. HRI/GEN/3 at p. 129.
[86] Rules of Procedure of the Committee on the Elimination of Discrimination Against Women, Rules 77–
79, United Nations Doc. HRI/GEN/3 at p. 129.
[87] Rules of Procedure of the Committee on the Elimination of Discrimination Against Women, Rule 82,
United Nations Doc. HRI/GEN/3 at p. 130.
[88] Rules of Procedure of the Committee on the Elimination of Discrimination Against Women, Rule 783,
United Nations Doc. HRI/GEN/3 at p. 130.
[89] Rules of Procedure of the Committee on the Elimination of Discrimination Against Women, Rule 83,
United Nations Doc. HRI/GEN/3 at pp. 130–131.
[90] Rules of Procedure of the Committee on the Elimination of Discrimination Against Women, Rules 84–
86 and 88, United Nations Doc. HRI/GEN/3 at pp. 131–133.

State Party may be informed by the Committee that it shall take all appropriate steps to ensure that those heard are not intimidated or subjected to ill-treatment.[91]

During the period of an inquiry the Committee may defer the consideration of any report of a State Party submitted under article 18 of the Convention.[92]

After examining the findings of the inquiry, the Committee transmits the findings, together with its comments and recommendation, to the State Party, inviting it to indicate, within six months, measures taken in response thereto.[93] The Committee may also request a State Party to include details of such measures in its reports under Article 18 of the Convention.[94]

7. GENERAL RECOMMENDATIONS

The Committee continues to elaborate General Recommendations based on the various articles and provisions of the Convention with a view to assisting States Parties in fulfilling their reporting obligation, and elucidating the full significance for law and practice of the Convention. By the end of 2000, the Committee had adopted twenty-four General Recommendations. In 1997 the Committee adopted a structured approach to the drafting of General Recommendations, intended to enhance input and use of the expertise of members and others, including NGOs. The drafting process comprises three stages,[95] with a duration of some one to three years:

(a) A general discussion and exchange of views on the subject of the proposed general recommendation, in an open meeting of the Committee. Specialised UN agencies and NGOs are encouraged to participate as well as to submit informal background papers.

(b) A designated Committee member, with the assistance of the Secretariat, draws the results of the discussion into an initial draft. This draft is then discussed during the next session of the Committee by a Working Group which may invite resource persons and NGOs to participate in the discussions.

(c) A revised draft is compiled and distributed to Committee members before the next session, where it is considered in closed meetings with a view to adoption.

The annual reports of the Committee provide information regarding the Committee's programme of work for the drafting of General Recommendations. This information can be supplemented by the Secretariat which will also be in a position to advise NGOs as to how best to input the drafting process, including through participation in the discussions within the Committee and its Working Groups.

---

[91] Rules of Procedure of the Committee on the Elimination of Discrimination Against Women, Rule 87, United Nations Doc. HRI/GEN/3 at p. 132.

[92] Rules of Procedure of the Committee on the Elimination of Discrimination Against Women, Rule 84, United Nations Doc. HRI/GEN/3 at pp. 131.

[93] Rules of Procedure of the Committee on the Elimination of Discrimination Against Women, Rule 89, United Nations Doc. HRI/GEN/3 at p. 131.

[94] Rules of Procedure of the Committee on the Elimination of Discrimination Against Women, Rule 90, United Nations Doc. HRI/GEN/3 at p. 133.

[95] United Nations Doc. A/52/38/Rev.1, at para. 480.

CHAPTER 6

THE COMMITTEE AGAINST TORTURE

1. THE SUBSTANTIVE PROVISIONS OF THE CONVENTION AGAINST TORTURE AND OTHER CRUEL, INHUMAN OR DEGRADING TREATMENT OR PUNISHMENT[1]

Article 1

1. *For the purposes of this Convention, the term "torture" means any act by which severe pain or suffering, whether physical or mental, is intentionally inflicted on a person for such purposes as obtaining from him or a third person information or a confession, punishing him for an act he or a third person has committed or is suspected of having committed, or intimidating or coercing him or a third person, or for any reason based on discrimination of any kind, when such pain or suffering is inflicted by or at the instigation of or with the consent or acquiescence of a public official or other person acting in an official capacity. It does not include pain or suffering arising only from, inherent in or incidental to lawful sanctions.*
2. *This article is without prejudice to any international instrument or national legislation which does or may contain provisions of wider application.*

Article 2

1. *Each State Party shall take effective legislative, administrative, judicial or other measures to prevent acts of torture in any territory under its jurisdiction.*
2. *No exceptional circumstances whatsoever, whether a state of war or a threat of war, internal political in stability or any other public emergency, may be invoked as a justification of torture.*

---

[1] J. Voyame and P. Burns, "The Convention against Torture and Other Cruel, Inhuman or Degrading Treatment or Punishment", in *Manual on Human Rights Reporting*, (United Nations, 1997), pp. 367–392; *Fact Sheet 17, The Committee against Torture*, (United Nations); A. Cassesse, Ed., *The International Fight Against Torture*, (1991); H. Burgers and H. Danelius, *The United Nations Convention Against Torture*, (1988); M. E. Tardu, "The UN Convention Against Torture and other Cruel, Inhuman or Degrading Treatment or Punishment", Nordic Journal of International Law, Vol. 56, (1987), pp. 303–321; N. Lerner, "The UN Convention on Torture", Israel Yearbook of Human Rights, Vol. 16, (1986), pp. 126–142; N. Rodley, *The Treatment of Prisoners under International Law*, (1999).

3. *An order from a superior officer or a public authority may not be invoked as a justification of torture.*

Article 3

1. *No State Party shall expel, return ("refouler") or extradite a person to another State where there are substantial grounds for believing that he would be in danger of being subjected to torture.*
2. *For the purpose of determining whether there are such grounds, the competent authorities shall take into account all relevant considerations including, where applicable, the existence in the State concerned of a consistent pattern of gross, flagrant or mass violations of human rights.*

Note

In General Comment 1[2] the Committee states that "article 3 is confined in its application to cases where there are substantial grounds for believing that the author would be in danger of being subjected to torture as defined in article 1 of the Convention" and that it is mainly the task of the author to establish a *prima facie* case for the purpose of admissibility. The Committee further observes that the phrase "another State" in article 3 refers to the State to which the individual concerned is being expelled, returned or extradited, as well as to any State to which the author may subsequently be expelled, returned or extradited. The criterion of a consistent pattern or gross, flagrant or mass violations of human rights, instead, is meant to refer only to violations by or at the instigation of or with the consent or acquiescence of a public official or other person acting in an official capacity.

Article 4

1. *Each State Party shall ensure that all acts of torture are offences under its criminal law. The same shall apply to an attempt to commit torture and to an act by any person which constitutes complicity or participation in torture.*
2. *Each State Party shall make these offences punishable by appropriate penalties which take into account their grave nature.*

Article 5

1. *Each State Party shall take such measures as may be necessary to establish its jurisdiction over the offences referred to in article 4 in the following cases:*
   (a) *When the offences are committed in any territory under its jurisdiction or on board a ship or aircraft registered in that State;*
   (b) *When the alleged offender is a national of that State;*

---

2   United Nations Doc. HRI/GEN/1/Rev.5, p. 253. At the time of writing this was the only General Comment adopted by the Committee Against Torture.

(c) When the victim is a national of that State if that State considers it appropriate.

2. *Each State Party shall likewise take such measures as may be necessary to establish its jurisdiction over such offences in cases where the alleged offender is present in any territory under its jurisdiction and it does not extradite him pursuant to article 8 to any of the States mentioned in paragraph I of this article.*

3. *This Convention does not exclude any criminal jurisdiction exercised in accordance with internal law.*

Article 6

1. *Upon being satisfied, after an examination of information available to it, that the circumstances so warrant, any State Party in whose territory a person alleged to have committed any offence referred to in article 4 is present shall take him into custody or take other legal measures to ensure his presence. The custody and other legal measures shall be as provided in the law of that State but may be continued only for such time as is necessary to enable any criminal or extradition proceedings to be instituted.*

2. *Such State shall immediately make a preliminary inquiry into the facts.*

3. *Any person in custody pursuant to paragraph I of this article shall be assisted in communicating immediately with the nearest appropriate representative of the State of which he is a national, or, if he is a stateless person, with the representative of the State where he usually resides.*

4. *When a State, pursuant to this article, has taken a person into custody, it shall immediately notify the States referred to in article 5, paragraph 1, of the fact that such person is in custody and of the circumstances which warrant his detention. The State which makes the preliminary inquiry contemplated in paragraph 2 of this article shall promptly report its findings to the said States and shall indicate whether it intends to exercise jurisdiction.*

Article 7

1. *The State Party in the territory under whose jurisdiction a person alleged to have committed any offence referred to in article 4 is found shall in the cases contemplated in article 5, if it does not extradite him, submit the case to its competent authorities for the purpose of prosecution.*

2. *These authorities shall take their decision in the same manner as in the case of any ordinary offence of a serious nature under the law of that State. In the cases referred to in article 5, paragraph 2, the standards of evidence required for prosecution and conviction shall in no way be less stringent than those which apply in the cases referred to in article 5, paragraph 1.*

3. *Any person regarding whom proceedings are brought in connection with any of the offences referred to in article 4 shall be guaranteed fair treatment at all stages of the proceedings.*

Article 8

1. *The offences referred to in article 4 shall be deemed to be included as extraditable offences in any extradition treaty existing between States Parties. States Parties undertake to include such offences as extraditable offences in every extradition treaty to be concluded between them.*
2. *If a State Party which makes extradition conditional on the existence of a treaty receives a request for extradition from another. State Party with which it has no extradition treaty, it may consider this Convention as the legal basis for extradition in respect of such offences. Extradition shall be subject to the other conditions provided by the law of the requested State.*
3. *States Parties which do not make extradition conditional on the existence of a treaty shall recognize such offences as extraditable offences between themselves subject to the conditions provided by the law of the requested State.*
4. *Such offences shall be treated, for the purpose of extradition between States Parties, as if they had been committed not only in the place in which they occurred but also in the territories of the States required to establish their jurisdiction in accordance with article 5, paragraph 1.*

Article 9

1. *States Parties shall afford one another the greatest measure of assistance in connection with criminal proceedings brought in respect of any of the offences referred to in article 4, including the supply of all evidence at their disposal necessary for the proceedings.*
2. *States Parties shall carry out their obligations under paragraph I of this article in conformity with any treaties on mutual judicial assistance that may exist between them.*

Article 10

1. *Each State Party shall ensure that education and information regarding the prohibition against torture are fully included in the training of law enforcement personnel, civil or military, medical personnel, public officials and other persons who may be involved in the custody, interrogation or treatment of any individual subjected to any form of arrest, detention or imprisonment.*
2. *Each State Party shall include this prohibition in the rules or instructions issued in regard to the duties and functions of any such person.*

Article 11

Each State Party shall keep under systematic review interrogation rules, instructions, methods and practices as well as arrangements for the custody and treatment of persons subjected to any form of arrest, detention or imprisonment in any territory under its jurisdiction, with a view to preventing any cases of torture.

Article 12

Each State Party shall ensure that its competent authorities proceed to a prompt and impartial investigation, wherever there is reasonable ground to believe that an act of torture has been committed in any territory under its jurisdiction.

Article 13

Each State Party shall ensure that any individual who alleges he has been subjected to torture in any territory under its jurisdiction has the right to complain to, and to have his case promptly and impartially examined by, its competent authorities. Steps shall be taken to ensure that the complainant and witnesses are protected against all ill-treatment or intimidation as a consequence of his complaint or any evidence given.

Article 14

1. Each State Party shall ensure in its legal system that the victim of an act of torture obtains redress and has an enforceable right to fair and adequate compensation, including the means for as full rehabilitation as possible. In the event of the death of the victim as a result of an act of torture, his dependants shall be entitled to compensation.

2. Nothing in this article shall affect any right of the victim or other persons to compensation which may exist under national law.

Article 15

Each State Party shall ensure that any statement which is established to have been made as a result of torture shall not be invoked as evidence in any proceedings, except against a person accused of torture as evidence that the statement was made.

Article 16

1. Each State Party shall undertake to prevent in any territory under its jurisdiction other acts of cruel, inhuman or degrading treatment or punishment which do not amount to torture as defined in article I, when such acts are committed by or at the instigation of or with the consent or acquiescence of a public official or other person acting in an official capacity. In particular, the obligations contained in articles 10, 11, 12 and 13 shall apply with the substitution for references to torture of references to other forms of cruel, inhuman or degrading treatment or punishment.

2. The provisions of this Convention are without prejudice to the provisions of any other international instrument or national law which prohibits cruel, inhuman or degrading treatment or punishment or which relates to extradition or expulsion.

2. COMMITTEE AGAINST TORTURE[3]

The Committee is established pursuant to the provisions of article 17 of the Convention. There are 10 members, elected by the States Parties for terms of four years.[4] Members, though all nationals of States Parties, serve in their private capacities and make a solemn declaration of impartiality upon taking up office. The Committee presently meets twice each year, in November and April/May for sessions of two/three working weeks each. All sessions take place in Geneva. Secretariat services are provided by the United Nations Office of the High Commissioner for Human Rights.[5]

Three of the activities of the Committee are of particular interest for NGOs and individuals: the reporting procedure, the investigation procedure under article 20 and the consideration of communications from individuals under article 22.

3. THE REPORTING PROCEDURE[6]

(a) The obligation on the State

Under article 19 of the Convention, States are obliged to submit reports to the Committee one year after the Convention comes into effect for the State and thereafter every four years, on the measures they have taken to give effect to their undertakings under the Convention. Periodic reports should provide information

---

[3] A. Byrnes, "The Committee against Torture", in *The United Nations and Human Rights* (P. Alston Ed. 1992), pp. 509–546; A. Dormenval, "United Nations Committee against Torture: Practice and Perspective", 8 *Netherlands Quarterly of Human Rights*, Vol. 8, (1990) pp. 26–44; M. Mohr and R. Kampa, "On the United Nations Anti-Torture Convention: Committee against Torture started its Work", 15 GDR Committee Hum. Rts. Bull., (1989), pp. 208–222; N. Rodley, *The Treatment of Prisoners under International Law*, (1999), pp. 150–161; R. Bank, "Country-oriented Procedures under the Convention Against Torture: Towards a new Dynamism", in *The Future of UN Human Rights Treaty Monitoring*, (P. Alston and J. Crawford Eds., 2000) 145–174; *Fact Sheet 17, The Committee against Torture*, (United Nations). See, generally, the following studies by P. Alston, *Long Term Approaches to Enhancing the Effectiveness of the United Nations Human Rights Treaty Bodies*, United Nations Doc. A/44/668; *Interim Report on Updated Study*, United Nations Doc. A/CONF.157/PC/62/Add.11/Rev.1; *Final Report on Enhancing the Long Term Effectiveness of the United Nations Human Rights Treaty System*, United Nations Doc. E/CN.4/1997/74; and, also, A. Bayefsky, *Report: The UN Human Rights Treaty System: Universality at the Crossroads*, (2001); P. Alston and J. Crawford Eds., *The Future of UN Human Rights Treaty Monitoring*, (2000); A. Bayefsky, Ed., *The UN Human Rights System in the 21st Century*, (2000).

[4] Membership as of October 2001: Peter Thomas Burns (Canada), Guibril Camara (Senegal), Sayed Kassem El Masry (Egypt), Felice Gaer (United States of America), Alejandro Gonzales Poblete (Chile), Antonio Silva Henriques Gaspar (Portugal), Andreas Mavrommatis (Cyprus), Ole Vedel Rasmussen (Denmark), Alexander M. Yakovlev (Russian Federation), Yu Mengzia (China).

[5] Secretariat of the Committee against Torture, Support Services Branch, Office of the High Commissioner for Human Rights, UNOG, 1211 Geneva 10, Switzerland (Tel.: 41 22 917 1234; Fax 41 22 917 0099).

additional to that in initial reports on new measures taken and on compliance with the Committee's Conclusions and Recommendations. States Parties are also obliged to submit any other reports which the Committee may request.[7]

The Committee has stipulated[8] that initial reports should be submitted in two parts. The first part[9] should:

(a) Describe the general legal framework to prohibit and eliminate torture and cruel, inhuman or degrading treatment;

(b) Indicate national or international binding obligations on the State to provide greater protection than that afforded by the Convention;

(c) Indicate the national redress procedures for victims of violations of the Convention and provide information on cases dealt with by those authorities during the reporting period.

The second part of the report[10] should provide information on implementation of articles 1 to 16 of the Convention, indicating:

(a) The legislative, judicial, administrative or other measures in force which give effect to the relevant provisions;

(b) Any factors and difficulties affecting the practical implementation of the provisions;

(c) Statistical data on cases where measures giving effect to the respective provisions have been enforced. The actual cases should also be described;

(d) The actual situation as regards the practical implementation of the Convention as well as any factors and difficulties affecting the degree of fulfilment of the obligations under the Convention.

Subsequent periodic reports should be presented in three parts.[11] The first part should describe in detail any new measures taken by the State Party to implement the Convention during the period since submission of the previous report, together with any new developments occurring in that period and relevant to implementation of

---

[6] J. Voyame and P. Burns, "The Convention against Torture and Other Cruel, Inhuman or Degrading Treatment or Punishment", in *Manual on Human Rights Reporting*, (United Nations, 1997), pp. 367–392; A. Byrnes, "The Committee against Torture" in *The United Nations and Human Rights* (P. Alston Ed. 1992); K. English and A. Stapleton, *The Human Rights Handbook – A Practical Guide to Monitoring Human Rights*, (1995), p. 179; S. Guillet, *Nous, Peuples des Nations Unies – L'action des ONG au sein du système de protection international des droits de l'homme*, (1995), pp. 66–67.

[7] Rules of Procedure of the Committee Against Torture, Rule 64, United Nations Doc. HRI/GEN/3 p. 156.

[8] United Nations Doc. HRI/GEN/2/Rev.1 pp. 44–46.

[9] The first part of reports should also comply with the consolidated guidelines relating to the preparation of the initial part of reports under the various international human rights instruments. See United Nations Doc. HRI/CORE/1.

[10] The article-by-article reporting obligation is analysed in J. Voyame and P. Burns, "The Convention against Torture and Other Cruel, Inhuman or Degrading Treatment or Punishment", in *Manual on Human Rights Reporting*, (United Nations, 1997), pp. 367–392.

[11] United Nations Doc. HRI/GEN/2/Rev.1 pp. 44–46.

the Convention. It is stipulated that information should, in particular, be provided concerning:

(a) Any change in legislation and institutions affecting implementation of the Convention;
(b) New case law relevant to implementation together with details of complaints and all other relevant proceedings and their outcome;
(c) Difficulties impeding implementation of the Convention.

The second part of the report should comprise information specifically requested by the Committee on the occasion of the previous consideration of a report unless that information has been otherwise furnished. The third part of the report should provide information on measures taken by the State to comply with the Committee's previous Conclusions and Recommendations adopted regarding the State.

(b) The procedure

i. The scheduling process
The Committee usually takes up reports within twelve months of their submission. As a matter of practice it is usually possible to obtain from the OHCHR website the proposed programme of reports to be considered no later than 10 weeks before each session. It is unusual, though not unknown, for the scheduling to be changed after this point. Occasionally adjustments to timetabling occur within sessions. The Committee occasionally encourages States to withdraw what it considers to be inadequate reports and to submit revised versions.[12] State Party reports, once published as United Nations documents, can be ordered from the United Nations Documents Distribution and Sales Section. The symbol number can be obtained from the Secretariat. Reports are usually available in all of the working languages of the Committee (English, French, Spanish and Russian). Reports are also posted on the OHCHR website.

ii. Before the session
Each report receives the attention of members designated as Country Rapporteur and alternate Country Rapporteur.[13] They are expected to undertake a detailed study of the report in preparation for the consideration by the Committee and to both identify key issues and prepare questions and comments to be put to the representatives of the Government. Country Rapporteurs base their analysis on the report itself, previous reports of the State, the records of the Committee's consideration of previous reports and other information which the Country Rapporteur considers to be of use. The latter may include reports of the United

---

[12] Rules of Procedure of the Committee against Torture, Rule 67, United Nations Doc.HRI/GEN/3 p. 157. As in the case of the initial report of Belize. See United Nations Doc. A/48/44, para. 45 with the explanation in United Nations Doc., CAT/C/SR.230, para. 5.
[13] See United Nations Doc. A/55/44, at Annex VII.

Nations Commission on Human Rights Special Rapporteurs, in particular the Special Rapporteur on Torture, and submissions of NGOs. The Country Rapporteur also makes use of a "country analysis" prepared by the Secretariat. This text, usually of some 15 to 20 pages in length, contains an in-depth analysis, based on any relevant information sources available to the drafters, including NGO inputs.

iii. Consideration by the Committee
The Committee considers reports in public session and in dialogue with representatives of the State.[14] Reports are introduced by representatives of the Government who will often use the occasion to provide further information or elaborate on aspects of the report.[15] The Country Rapporteur and alternate then take the floor and usually present an exhaustive analysis regarding the entire report and all provisions of the Convention. Whichever of the members who wish then pose their questions or make comments. Once the members have spoken the representative has the opportunity to reply. The exchange between Committee and representatives ends with the concluding remarks of the Country Rapporteur, the alternate and the members. Two or three days after the scrutiny, which usually extends over two three-hour meetings on consecutive days, the Committee adopts in private its "Conclusions and Recommendations",[16] and reads them out to the representatives of the State concerned during a subsequent public meeting. The Conclusions and Recommendations comprise a critique of the State report and of the response of the State representative to the scrutiny of the Committee, noting positive factors, occasionally identifying factors and difficulties impeding implementation of the Convention,[17] drawing attention to subjects of concern and making recommendations.[18] The Committee also, occasionally, requests additional information to be submitted for consideration at a future session.[19] Conclusions and Recommendations are adopted immediately following the examination of a report and made public in a subsequent meeting during the same session by means initially of being read out in the presence of representatives of the State. Conclusions and Recommendations are included in the annual report to the General Assembly of the United Nations, and are posted on the OHCHR website (initially solely in the language of adoption).

---

[14] Rules of Procedure of the Committee against Torture, Rules 64–68, United Nations Doc. HRI/GEN/3 p. 156–157.
[15] Rules of Procedure of the Committee against Torture, Rule 66, United Nations Doc. HRI/GEN/3 p. 157.
[16] See United Nations Doc. A/49/44, para. 14.
[17] Though the Committee had decided in 1994 that this category of comment be included in all Conclusions and Recommendations. See United Nations Doc. A/49/44, para. 14.
[18] A sample set of Conclusions and Recommendations (for The Netherlands) is reproduced in Appendix II.
[19] Rules of Procedure of the Committee Against Torture, Rule 67, United Nations Doc. HRI/GEN/3 p. 157.

(c) The role of non-governmental organisations[20]

Rule 62[21] of the Committee's Rules of Procedure states that the Committee may invite, *inter alia,* non-governmental organisations in consultative status with the Economic and Social Council, to submit to it information, documentation and written statements, relevant to the Committee's activities under the Convention. Notwithstanding this provision, NGOs, even if in consultative status with the Economic and Social Council, are not, in practice, accorded any official role in the process of consideration of reports. Thus, they may not have their documents received and processed as "United Nations documents" and they may not formally address the proceedings. NGOs do, however, have a wide range of opportunities to convey information informally to Committee members.[22]

Once a State's report has been scheduled for consideration, NGOs should indicate their interest to the Secretariat and send a submission for transmission to the Country Rapporteur, the alternate Rapporteur and other members, as well as for use by the Secretariat in the preparation of the "country analysis". Rather then rely on the Secretariat to copy these submissions for distribution, multiple copies (20) should be sent. Certain Counry Rapporteurs and members may also be happy to establish direct contact with NGOs.

About six weeks before the session, NGOs should send to the Secretariat a final version of their written submission with the request that it be distributed to members. At least 20 copies should be provided. Material submitted during the session may only be distributed to the Committee members by the Secretariat with the agreement of the Committee Chairperson.

A small number of NGOs have developed particular expertise in dealing with the Committee and their advice might usefully be sought. These NGOs might also consider accepting information for inclusion in their own submissions. Among the principle experienced NGOs are Amnesty International,[23] SOS Torture (OMCT),[24] the Association for the Prevention of Torture,[25] and the International Federation of Human Rights.[26]

If at all possible, NGOs should send representatives to attend the Committee meetings. Presence at the meetings permits informal contact with members, provision of updated submissions and other documentation, the channelling of information back to the country and the making of a comprehensive record of the proceedings. Opportunities may also arise for useful meetings with the Government

---

[20] See further at Chapter 1.
[21] Rules of Procedure of the Committee Against Torture, Rule 62, United Nations Doc. HRI/GEN/3 p. 155.
[22] See further, United Nations Doc. CAT/C/SR40, of 27 November 1995.
[23] Easton Street, London WCIX 8DJ, United Kingdom, (Tel. 44 207 413 5500, Fax 44 207 956 1157), www.amnesty.org.
[24] P. O. Box 119, 1211 Geneva, Switzerland, (Tel. 41 22 733 3140, Fax 41 22 733 1051), www.omct.org.
[25] Case Postale 2267, 1211 Geneva 2, Switzerland, (Tel. 41 22 734 2088, Fax 41 22 734 5649), www.apt.ch.
[26] 14 passage Dubail, 75010 Paris, France, (Tel. 33 1 4037 5426, Fax 33 1 4472 0586), www.fidh.org.

representatives, with international media in Geneva and with the international
human rights NGOs.

Access to the United Nations buildings in Geneva can be arranged in advance
with the Secretary of the Committee.

The role of NGOs following the conclusion of the Committee proceedings is
described in chapter one.

4. TABLE OF STATES PARTIES INDICATING WHEN A REPORT WAS LAST CONSIDERED AND IS NEXT DUE[27]

State Party	Entry into force	Last report considered	Next report due	Date due or overdue since
Afghanistan	26.06.87	Initial (1992)	2nd–4th periodic	25.06.92
Albania	10.06.94		Initial–2nd periodic	09.06.95
Algeria	12.10.89	2nd periodic (1996)	3rd periodic	11.10.98
Antigua Barbuda	18.8.93		Initial–2nd periodic	17.08.94
Argentina	26.06.87	3rd periodic (1997)	4th periodic	25.06.00
Armenia	13.10.93	2nd periodic (2000)	3rd periodic	12.10.02
Australia	07.09.89	2nd periodic (2000)	3rd periodic	06.11.04
Austria	28.08.87	5th periodic (2000)	6th periodic	30.04.03
Azerbaijan	15.09.96	Initial (1999)	2nd periodic	14.09.01
Bahraiin	05.04.98		Initial	04.04.99
Bangladesh	04.11.98		Initial	04.11.99
Belarus	26.06.87	3rd periodic (2000)	4th periodic	25.06.00
Belgium	25.07.99		Initial	25.07.00
Belize	26.06.87	Initial (1993)	2nd–4th periodic	25.06.92
Benin	11.04.92	Initial (2001)*		
Bolivia	11.05.99	Initial (2001)*		
Bosnia and Herzegovina	06.03.92		Initial–3rd periodic	05.03.93
Brazil	28.10.89	Initial (2001)*		
Bulgaria	26.06.87	2nd periodic (1999)	3rd–4th periodic	25.06.00
Burkina Faso	03.02.99		Initial	02.02.00
Burundi	20.03.93		Initial–2nd periodic	19.03.94
Cambodia	14.11.92		Initial–2nd periodic	13.11.97
Cameroon	26.06.87	2nd periodic (2000)	3rd periodic	25.06.00
Canada	24.07.87	3rd periodic (2000)	4th periodic	23.07.00
Cape Verde	04.07.92		Initial–2nd periodic	03.07.97
Chad	10.07.95		Initial–2nd periodic	09.07.00
Chile	30.10.88	2nd periodic (1994)	3rd periodic	29.10.97
China	03.11.88	3rd periodic (2000)	4th periodic	02.11.01
Colombia	07.01.88	2nd periodic (1995)	3rd–4th periodic	06.01.97
Costa Rica	11.12.93	Initial (2001)*		
Cote d'Ivoire	17.01.96		Initial–2nd periodic	16.01.01

[27] As of July 2001.

134

State Party	Entry into force	Last report considered	Next report due	Date due or overdue since
Croatia	08.10.91	2nd periodic (1998)	3rd periodic	07.10.00
Cuba	16.06.95	Initial (1997)	2nd periodic	15.06.00
Cyprus	17.08.91	2nd periodic (1997)	3rd periodic	16.08.00
Czech Republic	01.01.93	2nd periodic (2001)*		
Democratic Republic of the Congo	17.04.96		Initial–2nd periodic	16.04.97
Denmark	26.06.87	4th periodic (2001)*		
Ecuador	29.04.88	2nd periodic (1993)§	3rd–4th periodic	28.04.97
Egypt	26.06.87	3rd periodic (1999)		
El Salvador	17.07.96	Initial (2000)	2nd periodic	16.07.01
Estonia	20.11.91		Initial–3rd periodic	19.11.92
Ethiopia	13.04.94	2nd periodic (1999)		
Finland	29.09.89	3rd periodic (1999)	4th periodic	28.09.02
France	26.06.87	2nd periodic (1998)	3rd–4th periodic	25.06.96
Georgia	25.11.94	2nd periodic (2001)*		
Germany	31.10.90	2nd periodic (1998)	3rd periodic	30.10.99
Greece	05.11.88	3rd periodic (2001)*		
Guatemala	04.02.90	3rd periodic (2000)	4th periodic	03.02.03
Guinea	09.11.89		Initial–3rd periodic	08.11.90
Guyana	18.06.88		Initial–3rd periodic	17.06.89
Honduras	04.01.97		Initial	03.01.98
Hungary	26.06.87	3rd periodic (19989	4th periodic	25.06.00
Iceland	22.11.96	Initial (1998)	2nd periodic	22.11.01
Indonesia	27.11.98	Initial (2001)*		
Israel	02.11.91	3rd periodic (2001)*		
Italy	11.02.89	3rd periodic (1999)	4th periodic	10.02.02
Japan	29.07.99		Initial	29.07.00
Jordan	13.12.91	Initial (1995)	2nd–3rd periodic	12.12.96
Kazakhstan	25.09.98	Initial (2001)*		
Kenya	23.03.97		Initial	22.03.98
Latvia	13.05.92			
Kuwait	06.04.97	Initial (1998)	2nd periodic	05.04.01
Kyrgyzstan	05.10.97	Initial (1999)	2nd periodic	04.10.02
Latvia	14.05.92		Initial–2nd periodic	13.05.93
Libyan Arab Jamahiriya	15.06.89	3rd periodic (1999)	4th periodic	14.06.02
Liechtenstein	02.12.90	2nd periodic (1999)	3rd periodic	01.12.99
Lithuania	01.02.96		Initial–2nd periodic	01.03.97
Luxembourg	29.10.87	3rd–5th periodic (2001)*		
Malawi	11.07.97		Initial	10.07.98
Mali	28.03.99		Initial	27.03.00
Malta	13.10.90	2nd periodic (1999)	3rd periodic	12.10.99
Mauritius	08.01.93	2nd periodic (1999)	3rd periodic	07.06.02
Mexico	26.06.87	3rd periodic (1997)	4th periodic	25.06.00
Monaco	05.01.92	Initial (1994)	2nd–3rd periodic	04.01.97
Morocco	21.07.93	2nd periodic (1999)	3rd periodic	20.07.02
Mozambique	14.09.99		Initial	14.10.00

135

State Party	Entry into force	Last report considered	Next report due	Date due or overdue since
Namibia	28.12.94	Initial (1997)	2nd periodic	27.12.99
Nepal	13.06.91	Initial (1994)	2nd–3rd periodic	12.06.96
Netherlands	20.01.89	3rd periodic on Antilles and Aruba (2000)*	4th periodic	19.01.02
New Zealand	09.01.90	2nd periodic (1998)	3rd periodic	08.01.99
Niger	04.11.98		Initial	04.11.99
Norway	26.06.87	4th periodic (2001)*		
Panama	23.09.87	3rd periodic (1998)	4th periodic	27.09.00
Paraguay	11.04.90	3rd periodic (2000)	4th periodic	10.04.03
Peru	06.08.88	3rd periodic (1999)	4th periodic	05.08.01
Philippines	26.06.87	Initial (1989)	2nd–4th periodic	25.06.92
Poland	25.08.89	3rd periodic (2000)	4th periodic	24.08.02
Portugal	11.03.89	3rd periodic (2000)	4th periodic	10.03.02
Qatar	10.02.00		Initial	10.02.00
Republic of Korea	08.02.95	Initial (1996)	2nd periodic	07.02.00
Republic of Moldova	28.12.95		Initial–2nd periodic	27.12.00
Romania	17.01.91	Initial (1992)	2nd–3rd periodic	16.01.96
Russian Federation	26.06.87	3rd periodic (2001)*		
Saudi Arabia	23.10.97	Initial (2001)		
Senegal	26.06.87	2nd periodic (1996)	3rd–4th periodic	25.06.96
Seychelles	04.06.92		Initial–2nd periodic	03.06.93
Slovakia	28.05.93	Initial (2001)		
Slovenia	15.08.93	Initial (2000)	2nd periodic	14.09.01
Somalia	23.02.90		Initial–3rd periodic	22.02.91
South Africa	09.01.99		Initial	08.01.00
Spain	20.11.87	4th periodic (2001)*		
Sri Lanka	02.02.94	Initial (1998)	2nd periodic	01.02.99
Sweden	26.06.87	4th periodic (2001)*		
Switzerland	26.06.87	3rd periodic (1997)	4th periodic	25.06.00
Tajikistan	10.02.95		Initial–2nd periodic	09.02.96
Togo	18.12.87		Initial–4th periodic	17.12.88
Tunisia	23.10.88	2nd periodic (1998)	3rd periodic	30.11.99
Turkey	01.09.88	Initial (1990)	2nd–3rd periodic	31.08.93
Turkmenistan	25.07.99		Initial	25.07.00
Uganda	26.06.87		Initial–4th periodic	25.06.88
Ukraine	26.06.87	4th periodic (2001)*		
United Kingdom of Great Britain and Northern Ireland	07.01.89	3rd periodic (1998)	4th periodic	06.01.02
United States of America	20.11.94	2nd periodic (1996)	3rd–4th periodic	25.06.96
Uruguay	26.06.87	2nd periodic (1996)	3rd–4th periodic	25.06.96
Uzbekistan	28.10.95	2nd periodic (2001)*		
Venezuela	28.08.91	2nd periodic (2001)*		
Yemen	05.12.91		Initial–3rd periodic	04.12.92
Yugoslavia	10.10.91	Initial (1998)	2nd periodic	30.11.99

(An asterisk indicates that a report has been submitted but has not yet been considered by the Committee)

5. THE INVESTIGATION PROCEDURE UNDER ARTICLE 20

This procedure provides for the investigation of well-founded indications of the systematic practice of torture in a State Party. The procedure is confidential but may result in the inclusion of a summary account of its application in the Committee's annual report to the General Assembly. To date, its application has been reported concerning just three States, Turkey, Egypt and Peru. Three other inquiries are currently being conducted by the Committee.

Article 20 provides that:

1. *If the Committee receives reliable information which appears to it to contain well-founded indications that torture is being systematically practised in the territory of a State Party, the Committee shall invite that State Party to cooperate in the examination of the information and to this end to submit observations with regard to the information concerned.*
2. *Taking into account any observations which may have been submitted by the State Party concerned, as well as any other relevant information available to it, the Committee may, if it decides that this is warranted, designate one or more of its members to make a confidential inquiry and to report to the Committee urgently.*
3. *If an inquiry is made in accordance with paragraph 2 of this article, the Committee shall seek the cooperation of the State Party concerned. In agreement with that State Party, such an inquiry may include a visit to its territory.*
4. *After examining the findings of its member or members submitted in accordance with paragraph 2 of this article, the Committee shall transmit these findings to the State Party concerned together with any comments or suggestions which seem appropriate in view of the situation.*
5. *All the proceedings of the Committee referred to in paragraphs 1 to 4 of this article shall be confidential and to all stages of the proceedings the cooperation of the State Party shall be sought. After such proceedings have been completed with regard to an inquiry made in accordance with paragraph 2, the Committee may after consultations with the State Party concerned, decide to include a summary account of the results of the proceedings in its annual report made in accordance with article 24.*

A State Party is bound by the terms of article 20 unless it has, at the time of ratification or accession, declared and not subsequently withdrawn such a declaration, that it does not recognise the competence of the Committee under the article.[28]

---

[28] Article 28, para. 2 of the Convention. As of January 2001 the following States had so declared: Afghanistan, Belarus, China, Cuba, Israel, Kuwait, Morocco, Saudi Arabia, Ukraine.

The Committee's Rules of Procedure[29] explain the manner in which article 20 is to be implemented. It is clear that the procedure can be instigated on the basis of information received from any source.[30] All such information which appears to be submitted under article 20 must be registered and "where necessary" summarised and circulated to members by the Secretariat.[31] The Committee may instruct the Secretariat to investigate the reliability of the information and to seek further or corroborating information.[32] There is no requirement that alleged victims of torture have already exhausted all domestic remedies before their cases can be presented under article 20.[33]

In order to initiate the article 20 procedure, information provided must indicate the systematic practice of torture (art. 20, para.1). The Committee has elaborated the content of this requirement as follows: "The Committee considers that torture is practised systematically when it is apparent that the torture cases reported have not occurred fortuitously in a particular place or at a particular time, but are seen to be habitual, widespread and deliberate in at least a considerable part of the territory of the country in question. Torture may in fact be of a systematic character without resulting from the direct intention of a Government. It may be the consequence of factors which the Government has difficulty in controlling, and its existence may indicate a discrepancy between policy as determined by the central government and its implementation by the local administration. Inadequate legislation which in practice allows room for the use of torture may also add to the systematic nature of this practice".[34]

Once the information is deemed to meet the criteria in article 20, paragraph 1, the Government concerned is invited to comment within a stated time limit.[35] Other possible sources of information including NGOs and individuals may also be invited to submit further information and the Committee "shall decide, on its initiative and on the basis of its Rules of Procedure, the form and the manner in which such additional information may be obtained".[36] The Committee may then decide to conduct an inquiry to be conducted by one or more of its members, assisted by appropriate independent specialists, and invite the Government to afford its

---

[29] Rules of Procedure of the Committee Against Torture, Rule 69–84, United Nations Doc. HRI/GEN/3 pp. 158–162.

[30] Rules of Procedure of the Committee Against Torture, Rule 69, United Nations Doc. HRI/GEN/3 p. 158.

[31] Rules of Procedure of the Committee Against Torture, Rule 71, United Nations Doc. HRI/GEN/3 p. 158.

[32] Rules of Procedure of the Committee Against Torture, Rule 75, United Nations Doc. HRI/GEN/3 p. 159.

[33] See A. Byrnes, "The Committee against Torture" in *The United Nations and Human Rights*, (P. Alston Ed. 1992), pp. 530–533.

[34] United Nations Doc. A/48/44/Add.1. para. 39.

[35] Rules of Procedure of the Committee Against Torture, Rule 76 (2), United Nations Doc. HRI/GEN/3 p. 159.

[36] Rules of Procedure of the Committee Against Torture, Rule 76 (4)(5), United Nations Doc. HRI/GEN/3 pp. 159–160.

cooperation, including, if appropriate, the provision of facilities for the conducting of one or more visiting missions.[37] The inquiry may involve the conducting by the designated members of sworn hearings and the relevant Governments are requested to ensure that such proceedings are not interfered with and that those heard are not intimidated.[38]

After examining the findings of the inquiry, the Committee transmits the findings, together with its comments and recommendation, to the State Party, inviting it to indicate action which it intends to take in response thereto.[39] Finally, after consultation with the State Party, the Committee may decide to publish a summary of the proceedings in its annual report. This summary is first shared with the State Party.[40]

The summary which has been reported regarding Turkey provides indications as to the role of NGOs and others and the speed of the process.[41] The process was initiated by the submission of written information by Amnesty International. Subsequently, account was taken of written information from other NGOs and from the U.N. Special Rapporteur on Torture. The information was first examined in April 1990 and transmitted to the Government concerned in May. The Government stated that the Committee was acting outside its competence. In April 1991, the Committee appointed two members to make recommendations for further action. In November of that year, a two-member team of inquiry was established and requested the Government's consent to a mission in February 1992. The mission took place in June 1992. The inquiry team, assisted by a medical doctor, met with the national and local government officials, visited places of detention and interviewed many NGO representatives and individuals. Alleged victims of torture were interviewed and subjected to medical examinations. The team reported to the Committee in November 1992. Their findings were endorsed and transmitted to the Government which was invited to indicate by January 1993 any action it would take in response. The Government responded and the matter was again considered by the Committee in April 1993. The Committee then sought the views of the Government as to publication in the annual report of a summary of the proceedings. Despite the Government's objections, the Committee decided to publish the summary. It stated its reasons as follows: "The Committee, in view of the number and seriousness of the

---

[37] Rules of Procedure of the Committee Against Torture, Rules 78–80, United Nations Doc. HRI/GEN/3 pp. 160–161.

[38] Rules of Procedure of the Committee Against Torture, Rule 81, United Nations Doc. HRI/GEN/3 p. 161.

[39] Rules of Procedure of the Committee Against Torture, Rule 83, United Nations Doc. HRI/GEN/3 p. 162.

[40] Rules of Procedure of the Committee Against Torture, Rule 84, United Nations Doc. HRI/GEN/3 p. 162.

[41] United Nations Doc. A/48/44/Add.1. Regarding the Egypt proceedings see United Nations Doc. A/51/44, paras. 180–222, and, regarding Peru, United Nations Doc. A/55/44, paras. 219–224. See also R. Bank, "Country-oriented Procedures under the Convention Against Torture: Towards a new Dynamism", in *The Future of UN Human Rights Treaty Monitoring*, (P. Alston and J. Crawford Eds., 2000) 145–174.

allegations of torture … and in view of the findings on that question by the Committee members making the inquiry and the Committee's conclusions, and having considered the replies and observations of the … authorities, is convinced that such publication is necessary in order to encourage full respect for the provisions of the Convention in (the State Party)".

The summary appeared as an addendum to the annual report for that year, published on 15 November 1993.

The summary included the conclusions of the Committee. These constitute findings of fact as to the incidence of torture together with detailed recommendations directed to the Government.

There is no particular preferred format for NGO submissions which are made with a view towards initiation of an investigation under article 20. NGOs should, however, bear in mind that the procedure will only be employed in exceptional circumstances and on the basis of well-founded information indicating a widespread systematic incidence of torture. Submissions should therefore be prepared with great care and concern for accuracy. In general, NGOs would be advised, before attempting to have action initiated, to consult with both the Secretariat and those NGOs which have particular experience of the Committee and its work practices. Once an investigation has been initiated, NGOs which are invited to submit further information should take care to fully respect the confidentiality of the proceedings and to liaise closely with the Secretariat. They should also bear in mind that any delay by them in competently complying with requests of the Committee may delay or otherwise compromise the course of an investigation.

6. THE INDIVIDUAL COMPLAINTS PROCEDURE

The procedure permits individuals to complain directly or through representatives to the Committee about a State Party in circumstances where they are the alleged victims of violations of the Convention and the State Party has made the necessary declaration under article 22.[42] The function of the Committee is to gather all necessary information, primarily by means of written exchanges with the parties (the State and the complainant), to consider the admissibility and merits of complaints and to issue its "Views" or "Decisions" accordingly.[43]

---

[42] As of January 2001, 41 States: Algeria, Argentina, Australia, Austria, Belgium, Bulgaria, Canada, Croatia, Cyprus, Czech Republic, Denmark, Ecuador, Finland, France, Greece, Hungary, Iceland, Italy, Liechtenstein, Luxembourg, Malta, Monaco, Netherlands, New Zealand, Norway, Poland, Portugal, Russian Federation, Senegal, Slovakia, Slovenia, South Africa, Spain, Sweden, Switzerland, Togo, Tunisia, Turkey, Uruguay, Venezuela, Yugoslavia. Current information on the status of ratification of human rights instruments can be found at the OHCHR website: www.unhchr.ch.

[43] See, M. O'Flaherty, "Individual Communications: The Convention Against Torture and the Convention on the Elimination of All Forms of Racial Discrimination", in *Indigenous Peoples, the United Nations and Human Rights*, (S. Pritchard Ed., 1998); P. Burns, "Commentary on Complaint Processes by Human Rights Committee and Torture Committee Members, (b) The Committee Against Torture", and A. Byrnes, "An Effective Complaints Procedure in the Context of International Human Rights Law", in The UN Human Rights Treaty System in the 21st Century, (A.F. Bayefsky Ed.), 166–167 and 139–162.

Though not ineffective in having its Views respected by State Parties it should be noted that the Committee is not a court, does not issue "judgements" and has no means to enforce any Views which it might adopt. Furthermore, all exchanges with the Committee currently take only written form. The length of proceedings can vary from case to case. On average a period of two years may be envisaged, though in urgent situations, the Committee can dispose of a matter in a matter of months. It can be assumed that as the workload increases, there will be a corresponding delay in the processing of cases. There is no provision for the awarding of any financial assistance to needy applicants to assist them in taking a case to the Committee.

All steps of the procedure under article 22 are confidential until the point where the Committee adopts its Views or otherwise concludes a case. As a matter of practice Views are reported in the Committee's annual report together with a summary of the information made available to the Committee. Decisions on non-admissibility are also reported.[44]

By October 2000, the Committee had received 169 communications. Of these, 40 are at the pre-admissibility stage, 35 were deemed inadmissible, 45 were discontinued and, of 45 considered on the merits, 18 were found to indicate a violation of the Convention.

The first step in bringing a case to the attention of the Committee is to communicate with the Secretariat.[45] At this or any other stage complainants are free to maintain contact with members of the Secretariat to obtain advice and guidance.

Before a case can be considered on its merits it is necessary for it to have been found admissible.[46] The admissibility requirements are as follows:

i. A case may only be taken against a State and never an individual. The State must be a party to the Convention and have accepted the individual communication jurisdiction of article 22. Furthermore, the alleged violation of the Convention must have occurred since the date when article 22 came into force for that State.[47]

ii. Anonymous communications will not be accepted. However, the wish of the complainant to have his name withheld will be respected where the circumstances so warrant.

iii. Article 22 states that communications may be submitted by or on behalf of

---

[44] See Rules of Procedure of the Committee Against Torture, Rule 111, United Nations Doc. HRI/GEN/ 3 p. 172.

[45] Where the matter will be dealt with by a dedicated "petitions team" which handles all communications under the Optional Protocol to the International Covenant on Civil and Political Rights, the Convention Against Torture and the Convention on the Elimination of All Forms of Racial Discrimination.

[46] Rules of Procedure of the Committee Against Torture, Rule 107, United Nations Doc. HRI/GEN/3 p. 169.

[47] See Comm. No. 1, 2, 3/1998.

alleged victims. This provision has been translated into the Rules of Procedure as follows, "(t)he communication should be submitted by the individual himself or by his relatives or designated representatives or by others on behalf of an alleged victim when it appears that the victim is unable to submit the communication himself, and the author of the communication justifies his acting on the victim's behalf". This formulation leaves unclear the extent to which a case might be brought by non-relatives without the consent of an alleged victim, for instance by a well-meaning NGO in a situation where the victim is not in a position to give his consent.[48] In the case of *B. M'B v. Tunisia*, a communication from a person on behalf of a dead victim of torture was deemed inadmissible because the complainant was unable to provide "sufficient proof to establish his authority to act on behalf of the victim".

iv. Communications will be considered inadmissible if they are deemed to be an abuse of the right of petition or to be incompatible with the provisions of the Convention. These provisions are sufficiently unclear to allow for an overlapping of concern with other admissibility requirements. It is clear that they may cover a wide range of fact situations and would certainly preclude communications designed to subvert the work of the Committee, containing allegations of a frivolous nature, or abusive of the Committee or the Convention. Cases will also be deemed inadmissible if the complainant fails to provide a minimum amount of information indicating a possible violation of the Convention.[49] It may also be speculated that cases brought after excessively long delay following exhaustion of local remedies might also fall foul of these provisions.[50]

v. A communication will be considered inadmissible if the matter has been or is being considered under another procedure of international investigation or settlement. This provision clearly covers international redress procedures under the terms of human rights instruments. However, it is not clear to what extent it refers to non-conventional procedures such as those under Economic and Social Council resolution 1503 and the mandate of the Special Rapporteur on Torture and other mechanisms of the United Nations Commission on Human Rights. One may, however, presume that the Committee will follow the Human Rights Committee, which has held that such procedures do not fall foul of the

---

[48] *Fact Sheet No. 17, The Committee against Torture*, (United Nations), states that a non-governmental organisation may be entitled to take a case in circumstances where they can "justify their acting on the victim's behalf".

[49] The Committee in 1994 declared inadmissible two cases on the basis that the accounts provided by the complainants "lacked the minimum substantiation that would render (them) compatible with article 22 of the Convention", *X v. Switzerland*, and *Y v. Switzerland*. In both cases the Committee formed the view that the complainants had failed to indicate that they personally were endangered by a general situation of instability and human rights abuse in a third State (Zaire) to which they were at risk of being refouled. See also *A.M. v Switzerland*, Comm. No. 144/1999.

[50] There is no time limit within which a case must be brought following exhaustion of local remedies.

analogous provisions of the Optional Protocol to the International Covenant on Civil and Political Rights. It may indeed be noted that in at least two sets of cases to date, the States involved declined to argue that cases were inadmissible on the grounds that they arose within general situations which had already or were currently receiving the attention of Special Rapporteurs of the Commission on Human Rights.[51]

vi. Before a case can be taken to the Committee all domestic remedies should have been exhausted. However, this rule does not apply where the application of domestic remedies is unreasonably prolonged or is unlikely to bring effective relief to the victim. In the case of *Halimi-Nedzibi v. Austria*,[52] the Committee stated that "a delay of 15 months before an investigation of allegations of torture is initiated is unreasonably long". In another case, *R.E.G. v. Turkey*,[53] the alleged victim had taken no action to seek redress domestically and it was argued that he had no hope of justice in Turkey. The Committee was reluctant to accept such a sweeping generalisation and deemed the communication inadmissible. In *M.A. v. Canada*, an inadmissibility decision, the Committee further developed this point and stated that "in principle, it is not within the scope of the Committee's competence to evaluate the prospects of success of domestic remedies, but only whether they are proper remedies for determination of the author's claims".[54]

In the case of *Parot v. Spain*,[55] the Committee, in declaring the case admissible, noted that a genuine if misguided attempt to exhaust local remedies was sufficient "even if these attempts to engage available local remedies may not have complied with procedural formalities prescribed by law", in that the attempts made, "left no doubt as to Mr. Parot's wish to have the allegations investigated".

If the State chooses to argue that local remedies have not been exhausted it must offer substantiating evidence in support of this assertion.

If a communication is deemed inadmissible on the grounds of non-exhaustion of local remedies the option remains of re-submitting the matter subsequently when the remedies can be shown to be exhausted, unreasonably prolonged or ineffective.[56] To date the Committee has allowed the reopening of one case which it had previously deemed inadmissible, *I.U.B. v. Spain*.[57]

The first step in bringing a case to the Committee is to address a communication to its Secretariat. This first communication should include as much information as possible indicating both the satisfaction of the admissibility requirements and the

---

[51] Comm. No. 1, 2, 3/1988, and *Mutombo v. Switzerland,* Comm. No. 13/1993.
[52] Comm. No. 8/1991.
[53] Comm. No. 4/1990.
[54] See also *T.P. S. v Canada*, Comm. No. 99/1997.
[55] Comm. No. 6/1990.
[56] Rules of Procedure of the Committee Against Torture, Rule 109, United Nations Doc. HRI/GEN/3 p. 171.
[57] Comm. No. 6/1990.

applicability of the terms of the Convention to the specific matter being alleged.[58] Once the materials have arrived in Geneva, a staff member will open a dossier and make contact with the complainant to elicit in greater detail as much relevant information as possible.

Once the Secretariat is of the view that it has sufficient information, the case is given a reference number and listed in the register of cases. The Secretariat is obliged to duly register all cases where the complainants insist that they so do and where the impugned State Party has made a necessary declaration under article 22.[59]

At this stage, the file will probably be allocated to a member of the Committee known as a Special Rapporteur, whose task is to elicit as much information as possible in order to bring the case to the attention of the Committee, to refer the case for comment to the State Party as appropriate and to decide on any interim decisions or actions which may be required.[60] In practice the Special Rapporteur will from the outset seek information on both admissibility issues and the merits of the case. The view of the State Party will be sought and the communication brought to its attention, though, if the complainant so requests, his identity will not be disclosed. Both the State Party and the complainant must provide requested information within stated time limits of normally two months. Where information on the merits of the case is requested from the State Party there is a time limit for replying of six months.[61] Failure to abide by these time limits may result in the case proceeding without the requested information.[62]

If the circumstances so warrant, the Special Rapporteur (and of course the Committee itself) are empowered to request the State Party to take certain actions to protect the alleged victim.[63] Such requests are made without any prejudice to the eventual decision of the Committee on admissibility or the merits of a case. Urgent requests of this nature have been made on a number of occasions when the complainants indicated that they were likely to be deported to a State in circumstances where they believed that their lives would be thus endangered. In the case of *TPS v Canada*, the Committee, in expressing concern regarding the refusal of the State to comply with such a request, indicated that, "the State party, in ratifying the Convention and voluntarily accepting the Committee's competence under article 22, undertook to cooperate with it in good faith in applying the

---

[58] A model communication form is reproduced in Appendix III.

[59] Rules of Procedure of the Committee against Torture, Rule 98, United Nations Doc. HRI/GEN/3 p. 166.

[60] The Rules of Procedure also allow for the establishment of a Working Group of the Committee which may meet inter-sessionally if it so chooses. However, no such Group has yet been convened and the Committee has instead made use of Special Rapporteurs, who have equal authority to Working Groups. During 2001 this practice has been under review and it is likely that, from 2002, the role of the Rapporteur will be significantly supplanted by a pre-sessional Working Group of the Committee.

[61] Rules of Procedure of the Committee Against Torture, Rule 110, United Nations Doc. HRI/GEN/3 p. 171.

[62] Rules of Procedure of the Committee Against Torture, Rules 108 and 110, United Nations Doc. HRI/GEN/3 pp. 170–172.

[63] *Ibid.*

procedure. Compliance with the provisional measures called for by the Committee in cases it considers reasonable is essential to protect the person in question from irreparable harm, which could, moreover, nullify the end result of the proceedings before the Committee".[64]

When the Special Rapporteur is of the view that he has gathered sufficient information to form a view on admissibility he puts the case to the Committee for its consideration. The Committee has indicated that it is not constrained to address only the arguments made by the parties, but may itself, *ex officio*, address other matters which it considers of relevance. Thus, in its first three cases considered together, it examined questions arising under the provisions of article 14, which had not been raised by the parties.[65] As already noted, a decision of inadmissibility may also be reviewed subsequently by the Committee in the light of new information made available to it following a written request from the complainant.[66]

The Committee may choose to make its decision on the merits of a case simultaneously with its decision on admissibility.[67] Such a circumstance might arise where the State does not dispute admissibility and all relevant information has already been gathered. It might also occur in especially urgent cases such as *Mutombo v. Switzerland*.[68] In that case the State Party did not dispute admissibility and the entire case was disposed of within five months.

In its consideration of the merits, the Committee may defer decision pending receipt of further information. In all cases where further information is requested, the State Party and the complainant are kept fully informed. All requests for further information are subject to a time limit in which to reply.[69]

The Rules of Procedure of the Committee allow for the conducting of confidential oral hearings by the Committee in cases where it is of the view that these would be of assistance to it in gathering necessary information concerning the merits of a case.[70] There is no provision with regard to cases which are only at the admissibility stage. No hearings have as yet occurred. The Committee is also empowered to make reference to information made available to it by the United Nations bodies or specialised agencies which have a bearing on the determination of the merits of a case.[71]

When the Committee is of the view that it has gathered sufficient information, it proceeds to a consideration of the merits and the adoption of its Views.[72]

---

[64] Comm. No 99/1997, United Nations Doc. A/55/40 para. 242.

[65] Comm. No. 1, 2, 3/1998.

[66] Rules of Procedure of the Committee Against Torture, Rule 109, United Nations Doc. HRI/GEN/3 p. 171.

[67] Rules of Procedure of the Committee Against Torture, Rule 105, United Nations Doc. HRI/GEN/3 p. 168.

[68] Comm. No. 13/1993.

[69] Rules of Procedure of the Committee Against Torture, Rule 110, United Nations Doc. HRI/GEN/3 p. 171.

[70] *Ibid.*

[71] Rules of Procedure of the Committee Against Torture, Rule 111, United Nations Doc. HRI/GEN/3 p. 172.

[72] *ibid.*

The practice of the Committee is to adopt Views by consensus.[73] Members are free however, to append individual views to those of the Committee.[74] Though the Committee has no power to make awards, pecuniary or otherwise, it is free to make recommendations to the State Party regarding such matters.

The views of the Committee are communicated to the State Party and the complainant. Further to the Rules of Procedure, the State Party is invited to inform the Committee in due course of the action it takes in conformity with the Committee's Views.[75] In the case *Halimbi-Nedzibi v. Austria*,[76] "due course of time" was deemed by the Committee to be 90 days. The Committee has stipulated that, whenever a State fails to report on the remedial action taken, the Secretariat should, in consultation with the Special Rapporteur, send a reminder to the State concerned. If the State fails to respond, the matter will be taken up by the Committee at its subsequent session and may be referred to in the Committee's annual report to the General Assembly[77]

---

[73] On this practice, see M. Schmidt, "Individual Human Rights Complaints Procedures Based on United Nations Treaties and the Need For Reform" 41 ICLQ (1992), p. 645.

[74] Rules of Procedure of the Committee Against Torture, Rule 111, United Nations Doc. HRI/GEN/3 p. 172. See Comm. No. 99/1999, *TPS v Canada*.

[75] *Ibid.*

[76] Comm. No. 8/1991.

[77] United Nations Doc. A/55/44 para.19.

CHAPTER 7

THE COMMITTEE ON THE RIGHTS OF THE CHILD

1. THE SUBSTANTIVE PROVISIONS OF THE CONVENTION ON THE RIGHTS OF THE CHILD[1]

Article 1

For the purposes of the present Convention, a child means every human being below the age of eighteen years unless under the law applicable to the child, majority is attained earlier.

Article 2

1. *States Parties shall respect and ensure the rights set forth in the present Convention to each child within their jurisdiction without discrimination of any kind, irrespective of the child's or his or her parent's or legal guardian's race, colour, sex, language, religion, political or other opinion, national, ethnic or social origin, property, disability, birth or other status.*
2. *States Parties shall take all appropriate measures to ensure that the child is protected against all forms of discrimination or punishment on the basis of the status, activities, expressed opinions, or beliefs of the child's parents, legal guardians, or family members.*

Article 3

1. *In all actions concerning children, whether undertaken by public or private social*

---

[1] A. Lopatka, "An Introduction to the United Nations Convention on the Rights of the Child", in *Transnational Law and Contemporary Problems*, 6(1996) 2, pp. 263–286 and 251–262; S. Detrick, *A Commentary on the United Nations Convention on the Rights of the Child*, (1999); *Implementation Handbook for the Convention on the Rights of the Child*, (UNICEF, 1998) pp. 569–584; M. Santos Pais, "The Convention on the Rights of the Child", in *Manual on Human Rights Reporting*, (United Nations 1997), pp. 393–504; "Jurisprudence of the Committee on the Rights of the Child: A Guide for Research and Analysis", in Michigan Journal of International Law, 19 (1998) 3, pp. 633–728; J. Todres, "Emerging Limitations on the Rights of the Child: the UN Convention on the Rights of the Child and ite Early Case Law", in Colombia Human Rights Law Review, 30 (1998) 1, pp. 159–200.

welfare institutions, courts of law, administrative authorities or legislative bodies, the best interests of the child shall be a primary consideration.

2. States Parties undertake to ensure the child such protection and care as is necessary for his or her well-being, taking into account the rights and duties of his or her parents, legal guardians, or other individuals legally responsible for him or her, and, to this end, shall take all appropriate legislative and administrative measures.

3. States Parties shall ensure that the institutions, services and facilities responsible for the care or protection of children shall conform with the standards established by competent authorities, particularly in the areas of safety, health, in the number and suitability of their staff, as well as competent supervision.

Article 4

States Parties shall undertake all appropriate legislative, administrative, and other measures for the implementation of the rights recognized in the present Convention. With regard to economic, social and cultural rights, States Parties shall undertake such measures to the maximum extent of their available resources and, where needed, within the framework of international co-operation.

Article 5

States Parties shall respect the responsibilities, rights and duties of parents or, where applicable, the members of the extended family or community as provided for by local custom, legal guardians or other persons legally responsible for the child, to provide, in a manner consistent with the evolving capacities of the child, appropriate direction and guidance in the exercise by the child of the rights recognized in the present Convention.

Article 6

1. States Parties recognize that every child has the inherent right to life.

2. States Parties shall ensure to the maximum extent possible the survival and development of the child.

Article 7

1. The child shall be registered immediately after birth and shall have the right from birth to a name, the right to acquire a nationality and. as far as possible, the right to know and be cared for by his or her parents.

2. States Parties shall ensure the implementation of these rights in accordance with their national law and their obligations under the relevant international instruments in this field, in particular where the child would otherwise be stateless.

Article 8

1. States Parties undertake to respect the right of the child to preserve his or her identity, including nationality, name and family relations as recognized by law without unlawful interference.
2. Where a child is illegally deprived of some or all of the elements of his or her identity, States Parties shall provide appropriate assistance and protection, with a view to re-establishing speedily his or her identity.

Article 9

1. States Parties shall ensure that a child shall not be separated from his or her parents against their will, except when competent authorities subject to judicial review determine, in accordance with applicable law and procedures, that such separation is necessary for the best interests of the child. Such determination may be necessary in a particular case such as one involving abuse or neglect of the child by the parents, or one where the parents are living separately and a decision must be made as to the child's place of residence.
2. In any proceedings pursuant to paragraph 1 of the present article, all interested parties shall be given an opportunity to participate in the proceedings and make their views known.
3. States Parties shall respect the right of the child who is separated from one or both parents to maintain personal relations and direct contact with both parents on a regular basis, except if it is contrary to the child's best interests. 4. Where such separation results from any action initiated by a State Party, such as the detention, imprisonment, exile, deportation or death (including death arising from any cause while the person is in the custody of the State) of one or both parents or of the child, that State Party shall, upon request, provide the parents, the child or, if appropriate, another member of the family with the essential information concerning the whereabouts of the absent member(s) of the family unless the provision of the information would be detrimental to the well-being of the child. States Parties shall further ensure that the submission of such a request shall of itself entail no adverse consequences for the person(s) concerned.

Article 10

1. In accordance with the obligation of States Parties under article 9, paragraph 1, applications by a child or his or her parents to enter or leave a State Party for the purpose of family reunification shall be dealt with by States Parties in a positive, humane and expeditious manner. States Parties shall further ensure that the submission of such a request shall entail no adverse consequences for the applicants and for the members of their family.
2. A child whose parents reside in different States shall have the right to maintain on a regular basis, save in exceptional circumstances personal relations and direct contacts with both parents. Towards that end and in accordance with the obligation

of States Parties under article 9, paragraph 1, States Parties shall respect the right of the child and his or her parents to leave any country, including their own, and to enter their own country. The right to leave any country shall be subject only to such restrictions as are prescribed by law and which are necessary to protect the national security, public order (ordre public), public health or morals or the rights and freedoms of others and are consistent with the other rights recognized in the present Convention.

Article 11

1. States Parties shall take measures to combat the illicit transfer and non-return of children abroad.
2. To this end, States Parties shall promote the conclusion of bilateral or multilateral agreements or accession to existing agreements.

Article 12

1. States Parties shall assure to the child who is capable of forming his or her own views the right to express those views freely in all matters affecting the child, the views of the child being given due weight in accordance with the age and maturity of the child.
2. For this purpose, the child shall in particular be provided the opportunity to be heard in any judicial and administrative proceedings affecting the child, either directly, or through a representative or an appropriate body, in a manner consistent with the procedural rules of national law.

Article 13

1. The child shall have the right to freedom of expression; this right shall include freedom to seek, receive and impart information and ideas of all kinds, regardless of frontiers, either orally, in writing or in print, in the form of art, or through any other media of the child's choice.
2. The exercise of this right may be subject to certain restrictions, but these shall only be such as are provided by law and are necessary:
   (a) For respect of the rights or reputations of others; or
   (b) For the protection of national security or of public order (ordre public), or of public health or morals.

Article 14

1. States Parties shall respect the right of the child to freedom of thought, conscience and religion.
2. States Parties shall respect the rights and duties of the parents and, when applicable, legal guardians, to provide direction to the child in the exercise of his or her right in a manner consistent with the evolving capacities of the child.
3. reedom to manifest one's religion or beliefs may be subject only to such limitations as

are prescribed by law and are necessary to protect public safety, order, health or morals, or the fundamental rights and freedoms of others.

Article 15

1. States Parties recognize the rights of the child to freedom of association and to freedom of peaceful assembly.
2. No restrictions may be placed on the exercise of these rights other than those imposed in conformity with the law and which are necessary in a democratic society in the interests of national security or public safety, public order (ordre public), the protection of public health or morals or the protection of the rights and freedoms of others.

Article 16

1. No child shall be subjected to arbitrary or unlawful interference with his or her privacy, family, home or correspondence, nor to unlawful attacks on his or her honour and reputation.
2. The child has the right to the protection of the law against such interference or attacks.

Article 17

States Parties recognize the important function performed by the mass media and shall ensure that the child has access to information and material from a diversity of national and international sources, especially those aimed at the promotion of his or her social, spiritual and moral well-being and physical and mental health. To this end, States Parties shall:

(a) Encourage the mass media to disseminate information and material of social and cultural benefit to the child and in accordance with the spirit of article 29;
(b) Encourage international co-operation in the production, exchange and dissemination of such information and material from a diversity of cultural, national and international sources;
(c) Encourage the production and dissemination of children's books;
(d) Encourage the mass media to have particular regard to the linguistic needs of the child who belongs to a minority group or who is indigenous;
(e) Encourage the development of appropriate guidelines for the protection of the child from information and material injurious to his or her well-being, bearing in mind the provisions of articles 13 and 18.

Article 18

1. States Parties shall use their best efforts to ensure recognition of the principle that both parents have common responsibilities for the upbringing and development of the

child. Parents or, as the case may be, legal guardians, have the primary responsibility for the upbringing and development of the child. The best interests of the child will be their basic concern.

2. For the purpose of guaranteeing and promoting the rights set forth in the present Convention, States Parties shall render appropriate assistance to parents and legal guardians in the performance of their child-rearing responsibilities and shall ensure the development of institutions, facilities and services for the care of children.

3. States Parties shall take all appropriate measures to ensure that children of working parents have the right to benefit from child-care services and facilities for which they are eligible.

Article 19

1. States Parties shall take all appropriate legislative, administrative, social and educational measures to protect the child from all forms of physical or mental violence, injury or abuse, neglect or negligent treatment, maltreatment or exploitation, including sexual abuse, while in the care of parent(s), legal guardian(s) or any other person who has the care of the child.

2. Such protective measures should, as appropriate, include effective procedures for the establishment of social programmes to provide necessary support for the child and for those who have the care of the child, as well as for other forms of prevention and for identification, reporting, referral, investigation, treatment and follow-up of instances of child maltreatment described heretofore, and, as appropriate, for judicial involvement.

Article 20

1. A child temporarily or permanently deprived of his or her family environment, or in whose own best interests cannot be allowed to remain in that environment, shall be entitled to special protection and assistance provided by the State.

2. States Parties shall in accordance with their national laws ensure alternative care for such a child.

3. Such care could include, inter alia, foster placement, kafalah of Islamic law, adoption or if necessary placement in suitable institutions for the care of children. When considering solutions, due regard shall be paid to the desirability of continuity in a child's upbringing and to the child's ethnic, religious, cultural and linguistic background.

Article 21

States Parties that recognize and/or permit the system of adoption shall ensure that the best interests of the child shall be the paramount consideration and they shall:

(a) Ensure that the adoption of a child is authorized only by competent authorities who determine, in accordance with applicable law and procedures and on the basis of all *pertinent and reliable information, that the adoption is permissible in view of the child's status concerning parents, relatives and legal guardians and that, if required, the persons concerned have given their informed consent to the adoption on the basis of such counselling as may be necessary;*

(b) Recognize that inter-country adoption may be considered as an alternative means of child's care, if the child cannot be placed in a foster or an adoptive family or cannot in any suitable manner be cared for in the child's country of origin; (c) Ensure that the child concerned by inter-country adoption enjoys safeguards and standards equivalent to those existing in the case of national adoption;

(d) Take all appropriate measures to ensure that, in inter-country adoption, the placement does not result in improper financial gain for those involved in it;

(e) Promote, where appropriate, the objectives of the present article by concluding bilateral or multilateral arrangements or agreements, and endeavour, within this framework, to ensure that the placement of the child in another country is carried out by competent authorities or organs.

Article 22

1. *States Parties shall take appropriate measures to ensure that a child who is seeking refugee status or who is considered a refugee in accordance with applicable international or domestic law and procedures shall, whether unaccompanied or accompanied by his or her parents or by any other person, receive appropriate protection and humanitarian assistance in the enjoyment of applicable rights set forth in the present Convention and in other international human rights or humanitarian instruments to which the said States are Parties.*

2. *For this purpose, States Parties shall provide, as they consider appropriate, co-operation in any efforts by the United Nations and other competent intergovern-mental organizations or non-governmental organizations co-operating with the United Nations to protect and assist such a child and to trace the parents or other members of the family of any refugee child in order to obtain information necessary for reunification with his or her family. In cases where no parents or other members of the family can be found, the child shall be accorded the same protection as any other child permanently or temporarily deprived of his or her family environment for any* reason , as set forth in the present Convention.

Article 23

1. *States Parties recognize that a mentally or physically disabled child should enjoy a full and decent life, in conditions which ensure dignity, promote self-reliance and facilitate the child's active participation in the community.*

2. *States Parties recognize the right of the disabled child to special care and shall encourage and ensure the extension, subject to available resources, to the eligible child and those responsible for his or her care, of assistance for which application is made and which is appropriate to the child's condition and to the circumstances of the parents or others caring for the child. 3. Recognizing the special needs of a*

disabled child, assistance extended in accordance with paragraph 2 of the present article shall be provided free of charge, whenever possible, taking into account the financial resources of the parents or others caring for the child, and shall be designed to ensure that the disabled child has effective access to and receives education, training, health care services, rehabilitation services, preparation for employment and recreation opportunities in a manner conducive to the child's achieving the fullest possible social integration and individual development, including his or her cultural and spiritual development

3. *States Parties shall promote, in the spirit of international cooperation, the exchange of appropriate information in the field of preventive health care and of medical, psychological and functional treatment of disabled children, including dissemination of and access to information concerning methods of rehabilitation, education and vocational services, with the aim of enabling States Parties to improve their capabilities and skills and to widen their experience in these areas. In this regard, particular account shall be taken of the needs of developing countries.*

Article 24

1. *States Parties recognize the right of the child to the enjoyment of the highest attainable standard of health and to facilities for the treatment of illness and rehabilitation of health. States Parties shall strive to ensure that no child is deprived of his or her right of access to such health care services.*

2. *States Parties shall pursue full implementation of this right and, in particular, shall take appropriate measures:*

   (a) To diminish infant and child mortality;

   (b) To ensure the provision of necessary medical assistance and health care to all children with emphasis on the development of primary health care;

   (c) To combat disease and malnutrition, including within the framework of primary health care, through, inter alia, the application of readily available technology and through the provision of adequate nutritious foods and clean drinking-water, taking into consideration the dangers and risks of environmental pollution;

   (d) To ensure appropriate pre-natal and post-natal health care for mothers;

   (e) To ensure that all segments of society, in particular parents and children, are informed, have access to education and are supported in the use of basic knowledge of child health and nutrition, the advantages of breastfeeding, hygiene and environmental sanitation and the prevention of accidents;

   (f) To develop preventive health care, guidance for parents and family planning education and services.

3. *States Parties shall take all effective and appropriate measures with a view to abolishing traditional practices prejudicial to the health of children.*

4. *States Parties undertake to promote and encourage international co-operation with a view to achieving progressively the full realization of the right recognized in the present article. In this regard, particular account shall be taken of the needs of developing countries.*

Article 25

States Parties recognize the right of a child who has been placed by the competent authorities for the purposes of care, protection or treatment of his or her physical or mental health, to a periodic review of the treatment provided to the child and all other circumstances relevant to his or her placement.

Article 26

1. States Parties shall recognize for every child the right to benefit from social security, including social insurance, and shall take the necessary measures to achieve the full realization of this right in accordance with their national law.
2. The benefits should, where appropriate, be granted, taking into account the resources and the circumstances of the child and persons having responsibility for the maintenance of the child, as well as any other consideration relevant to an application for benefits made by or on behalf of the child.

Article 27

1. States Parties recognize the right of every child to a standard of living adequate for the child's physical, mental, spiritual, moral and social development.
2. The parent(s) or others responsible for the child have the primary responsibility to secure, within their abilities and financial capacities, the conditions of living necessary for the child's development.
3. States Parties, in accordance with national conditions and within their means, shall take appropriate measures to assist parents and others responsible for the child to implement this right and shall in case of need provide material assistance and support programmes, particularly with regard to nutrition, clothing and housing.
4. States Parties shall take all appropriate measures to secure the recovery of maintenance for the child from the parents or other persons having financial responsibility for the child, both within the State Party and from abroad. In particular, where the person having financial responsibility for the child lives in a State different from that of the child, States Parties shall promote the accession to international agreements or the conclusion of such agreements, as well as the making of other appropriate arrangements.

Article 28

1. States Parties recognize the right of the child to education, and with a view to achieving this right progressively and on the basis of equal opportunity, they shall, in particular:

    (a) Make primary education compulsory and available free to all;
    (b) Encourage the development of different forms of secondary education, including general and vocational education, make them available and accessible to every

155

child, and take appropriate measures such as the introduction of free education
and offering financial assistance in case of need;

(c) Make higher education accessible to all on the basis of capacity by every
appropriate means;

(d) Make educational and vocational information and guidance available and
accessible to all children;

(e) Take measures to encourage regular attendance at schools and the reduction of
drop-out rates.

2. States Parties shall take all appropriate measures to ensure that school discipline is
administered in a manner consistent with the child's human dignity and in conformity
with the present Convention.

3. States Parties shall promote and encourage international cooperation in matters
relating to education, in particular with a view to contributing to the elimination of
ignorance and illiteracy throughout the world and facilitating access to scientific and
technical knowledge and modern teaching methods. In this regard, particular
account shall be taken of the needs of developing countries.

Article 29

1. States Parties agree that the education of the child shall be directed to:

(a) The development of the child's personality, talents and mental and physical
abilities to their fullest potential;

(b) The development of respect for human rights and fundamental freedoms, and for
the principles enshrined in the Charter of the United Nations;

(c) The development of respect for the child's parents, his or her own cultural
identity, language and values, for the national values of the country in which the
child is living, the country from which he or she may originate, and for
civilizations different from his or her own;

(d) The preparation of the child for responsible life in a free society, in the spirit of
understanding, peace, tolerance, equality of sexes, and friendship among all
peoples, ethnic, national and religious groups and persons of indigenous origin;

(e) The development of respect for the natural environment.

2. No part of the present article or article 28 shall be construed so as to interfere with
the liberty of individuals and bodies to establish and direct educational institutions,
subject always to the observance of the principle set forth in paragraph 1 of the
present article and to the requirements that the education given in such institutions
shall conform to such minimum standards as may be laid down by the State.

Note

In its General Comment 1[2] the Committee notes that article 29 (1) not only adds to

---

[2]   United Nations Doc. HRI/GEN/1/Rev.5, p. 255. This General Comment is the only one which has
been adopted to date by the Committee on the Rights of the Child.

the right to education recognized in article 28 a qualitative dimension which reflects the rights and inherent dignity of the child; it also insists upon the need for education to be child-centred, child-friendly and empowering, and it highlights the need for educational processes to be based upon the very principles it enunciates. Consequently, "education in this context goes far beyond formal schooling to embrace the broad range of life experiences and learning processes which enable children, individually and collectively, to develop their personalities, talents and abilities and to live a full and satisfying life within society." Moreover, the Committee also highlighted the links between article 29 (1) and the struggle against racism, racial discrimination, xenophobia and related intolerance. Even in this respect, the media play a relevant role, insofar as they shall take all appropriate steps to encourage the mass media to disseminate information and material of social and cultural benefit to the child.

The Committee also called upon the States Parties to establish a review procedure which responds to complaints that existing policies or practices are not consistent with article 29 (1). This may also be entrusted to national human rights institutions or to existing administrative bodies.[3] The Committee requests each State Party when reporting on this article to identify the genuine possibilities that exist at the national or local level to obtain a review of existing approaches which are claimed to be incompatible with the Convention. Information should be provided as to how such reviews can be initiated and how many such review procedures have been undertaken within the reporting period.

Article 30

In those States in which ethnic, religious or linguistic minorities or persons of indigenous origin exist, a child belonging to such a minority or who is indigenous shall not be denied the right, in community with other members of his or her group, to enjoy his or her own culture, to profess and practise his or her own religion, or to use his or her own language.

Article 31

1. *States Parties recognize the right of the child to rest and leisure, to engage in play and recreational activities appropriate to the age of the child and to participate freely in cultural life and the arts.*
2. *States Parties shall respect and promote the right of the child to participate fully in cultural and artistic life and shall encourage the provision of appropriate and equal opportunities for cultural, artistic, recreational and leisure activity.*

---

[3] *Ibid*, at p. 261.

Article 32

1. States Parties recognize the right of the child to be protected from economic exploitation and from performing any work that is likely to be hazardous or to interfere with the child's education, or to be harmful to the child's health or physical, mental, spiritual, moral or social development.
2. States Parties shall take legislative, administrative, social and educational measures to ensure the implementation of the present article. To this end, and having regard to the relevant provisions of other international instruments, States Parties shall in particular:

   (a) Provide for a minimum age or minimum ages for admission to employment;
   (b) Provide for appropriate regulation of the hours and conditions of employment;
   (c) Provide for appropriate penalties or other sanctions to ensure the effective enforcement of the present article.

Article 33

States Parties shall take all appropriate measures, including legislative, administrative, social and educational measures, to protect children from the illicit use of narcotic drugs and psychotropic substances as defined in the relevant international treaties, and to prevent the use of children in the illicit production and trafficking of such substances.

Article 34

States Parties undertake to protect the child from all forms of sexual exploitation and sexual abuse. For these purposes, States Parties shall in particular take all appropriate national, bilateral and multilateral measures to prevent:

(a) The inducement or coercion of a child to engage in any unlawful sexual activity;
(b) The exploitative use of children in prostitution or other unlawful sexual practices;
(c) The exploitative use of children in pornographic performances and materials.

Article 35

States Parties shall take all appropriate national, bilateral and multilateral measures to prevent the abduction of, the sale of or traffic in children for any purpose or in any form.

Article 36

States Parties shall protect the child against all other forms of exploitation prejudicial to any aspects of the child's welfare.

Article 37

States Parties shall ensure that:

(a) No child shall be subjected to torture or other cruel, inhuman or degrading treatment or punishment. Neither capital punishment nor life imprisonment without possibility of release shall be imposed for offences committed by persons below eighteen years of age;

(b) No child shall be deprived of his or her liberty unlawfully or arbitrarily. The arrest, detention or imprisonment of a child shall be in conformity with the law and shall be used only as a measure of last resort and for the shortest appropriate period of time;

(c) Every child deprived of liberty shall be treated with humanity and respect for the inherent dignity of the human person, and in a manner which takes into account the needs of persons of his or her age. In particular, every child deprived of liberty shall be separated from adults unless it is considered in the child's best interest not to do so and shall have the right to maintain contact with his or her family through correspondence and visits, save in exceptional circumstances;

(d) Every child deprived of his or her liberty shall have the right to prompt access to legal and other appropriate assistance, as well as the right to challenge the legality of the deprivation of his or her liberty before a court or other competent, independent and impartial authority, and to a prompt decision on any such action.

Article 38

1. States Parties undertake to respect and to ensure respect for rules of international humanitarian law applicable to them in armed conflicts which are relevant to the child.
2. States Parties shall take all feasible measures to ensure that persons who have not attained the age of fifteen years do not take a direct part in hostilities.
3. States Parties shall refrain from recruiting any person who has not attained the age of fifteen years into their armed forces. In recruiting among those persons who have attained the age of fifteen years but who have not attained the age of eighteen years, States Parties shall endeavour to give priority to those who are oldest.
4. In accordance with their obligations under international humanitarian law to protect the civilian population in armed conflicts, States Parties shall take all feasible measures to ensure protection and care of children who are affected by an armed conflict.

Article 39

States Parties shall take all appropriate measures to promote physical and psychological recovery and social reintegration of a child victim of: any form of neglect, exploitation, or abuse; torture or any other form of cruel, inhuman or degrading treatment or punishment; or armed conflicts. Such recovery and reintegra-

tion shall take place in an environment which fosters the health, self-respect and dignity of the child.

Article 40

1. *States Parties recognize the right of every child alleged as, accused of, or recognized as having infringed the penal law to be treated in a manner consistent with the promotion of the child's sense of dignity and worth, which reinforces the child's respect for the human rights and fundamental freedoms of others and which takes into account the child's age and the desirability of promoting the child's reintegration and the child's assuming a constructive role in society.*

2. *To this end, and having regard to the relevant provisions of international instruments, States Parties shall, in particular, ensure that:*

   (a) *No child shall be alleged as, be accused of, or recognized as having infringed the penal law by reason of acts or omissions that were not prohibited by national or international law at the time they were committed;*

   (b) *Every child alleged as or accused of having infringed the penal law has at least the following guarantees:*

   (i) *To be presumed innocent until proven guilty according to law;*

   (ii) *To be informed promptly and directly of the charges against him or her, and, if appropriate, through his or her parents or legal guardians, and to have legal or other appropriate assistance in the preparation and presentation of his or her defence;*

   (iii) *To have the matter determined without delay by a competent, independent and impartial authority or judicial body in a fair hearing according to law, in the presence of legal or other appropriate assistance and, unless it is considered not to be in the best interest of the child, in particular, taking into account his or her age or situation, his or her parents or legal guardians;*

   (iv) *Not to be compelled to give testimony or to confess guilt; to examine or have examined adverse witnesses and to obtain the participation and examination of witnesses on his or her behalf under conditions of equality;*

   (v) *If considered to have infringed the penal law, to have this decision and any measures imposed in consequence thereof reviewed by a higher competent, independent and impartial authority or judicial body according to law;*

   (vi) *To have the free assistance of an interpreter if the child cannot understand or speak the language used;*

   (vii) *To have his or her privacy fully respected at all stages of the proceedings.*

   3. *States Parties shall seek to promote the establishment of laws, procedures, authorities and institutions specifically applicable to children alleged as, accused of, or recognized as having infringed the penal law, and, in particular:*

   (a) *The establishment of a minimum age below which children shall be presumed not to have the capacity to infringe the penal law;*

(b) *Whenever appropriate and desirable, measures for dealing with such children without resorting to judicial proceedings, providing that human rights and legal safeguards are fully respected.*

4. *A variety of dispositions, such as care, guidance and supervision orders; counselling; probation; foster care; education and vocational training programmes and other alternatives to institutional care shall be available to ensure that children are dealt with in a manner appropriate to their well-being and proportionate both to their circumstances and the offence.*

Article 41

Nothing in the present Convention shall affect any provisions which are more conducive to the realization of the rights of the child and which may be contained in:

(a) *The law of a State party; or*
(b) *International law in force for that State.*

Article 42

States Parties undertake to make the principles and provisions of the Convention widely known, by appropriate and active means, to adults and children alike.

2. The Committee on the Rights of the Child[4]

The Committee is established pursuant to the provisions of article 43 of the Convention. There are 10 members,[5] elected by the States Parties for terms of four

---

[4] M. Sardenberg, "Committee on the Rights of the Child: Basic Processes", A. Lopatka, "An Introduction to the United Nations Convention on the Rights of the Child", in *Transnational Law and Contemporary Problems*, 6(1996) 2, pp. 263–286 and 251–262; S. Detrick, *A Commentary on the United Nations Convention on the Rights of the Child*, (1999); *Implementation Handbook for the Convention on the Rights of the Child*, (UNICEF, 1998) pp. 569–584; M. Santos Pais, "The Convention on the Rights of the Child", in *Manual on Human Rights Reporting*, (United Nations 1997), pp. 393–504; J. Karp, "Reporting and the Committee on the Rights of the Child", *in The UN Human Rights Treaty System in the 21st Century*, (A.F. Bayefsky Ed. 2000); S. Guillet, *Nous, Peuples des Nations Unies – L'action des ONG au sein du système de protection international des droits de l'homme*, (1995), pp. 67–70; M. Santos Pais, "The Committee on the Rights of the Child", *International Commission of Jurists Review*, No. 47, (Dec. 1991), pp. 36–43. See, generally, the following studies by P. Alston, *Long Term Approaches to Enhancing the Effectiveness of the United Nations Human Rights Treaty Bodies*, United Nations Doc. A/44/668; *Interim Report on Updated Study*, United Nations Doc. A/CONF.157/PC/62/Add.11/Rev.1; *Final Report on Enhancing the Long Term Effectiveness of the United Nations Human Rights Treaty System*, United Nations Doc. E/CN.4/1997/74; and, also, A. Bayefsky, *Report: The UN Human Rights Treaty System: Universality at the Crossroads*, (2001); P. Alston and J. Crawford Eds., *The Future of UN Human Rights Treaty Monitoring*, (2000); A. Bayefsky, Ed., *The UN Human Rights System in the 21st Century*, (2000).

[5] Membership as of January 2001; Abdul Aziz Al-Sheddi (Saudi Arabia); Ghalia Mohd Bin Hamad (Qatar); Sasuree Chutikul (Thailand); Luigi Citarella (Italy); Jacob Egbert Doek (Netherlands); Amina Hamza El Guidi (Egypt); Awa N'Deye Ouedraogo (Burkina Faso); Marila Sardenberg (Brazil);

years. Members, though all nationals of States Parties, serve in their private capacities and make a solemn declaration of impartiality upon taking up office. The Committee presently meets three times each year, in January, May-June and September-October for sessions of three working weeks each. Each session is followed by a meeting of one week's duration of a Working Group to prepare for the following session. All sessions take place in Geneva. Secretariat services are provided by the United Nations Office of the High Commissioner for Human Rights.[6]

The role of non-governmental sources of information in the work of the Committee is highlighted in the Convention itself and is, accordingly, well reflected in the Rules of Procedure.[7] The Committee has made considerable use of these provisions and has accorded an important role in its activities for national and international NGOs and other appropriate sources of information.[8] An important initiative, taken by a number of NGOs has been the establishment of the NGO Group for the Convention on the Rights of the Child. This body, which has a full-time Geneva-based co-ordinator,[9] both facilitates flows of information to and from the Committee, and forges national and regional alliances of children's NGOs in order to render more effective their contributions to the work of the Committee.

Three of the activities of the Committee are of particular interest for NGOs: the reporting procedure, the thematic examinations of a range of issues concerning the rights of the child and the occasional regional and subregional missions by all or some of the Committee members.

3. THE REPORTING PROCEDURE[10]

(a) The obligation on the State

Under article 44 of the Convention, States are obliged to submit reports to the Committee two years after the Convention comes into effect for the State and

---

cont.

    Elisabeth Tigerstedt-Tahtela (Finland). An amendment to the Convention raising to 18 the membership of the Committee was adopted by a meeting of the States Parties in 1995. It has not yet come into effect.

[6] Secretariat of the Committee on the Rights of the Child, Support Services Branch, Office of the High Commissioner for Human Rights, UNOG, 1211 Geneva 10, Switzerland (Tel.: 41 22 917 1234; Fax 41 22 917 0099).

[7] Article 45. Rules of Procedure of the Committee on the Rights of the Child. Rules 34, 70 and 74. United Nations Doc. HRI/GEN3, pp. 186, 195, 197.

[8] See *A Guide for Non-Governmental Organisations Reporting to the Committee on the Rights of the Child*, (The NGO Group for the Convention on the Rights of the Child, 1998).

[9] NGO Group for the Convention on the Rights of the Child, c/o Defence for Children International, P.O. Box 88, 1211 Geneva 20, Switzerland. Tel: 41–22–7340558; fax: 41–22–7401145. Email: dci-ngo.group@pingnet.ch.

[10] M. Sardenberg, "Committee on the Rights of the Child: Basic Processes", A. Lopatka, "An Introduction to the United Nations Convention on the Rights of the Child" in, *Transnational Law and Contemporary Problems*, 6(1996) 2, pp. 263–286 and 251–262; S. Detrick, *A Commentary on the United Nations Convention on the Rights of the Child*, (1999*); Implementation Handbook for the Convention on*

thereafter every five years, on the measures they have adopted to give effect to the rights in the Convention and on the progress made in the enjoyment of those rights. It is also stipulated that reports should indicate factors and difficulties, if any, affecting the degree of fulfilment of the obligations. Reports should also contain sufficient information to provide the Committee with a comprehensive understanding of the implementation of the Convention in the State concerned.[11]

The General Guidelines for the Form and Content of Initial Reports[12] stipulate that Initial Reports should categorise material as follows:

(a) General measures of implementation. Information should be provided on implementation of articles 4, 42 and 44, paragraph 6.

(b) Definition of the Child. Information pursuant to article 1, including details of the legal minimum age for such purposes as the end of compulsory education full-time employment, sexual consent, marriage, voluntary enlistment to the armed forces, criminal liability, deprivation of liberty, imprisonment, and consumption of controlled substances such as alcohol.

(c) General principles. Information should be provided on effective implementation of articles 2, 3, 6 and 12. It is further stipulated that States Parties should provide relevant information on the application of these principles in the implementation of the other articles of the Convention.

(d) Civil rights and freedoms. Information should be provided on implementation of articles 7, 8, 13, 14, 15, 16, 17 and 37 (a).

(e) Family environment and alternative care. Information should be provided with particular attention paid to the principles of "the best interests of the child" and "respect for the views of the child" concerning articles 5, 18, paragraphs 1 and 2, 9, 10, 27, paragraphs 4, 20, 21, 11, 19, 39 and 25. Information should also be provided, disaggregated by age, group, sex, ethnic or national background and rural and urban environment concerning children who are homeless, abused,

---

cont.

the Rights of the Child, (UNICEF, 1998) pp. 569–584; M. Santos Pais, "The Convention on the Rights of the Child", in *Manual on Human Rights Reporting*, (United Nations 1997), pp. 393–504; J. Karp, "Reporting and the Committee on the Rights of the Child", *in The UN Human Rights Treaty System in the 21st Century*, (A.F. Bayefsky Ed. 2000); G. Lansdown, "The Reporting Process under the Convention on the Rights of the Child", in *The Future of UN Human Rights Treaty Monitoring*, (P. Alston and J. Crawford, Eds., 2000); *A Guide for Non-Governmental Organisations Reporting to the Committee on the Rights of the Child*, (The NGO Group for the Convention on the Rights of the Child, 1998); L. P Scherer and S. N. Hall, "Reporting to the UN Committee on the Rights of the Child – Analyses of the first 49 State Party Reports on the Education Articles of the Convention on the Rights of the Child", in, *The International Journal of Children's Rights*, 7(1999) 4, pp. 349–363; C. Prince Cohen, "States Report" United Nations Convention on the Rights of the Child", *New York Law School Journal of Human Rights*, 8 (2), (Spring 1991), pp. 367–382; *Overview of the Reporting Procedure*, United Nations Doc. CRC/C/33.

[11] The first part of reports should also comply with the consolidated guidelines relating to the preparation of the initial part of reports under the various international human rights instruments. See United Nations Doc. HRI/CORE/1.

[12] United Nations Doc. HRI/GEN/2/Rev.1 pp. 47–51.

neglected, in institutional or other care or who have been adopted domestically or internationally.
(f) Basic health and welfare. Information should be provided on implementation of articles 6, paragraph 2; 23; 24; 26; 18, paragraph 3; 27, paragraphs 1-3.
(g) Education, leisure and cultural activities. Information should be provided on implementation of articles 28, 29 and 31.
(h) Special protection measures. Information should be provided on implementation of articles 22, 38, 39, 40, 37 (b), (c) and (d), 37 (a), 39, 32, 33, 34, 36, 35 and 30.

The General Guidelines for the Form and Content of Periodic Reports[13] stipulate that such reports should provide information with respect to the period covered by the report on the measures adopted by the State Party, including the conclusion of and accession to bilateral and multilateral agreements in the field of children's rights, and changes which have occurred in legislation and practice at the national, regional and local levels, and where appropriate at the federal and provincial levels, such as mechanisms and structures to co-ordinate and monitor efforts to implement the Convention and overall or sectoral policies, programmes and services developed to implement the Convention. Reports should describe any progress achieved in the enjoyment of children's rights, the factors and difficulties encountered in the full implementation of children's rights and any plans envisaged to further improve the realisation of these rights. It is also stipulated that reports should include information on the consideration given to the Concluding Observations adopted by the Committee in relation to the previous report, including regarding the steps taken to widely disseminate the previous report and the Concluding Observations.[14]

Periodic reports should be structured in the same manner as initial reports, addressing the rights and issues within the clusters noted above. The General Guidelines offer highly detailed assistance regarding the reporting requirement within each of the clusters.

(b) The procedure

i. The scheduling process

At present, reports, once submitted, can be expected to be taken up by the Committee within 24 months.[15] Information regarding the session at which a report will be considered is usually posted some eight months in advance on the web site of the United Nations High Commissioner for Human Rights (OHCHR).[16] Scheduling arrangements may be subject to change at short notice, particularly with regard to the exact dates for consideration within a session. Full details of scheduling and any

---

[13] United Nations Doc. HRI/GEN/2/Rev.1 pp. 52–100.
[14] Article 44 (6) of the Convention stipulates that "States parties shall make their reports widely available to the public in their own countries".
[15] A delay which the Committee is endeavouring to considerably shorten.
[16] www.unhchr.ch.

changes which might occur can be obtained from the Secretary of the Committee. State party reports, once published as United Nations documents, can be ordered from the United Nations Documents Distribution and Sales Section. The symbol number can be obtained from the Secretariat. Reports are usually available in all of the working languages of the Committee (English, French and Spanish). Reports are also posted on the OHCHR website.

ii. *The Working Group*

Periodic reports first receive the attention of the members of the Committee assembled in an informal Working Group. The Working Group meets in unreported and closed meetings at the end of each session and considers reports scheduled for consideration at the next or another forthcoming session. The purpose of the consideration is to identify areas in the reports which require clarification or give cause for concern and to prepare a list of issues for transmission to the State Parties with a request for written replies to be considered together with the report. States Parties are not present at meetings of the Working Group.

To aid it in its task, the Working Group has before it draft lists of issues drawn up by members serving as "Country Rapporteurs",[17] together with "country analyses" prepared by the Secretariat. Country analyses, typically some 25-30 pages in length, may contain reference to material provided by a wide range of information sources, including intergovernmental entities/organisations, such as OHCHR, UNICEF, ILO and UNHCR, as well as by NGOs.

In adopting its lists of issues,[18] the Working Group may choose to consider both the written and oral interventions of intergovernmental organisations and NGOs (with regard to the role of NGOs, see below).

Lists of issues can be obtained from the Secretariat about a month after they are adopted (and on the OHCHR website after the dialogue). Replies received from State parties may also be obtained from the Secretariat or from the NGO Group for the Convention on the Rights of the Child.

iii. *Consideration by the Committee*

Reports are considered by the Committee in public session and in dialogue with representatives of the State, usually over two consecutive meetings, each of three hours duration.[19] Reports are introduced by representatives of the Government. The scrutiny which follows is structured to reflect the categories into which the rights under the Convention are assembled in the reporting guidelines. Thus, discussion of each category is introduced by comments of the State representative, followed by questions and comments of the Country Rapporteur and other members and concluded by responses of the representative. Towards the end of the overall

---

[17] The practice of appointing Country Rapporteurs had been in use in the early years of the Committee, fell into disuse and was revived in 1999. See United Nations Doc. A/55/41 at para. 1478.

[18] A sample List of Issues (for Denmark) is reproduced in Appendix I.

[19] Rules of Procedure of the Committee on the Rights of the Child, Rules 66–74, United Nations Doc. United Nations Doc. HRI/GEN3, pp. 194–197.

discussion, the Country Rapporteur and other Committee members summarise their observations and may make preliminary suggestions and recommendations.

The Committee has indicated that the replies to the lists of issues should serve to dispose of matters of fact and, accordingly, at the Committee meetings, the discussion should focus on progress achieved and on factors and difficulties impeding implementation of the Convention. Attention should also be paid to implementation priorities and to future goals.[20]

Following the consideration in public meetings, the Committee proceeds, in private session, to prepare its "Concluding Observations", based on an initial draft prepared by the Country Rapporteur. The Concluding Observations comprise a critique of the State report and of the response of the State representative to the scrutiny of the Committee, noting positive factors, identifying factors and difficulties impeding the implementation of the Covenant, drawing attention to matters of concern and making suggestions and recommendations. Concluding Observations are adopted and issued as public documents at the end of each session of the Committee, posted on the OHCHR website (initially solely in the language of adoption), sent to the NGO Group for the Convention on the Rights of the Child (for transmittal to national NGOs) and included in the Committee's biennial report to the General Assembly of the United Nations.

Concluding Observations frequently include recommendations for the provision to States Parties of technical cooperation and assistance in implementation of the Convention.[21] Pursuant to article 45 (b), such recommendations are transmitted to the relevant specialised bodies of the United Nations, such as the Office of the High Commissioner for Human Rights and UNICEF, as well as to "other competent bodies".[22]

If the Committee is of the view that the report and information furnished by a State Party has been insufficient, they may choose to issue only preliminary Concluding Observations and request that further information be provided for consideration at a future session, at which time definitive Concluding Observations may issue.[23] The Committee may also choose to adopt definitive Concluding Observations which include a request for the provision of further information.[24]

The Committee has stated that "in the spirit of article 44 (6), it is important that the Concluding Observations are made widely available within the State Party concerned."[25]

The Committee has not as yet established a particular procedure, with

---

[20] Overview of the Reporting Procedure, United Nations Doc. CRC/C/33.

[21] Rules of Procedure of the Committee on the Rights of the Child, Rule 74, United Nations Doc. HRI/GEN/3, p. 197.

[22] A sample set of Concluding Observations (for The Netherlands) is reproduced in Appendix II.

[23] Rules of Procedure of the Committee on the Rights of the Child, Rule 69, United Nations Doc. HRI/GEN/3, p. 195.

[24] With regard to the range of options available, see Overview of the Reporting Procedure, United Nations Doc. CRC/C/33.

[25] *Ibid*, para. 22.

implications for NGOs, concerning consideration of implementation of the Convention in States Parties, the reports of which are seriously overdue.[26]

(c) The role of non-governmental organisations[27]

Once NGOs become aware that a State's report has been received by the United Nations, and ideally no less than seven months before the report is scheduled to be considered, they should both indicate their interest to the Secretariat and establish contact with the NGO Group for the Convention on the Rights of the Child. The latter group may furnish much useful advice and also assist in the forging of appropriate regional or national alliances of NGOs. Where such alliances already exist, the NGO Group may encourage NGOs to associate themselves with these rather than attempting to individually gain the attention of the Committee. At this early stage, submissions may also be forwarded both to the Secretariat and the NGO Group. These submissions may be put to use by the Secretariat in preparing its country analyses and by the Country Rapporteur in writing draft lists of issues for eventual consideration by the Working Group. It is advisable to submit at least 15 copies of each submission to the Secretariat and to specifically request that the materials be distributed to members of the Committee.

It is very important that NGOs which wish to be invited to make oral submissions to the Working Group so indicate. They should, however, bear in mind that the Committee will only extend invitations to a small number of organisations in each State. NGOs must, accordingly, give evidence both of their competence and seriousness of intent. It may often be the case that alliances of NGOs will appear to the Committee to be the more worthy of invitation. With regard to all aspects of this matter, the advice of the NGO Group will prove invaluable. The NGO Group may also be in a position to channel limited amounts of financial assistance to NGOs which are invited to attend the Working Group.

NGOs are invited to the Working Group only for the one three-hour meeting at which the relevant country report is being considered. To gain access to the United Nations building in Geneva, it is sufficient to show the letter of invitation to the

---

[26] The Rules of Procedure allow to the Committee considerable discretion in determining appropriate ways to deal with States which are seriously overdue in submitting reports. See Rules of Procedure of the Committee on the Rights of the Child, Rule 67, United Nations Doc. HRI/GEN3, p. 195.

[27] See further at Chapter 1. See, also, *A Guide for Non-Governmental Organisations Reporting to the Committee on the Rights of the Child*, (The NGO Group for the Convention on the Rights of the Child, 1998); G. Lansdown, "The Reporting Process under the Convention on the Rights of the Child", in *The Future of UN Human Rights Treaty Monitoring*, (P. Alston and J. Crawford, Eds. 2000); U. Kilkelly, *"The United Nations Committee on the Rights of the Child – An Evaluation in the Light of Recent UK Experience"*, 8 Child an Family Law Quarterly, (1996) at 105; L. Theytaz-Bergman, "State Reporting and the Role of Non-Governmental Organisations", in, *The UN Human Rights Treaty System in the 21st Century*, (A.F. Bayefsky Ed. 2000) pp. 45–56; A. Edman, "NGOs and UN Human Rights Treaty Bodies: A Case Study of the Committee on the Rights of the Child", *in Human Rights, The United Nations and Nongovernmental Organisations*, (The Carter Center, undated), pp. 102–113.

Security personnel at the entrance. On arrival at the meeting room, NGOs should indicate their presence to the Secretariat in order to ensure that they are called on to speak. They will normally be called on immediately following the presentation by the Committee's Country Rapporteur. Oral contributions should be kept short (no more than 15 minutes) and to the point (focusing on the report and on the terms of the Convention) and may be made in any of the working languages of the Committee: English, French or Spanish. If an NGO wishes to employ audio visual aids, it should advise the Secretariat in good time. In general, NGOs should liaise closely with the NGO Group with regard to their deportment at the Working Groups. At the conclusion of the NGO presentations, Committee members make comments and may put questions to the NGOs.

Following the Working Group, NGOs can, either directly from the Secretariat or through the NGO Group, obtain copies of the List of Issues and eventually of the Replies of the Government. Using these and the report, final submissions can be prepared. The submissions should be sent to the Secretariat, directly or through the NGO Group, in good time for their distribution to the members prior to the scheduled dates for consideration of the report by the Committee. At least 15 copies should be provided.

If at all possible, NGOs should send representatives to attend the Committee meetings. Presence at the meetings permits informal contact with members, provision of updated submissions and other documentation, the channelling of information back to the country and the making of a comprehensive record of the proceedings. Opportunities may also arise for useful meetings with the Government representatives, with international media in Geneva, with staff of the Office of the High Commissioner for Human Rights and with the international human rights NGOs. Access to the United Nations buildings in Geneva can be arranged in advance with the Secretary of the Committee.

The role of NGOs following the conclusion of the Committee proceedings is described in chapter one.

5. TABLE OF STATES INDICATING WHEN A REPORT WAS LAST CONSIDERED AND IS NEXT DUE[28]

State Party	Entry into force	Last report considered	Next report due	Date due or overdue since
Afghanistan	27.04.94		Initial–2nd periodic	26.04.96
Albania	28.03.92		Initial–2nd periodic	27.03.94
Algeria	16.05.93	Initial (1997)	2nd periodic	15.05.00
Andorra	01.02.96	Initial (2002)*	2nd periodic	31.01.03
Angola	04.01.91		Initial–2nd periodic	03.01.93
Antigua Barbuda	04.11.93		Initial–2nd periodic	03.11.95
Argentina	03.01.91	2nd periodic (2002)*	3rd periodic	02.01.03
Armenia	23.07.93	Initial (2000)	2nd periodic	21.07.00
Australia	16.01.91	Initial (1997)	2nd periodic	15.01.98
Austria	05.09.92	Initial (1999)	2nd periodic	04.09.99
Azerbaijan	12.09.92	Initial (1997)	2nd periodic	11.09.1999
Bahamas	22.03.91		Initial	21.03.93
Bahrain	14.03.92	Initial (2002)*	2nd periodic	12.03.99
Bangladesh	02.09.90	Initial (1997)	2nd periodic	01.09.97
Barbados	08.11.90	Initial (1999)	2nd periodic	07.11.97
Belarus	31.10.90	2nd periodic (2002)*	3rd periodic	30.10.02
Belgium	15.01.92	2nd periodic (2002)*	3rd periodic	14.04.04
Belize	02.09.90	Initial (1999)	2nd periodic	01.09.97
Benin	02.09.90	Initial (1999)	2nd periodic	01.09.97
Bhutan	02.09.90	Initial (2001)	2nd periodic	01.09.97
Bolivia	02.09.90	2nd periodic (1998)	3rd periodic	02.09.02
Bosnia and Herzegovina	06.03.92		Initial–2nd periodic	05.03.94
Botswana	13.04.95		Initial	12.04.97
Brazil	24.10.90		Initial–2nd periodic	23.10.92
Brunei Darussalam	26.01.96		Initial	25.01.98
Bulgaria	03.07.91	Initial (1997)	2nd periodic	02.07.98
Burkina Faso	30.09.90	2nd periodic (2002)*	3rd periodic	29.09.02
Burundi	18.11.90	Initial (2000)	2nd periodic	17.11.97
Cambodia	14.11.92	Initial (2000)	2nd periodic	13.11.99
Cameroon	10.02.93	Initial (2001)	2nd periodic	09.02.00
Canada	12.01.92	Initial (1995)	2nd periodic	11.01.99
Cape Verde	04.07.92	Initial (2001)*	2nd periodic	03.07.99
Central African Republic	23.05.92	Initial (2000)	2nd periodic	23.05.99
Chad	01.11.90	Initial (1999)	2nd periodic	31.10.97
Chile	12.09.90	2nd periodic (2002)*	3rd periodic	11.09.02
China	01.04.92	Initial (1996)	2nd periodic	31.03.99
Colombia	27.02.91	2nd periodic (2000)	3rd periodic	26.02.03
Comoros	21.07.93	Initial (2000)	2nd periodic	21.07.00

---

[28] As of July 2001.

State Party	Entry into force	Last report considered	Next report due	Date due or overdue since
Congo	13.11.93		Initial–2nd periodic	12.11.00
Cook Islands	06.07.97		Initial	
	05.06.99			
Costa Rica	20.09.90	2nd periodic (2000)	3rd periodic	19.09.02
Cote d'Ivoire	06.03.91	Initial (2001)*	2nd periodic	05.03.98
Croatia	08.10.91	Initial (1996)	2nd periodic	07.10.98
Cuba	20.09.91	Initial (1997)	2nd periodic	19.09.98
Cyprus	09.03.91	2nd periodic (2003)*	3rd periodic	08.03.03
Czech Republic	01.01.93	2nd periodic (2003)*	3rd periodic	31.12.05
Democratic People's Republic of Korea	21.10.90	Initial (1998)	2nd periodic	20.10.97
Democratic Republic of the Congo	27.10.90	Initial (2001)*	2nd periodic	26.10.97
Denmark	18.08.91	2nd periodic (2001)	3rd periodic	17.08.03
Djibouti	05.01.91	Initial (2000)	2nd periodic	04.01.98
Dominica	12.04.91		Initial–2nd periodic	11.04.98
Dominican Republic	11.07.91	Initial (2001)	2nd periodic	10.07.98
Ecuador	02.09.90	Initial (1998)	2nd periodic	01.09.97
Egypt	02.09.90	2nd periodic (2001)	3rd periodic	01.09.02
El Salvador	02.09.90	Initial (1993)	2nd periodic	01.09.97
Equatorial Guinea	15.07.92		Initial–2nd periodic	14.07.99
Eritrea	02.09.94		Initial	01.09.96
Estonia	20.11.91		Initial–2nd periodic	19.11.93
Ethiopia	13.06.91	2nd periodic (2001)	3rd periodic	12.06.03
Federated States of Micronesia	04.06.93	Initial (1998)	2nd periodic	03.06.00
Fiji	12.09.93	Initial (1998)	2nd periodic	11.09.00
Finland	20.07.91	2nd periodic (2000)	3rd periodic	19.07.03
France	06.09.90	Initial (1994)	2nd periodic	05.09.97
Gabon	11.03.94	Initial (2002)*	2nd periodic	10.03.01
Gambia	07.09.90	Initial (2001)	2nd periodic	06.09.97
Georgia	02.07.94	Initial (2000)	2nd periodic	01.07.01
Germany	05.04.92	Initial (1995)	2nd periodic	04.04.99
Ghana	02.09.90	Initial (1997)	2nd periodic	01.09.97
Greece	10.06.93	Initial (2002)*	2nd periodic	09.06.00
Grenada	05.12.90	Initial (2000)	2nd periodic	04.12.97
Guatemala	02.09.90	2nd periodic (2001)*	3rd periodic	01.09.02
Guinea	02.09.90	Initial (1999)	2nd periodic	01.09.97
Guinea Bissau	19.09.90	Initial (2002)	2nd periodic	18.09.97
Guyana	13.02.91		Initial–2nd periodic	12.02.93
Haiti	08.07.95		2nd periodic	07.07.02
Holy See	02.09.90	Initial (1995)	2nd periodic	01.09.97
Honduras	09.09.90	2nd periodic (1999)	3rd periodic	08.09.02
Hungary	06.11.91	Initial (1998)	2nd periodic	05.11.98
Iceland	27.11.92	2nd periodic (2003 = *	3rd periodic	26.11.04
India	11.01.93	Initial (2000)	2nd periodic	10.01.00

State Party	Entry into force	Last report considered	Next report due	Date due or overdue since
Indonesia	05.10.90	Initial (1992)	2nd periodic	04.10.97
Islamic Republic of Iran	12.08.94	Initial (2000)	2nd periodic	11.08.01
Iraq	15.07.94	Initial (1998)	2nd periodic	14.07.01
Ireland	28.10.92	Initial (1998)	2nd periodic	27.10.99
Israel	02.11.91	Initial (2002)*	2nd periodic	01.11.98
Italy	05.10.91	2nd periodic (2003)*	3rd periodic	04.10.03
Jamaica	13.06.91	2nd periodic (2003)*	3rd periodic	12.06.03
Japan	22.05.94	Initial (1998)	2nd periodic	21.05.01
Jordan	23.06.91	2nd periodic (2000)	3rd periodic	22.06.03
Kazakhastan	11.09.94		Initial	10.09.96
Kenya	02.09.90	Initial (2001)*	2nd periodic	01.09.97
Kiribati	10.01.96		Initial	09.01.98
Kuwait	20.11.91	Initial (1998)	2nd periodic	19.11.98
Kyrgyzstan	06.11.94	Initial (2000)	2nd periodic	05.11.01
Lao People's Democratic Republic	07.06.91	Initial (1997)	2nd periodic	07.06.98
Latvia	14.05.92	Initial (2001)	2nd periodic	13.05.99
Lebanon	13.06.91	2nd periodic (2002)*	3rd periodic	23.06.03
Lesotho	09.04.92	Initial (2001)	2nd periodic	08.04.99
Liberia	04.07.93		Initial–2nd periodic	03.07.00
Libyan Arab Jamahiriya	15.05.93	2nd periodic (2003)*	3rd periodic	14.05.05
Liechtenstein	21.01.96	Initial (2001)	2nd periodic	20.01.03
Lithuania	01.03.92	Initial (2001)	2nd periodic	28.02.99
Luxembourg	06.04.94	Initial (1996)	3rd periodic	05.04.06
Madagascar	18.04.91	2nd periodic (2001)*	3rd periodic	17.04.03
Malawi	01.02.91	Initial (2002)"	2nd periodic	31.01.98
Malaysia	19.03.95		Initial	19.03.97
Maldives	13.03.91	Initial (1998)	2nd periodic	12.03.98
Mali	20.10.90	Initial (1999)	2nd periodic	18.10.97
Malta	30.10.90	Initial (2000)	2nd periodic	29.10.97
Marshall Islands	03.11.93	Initial (2000)	2nd periodic	02.11.00
Mauritania	15.06.91	Initial (2001)*	2nd periodic	14.06.98
Mauritius	02.09.90	Initial (1996)	2nd periodic	01.09.97
Mexico	21.10.90	2nd periodic (1999)	3rd periodic	19.10.02
Micronesia	04.06.93	Initial (1998)	2nd periodic	03.06.00
Monaco	21.07.93	Initial (2001)*	2nd periodic	20.07.00
Mongolia	02.09.90	Initial (1996)	2nd periodic	01.09.97
Morocco	21.07.93	2nd periodic (2003)*	3rd periodic	19.07.05
Mozambique	26.05.94		Initial	14.10.00
Myanmar	14.08.91	Initial (1997)	2nd periodic	13.08.98
Namibia	30.10.90	Initial (1994)	2nd periodic	29.10.97
Nauru	26.08.94		Initial	25.08.96
Nepal	14.10.90	Initial (1996)	2nd periodic	13.10.97

State Party	Entry into force	Last report considered	Next report due	Date due or overdue since
Netherlands	07.03.95	Initial–Antilles (2002)*	2nd periodic	06.03.02
New Zealand	06.05.93	Initial (1997)	2nd periodic	05.05.00
Nicaragua	04.11.90	2nd periodic (1999)	3rd periodic	03.11.02
Niger	30.10.90	Initial (2002)*	2nd periodic	29.10.97
Nigeria	19.05.91	Initial (1996)	2nd periodic	18.05.98
Niue	19.01.96		Initial	18.01.98
Norway	07.02.91	2nd periodic (2000)	3rd periodic	06.02.03
Oman	09.12.96	Initial (2001)*	2nd periodic	01.04.04
Pakistan	12.12.90	2nd periodic (2001)*	3rd periodic	11.12.02
Palau	03.09.95	Initial (2001)	2nd periodic	02.09.02
Panama	11.01.91	Initial (1997)	2nd periodic	10.01.98
Papua New Guinea	31.03.93		Initial–2nd periodic	31.03.00
Paraguay	25.10.90	2nd periodic (2001)*	3rd periodic	24.10.02
Peru	04.10.90	2nd periodic (2000)	3rd periodic	03.10.02
Philippines	20.09.90	Initial (1995)	2nd periodic	19.09.97
Poland	07.07.91	2nd periodic (2002)*	3rd periodic	07.07.03
Portugal	21.10.90	Initial (1995)	2nd- 3rd periodic	24.10.97
Qatar	03.05.95	Initial (2001)*	2nd periodic	02.05.02
Republic of Korea	20.12.91	2nd periodic (2003)*	3rd periodic	19.12.03
Republic of Moldova	25.02.93	Initial (2002)*	2nd periodic	24.02.00
Romania	28.10.90	2nd periodic (2003)	3rd periodic	27.10.02
Russian Federation	15.09.90	2nd periodic (1999)	3rd periodic	14.09.02
Rwanda	23.02.91	Initial (1993)	2nd periodic	22.02.98
Saint Kitts and Nevis	02.09.90	Initial (1999)	2nd periodic	01.09.97
Saint Lucia	16.07.93		Initial–2nd periodic	15.07.95
Saint Vincent and the Grenadines	25.11.93	Initial (2002)*	2nd periodic	21.11.00
Samoa	29.12.94		Initial	28.12.96
San Marino	25.12.91		Initial–2nd periodic	24.12.93
Sao Tome and Principe	13.06.91		Initial–2nd periodic	12.06.93
Saudi Arabia	25.02.96	Initial (2001)	2nd periodic	24.02.03
Senegal	02.09.90	Initial (1995)	2nd periodic	01.09.97
Seychelles	07.10.90	2nd periodic (2002)*	Initial–3rd periodic	06.10.92
Sierra Leone	02.09.90	Initial (2000)	2nd periodic	01.09.97
Singapore	04.11.95		Initial	03.11.97
Slovakia	01.01.93	Initial (2000)	2nd periodic	31.12.99
Slovenia	25.06.91	Initial (1996)	2nd periodic	24.06.98
Solomon Islands	10.05.95	Initial (2003)*	2nd periodic	09.05.02
South Africa	16.07.95	Initial (2000)	2nd periodic	15.07.02
Spain	05.01.91	2nd periodic (2002)*	3rd periodic	04.01.03
Sri Lanka	11.08.91	2nd periodic (2000)	3rd periodic	10.08.03
Sudan	02.09.90	2nd periodic (2002)*	3rd periodic	01.09.02
Suriname	31.03.93	Initial (2000)	2nd periodic	31.03.00
Swaziland	02.09.90		Initial	05.10.97
Sweden	14.08.93	2nd periodic (1999)	3rd periodic	01.09.02

State Party	Entry into force	Last report considered	Next report due	Date due or overdue since
Switzerland	26.03.97	Initial (2002)*	2nd periodic	23.03.04
Syrian Arab Republic	25.11.93	2nd periodic (2003)*	3rd periodic	13.08.05
Tajikistan	25.11.93	Initial (2000)	2nd periodic	24.11.00
Thailand	26.04.92	Initial (1998)	2nd periodic	25.04.99
The Former Yugoslav Republic of Macedonia	17.09.91	Initial (2000)	2nd periodic	16.09.98
Togo	02.09.90	Initial (1997)	2nd periodic	01.09.97
Tonga	06.12.95		Initial	06.12.97
Trinidad and Tobago	04.01.92	Initial (1997)	2nd periodic	03.01.99
Tunisia	29.02.92	2nd periodic (2002)*	3rd periodic	28.02.04
Turkey	04.05.95	Initial (2001)*	2nd periodic	03.05.02
Turkmenistan	19.10.93		Initial–2nd periodic	19.10.00
Tuvalu	22.10.95		Initial	21.12.97
Uganda	16.09.90	Initial (1997)	2nd periodic	15.09.97
Ukraine	27.09.91	2nd periodic (2002)*	3rd periodic	26.09.03
United Arab Emirates	02.02.97	Initial (2002)*	2nd periodic	07.03.04
United Kingdom of Great Britain and Northern Ireland	15.01.92	2nd periodic (2002)*	3rd periodic	14.09.04
United Republic of Tanzania	10.07.91	Initial (2001)	2nd periodic	09.07.98
United States of America	20.12.90	Initial (1996)	2nd periodic	19.12.97
Uruguay	20.12.90	Initial (1996)	2nd periodic	19.12.97
Uzbekistan	29.07.94	Initial (2001)*	2nd periodic	28.07.01
Vanuatu	06.08.93	Initial (1999)	2nd periodic	05.08.00
Venezuela	13.10.90	Initial (1999)	2nd periodic	12.10.97
Vietnam	02.09.90	2nd periodic (2003)*	3rd periodic	01.09.02
Yemen	31.05.91	2nd periodic (1999)	3rd periodic	30.05.03
Yugoslavia	02.02.91	Initial (1996)	2nd periodic	01.02.98
Zambia	05.01.92		Initial–2nd periodic	04.01.99
Zimbabwe	11.10.90	Initial (1995)	2nd periodic	10.10.97

(An asterisk indicates that a report has been submitted but has not yet been considered by the Committee)

5. THE THEMATIC CONSIDERATION OF ISSUES

Rule 75 of the Rules of Procedure stipulates that "in order to enhance a deeper understanding of the content and implications of the Convention, the Committee may devote one or more meetings of its regular sessions to a general discussion on one specific article of the Convention or related subject".[29] This provision has been the basis for a series of "Days of General Discussion" on a wide range of topics including children in armed conflict, the role of the family for promotion of child rights, the situation of the girl child, the requirements for an appropriate system of juvenile justice, the economic exploitation of children, the child and the media, the rights of children with disabilities, issues of children and HIV/AIDS and violence against children.[30] The discussions, participated in by members and representatives of national and international organisations, including NGOs, have proved useful in deepening the Committee's understanding of its task, in providing an international forum for the exchange of views and, occasionally, in having implications for practice outside the Committee. Thus, for instance, in 1995 the conclusions of the discussion on the girl child influenced the content of the final document of the Fourth World Conference on Women.[31]

Days of General Discussion are normally announced in the report of the session immediately preceding that in which it is proposed that they occur. The announcement may be accompanied by a paper of the Committee on the topic. All interested parties, including NGOs, are invited to make written contributions. NGOs may also be invited to make oral contributions to the discussion. NGOs wishing to make effective contributions to the discussions should liaise closely with the NGO Group, which can provide timetabling information, relay submissions and lobby for the issuing of invitations to make oral submissions.

The Committee has concluded recent Days of General Discussion with the putting in place of follow up procedures, such as the establishment of informal working groups to promote implementation of the recommendations adopted on the day. Membership of such working groups is not confined to Committee members and may include NGO representatives and independent experts.[32]

6. MISSIONS

With the assistance of UNICEF, the Committee, represented by a number of its members, has undertaken a number of regional and subregional missions.[33] In the course of such trips, members have had the opportunity to discuss all aspects of implementation of the Convention with representatives of States and international and national organisations, including NGOs. Committee missions have been of use

---

[29] Rules of Procedure of the Committee on the Rights of the Child, Rule 75, United Nations Doc. HRI/GEN3, p. 197.

[30] The proceedings are reported in the reports of the session and in the biennial report to the General Assembly.

[31] See Report of the Fourth World Conference on Women, United Nations Doc. A/CONF.177/20 at Annex II, chapter IV, part L, "The Girl Child"; the report of the Committee's Day of General Discussion on the girl child, United Nations Doc. CRC/C/38 at paras. 275–299; the report of Committee members on their participation in the World Conference, United Nations Doc. CRC/C/SR.242.

[32] See, for instance, United Nations Doc. A/53/41 at para. 1397.

[33] See, *inter alia*, United Nations Doc. A/53/41. Paras. 1341–1352.

in alerting the Committee to particular national and regional problems and challenges and also in indicating the existence and competencies of local organisations. They have also served to draw attention to matters which the Committee mission may wish to put to the respective Government representatives.

It is not clear at this time whether missions of this type will continue to occur on a regular basis. Information in this regard can be obtained from the Secretariat and arrangements to meet with Committee members are best put in place through the appropriate UNICEF representatives in the countries concerned.

7. THE COMMITTEE PROCEDURE FOR ADDRESSING URGENT SITUATIONS

The Committee has indicated that it is willing to consider the situation in a State Party on the basis of urgently requested reports.[34] But it has not as yet taken action in this regard. NGOs have a role in developing the procedure by bringing emergency situations of human rights violations to the attention of the Committee.[35]

---

[34] See United Nations Doc. A/49/41, paras. 372–381.

[35] In 1996 the Special Rapporteur of the Commission on Human Rights on the Situation of Human Rights in the Former Yugoslavia, Elisabeth Rehn, wrote to the Committee requesting it to urgently address the situation in Bosnia and Herzegovina. The Committee responded by inviting the Special Rapporteur to meet with it, which she did in January 1997. The Committee took no further action other than to invite the Special Rapporteur to compile a special report on the situation of children in the former Yugoslavia. See, M. O'Flaherty, "Treaty Bodies Responding to States of Emergency", in, *The Future of UN Human Rights Treaty Monitoring*, (P. Alston and J. Crawford, Eds., 2000) at p. 458.

SAMPLE LIST OF ISSUES FOR THE HUMAN RIGHTS COMMITTEE

NETHERLANDS (2001)

Constitutional and legal framework within which the Covenant and the Optional Protocol are implemented (art. 2)

1. Please provide information on the existing mechanisms to implement the Committee's recommendations expressed in its concluding observations and in Views on individual communications.

I. EUROPEAN PART OF THE KINGDOM

The right to life; prevention of torture and degrading treatment; liberty and security of the person; treatment of prisoners and other detainees (arts. 6 and 7, 9 and 10)

2. Please provide information on the practice of euthanasia and/or assisted suicide in the Netherlands. How is it regulated and under what conditions is it practised?
3. Please provide further information on the Medical Research Involving Human Subjects Act. Please provide more details on scientific research involving minors and incapacitated adults, in particular the non-prohibited therapeutic research referred to (paragraph 36 of the report).
4. Please provide information with regard to any measures that have been taken to improve the implementation of the right to notify family members or friends if an individual has been taken into custody.
5. Please explain what provisions apply to the right of any detained persons to have access to a lawyer, when access is granted and with what delays.
6. Please provide further details on the practice of electronic tagging as an alternative to implementation of custodial sentences (paragraph 71 b of the report). How many convicted persons have been the subject of such alternative sentencing?
7. Please comment on the new provisions of the Code of Criminal Procedure (April 1995), whereby pre-trial detention may be imposed in respect of a number of specific property offences and its compatibility with the provisions of article 9 of the Covenant (paragraph 58 of the report).

Rights of aliens (art. 13)

8. Please explain whether the new aliens bill, reportedly submitted to the Lower House of Parliament in September 1999, has come into force since the submission of the report. Please provide information about the main changes introduced by this new law, in comparison to the previous Act (paragraph 90 of the report).
9. Are female genital mutilation or other traditional practices that infringe the physical integrity or health of women taken into consideration when deciding on measures of expulsion to another country?

Protection of the child (art. 24)

10. Please provide updated statistics on cases of child abuse (paragraph 165 of the report). What specific measures have been adopted to combat this phenomenon? Have they proved effective in reducing reported incidents of child abuse?

Equality and the principle of non-discrimination (arts. 3 and 26)

11. Please provide statistics with regard to incidents of violence against women. What measures have been taken to prevent such incidents? Have there been any indictments and/or convictions for marital rape since 1991?
12. What measures are being taken to prevent or combat trafficking in women for the purpose of forced prostitution (paragraph 38 of the report)?
13. How many cases of discrimination have been investigated by the Equal Treatment Commission (paragraph 185 of the report)? Also please provide information on the outcome of the investigations.

Minorities (art. 27)

14. Please comment on any special measures, legislative or administrative, that have been taken for the protection of minorities, as provided for in article 27 of the Covenant.

II. The Netherlands Antilles

15. Has the new Civil Code for the Netherlands Antilles entered into force since the submission of the report (paragraph 379 of the report) and what would be its impact on the promotion of equality between men and women?
16. Taking into account the statements in paragraphs 230 and following of the report, please comment on the factual and legal equality of women with respect to men.
17. Has the Criminal Code been revised? If so, please indicate whether the references to the death penalty in articles 103.2 and 108.3 have been deleted. If it has not been revised yet, when is it expected that the revision will take place (paragraphs 46 and following of the report)?
18. Please provide further information on the functioning of the Police Complaints Committees (paragraphs 252 and 382 of the report). How many complaints have been submitted to these Committees, if any? Please indicate the results of the investigations undertaken by these Committees. Has anyone been brought to justice on the basis of the investigations undertaken by the Committees?

19. Please clarify the precise content and scope of the cooperation agreement between the Netherlands Antilles and the Netherlands concerning the reorganization of the prison system (paragraph 389 of the report). Does this agreement address issues such as improvement of detention conditions, particularly overcrowding and poor sanitary conditions in the prison system? Please comment specifically on the situation in Koraal Specht prison, in Curacao, and in police stations in St. Marteen and Bonaire.
20. Please inform the Committee of the existing mechanism for the investigation of allegations of ill-treatment in detention facilities.

III. ARUBA

21. Please clarify whether the Police Complaints Decree has now been amended and explain the main changes introduced by the amendments (paragraph 600 of the report).
22. Please explain the progress made since the submission of the report with regard to the drafting of a new national ordinance on the rules governing the prison system and forms of detention other than imprisonment (paragraphs 512 and 607)? When is this new national ordinance expected to enter into force?
23. The Country Ordinance on Admittance and Deportation entitles the legitimate family of Aruban males – but not of Aruban females – to be admitted to Aruba. Please provide information on whether the proposed Admission and Expulsion Ordinance designed to abolish this discriminatory treatment has entered into force, or when is it expected to do so (paragraph 596 of the report).
24. Please provide updated information about the participation of women in public life, the workforce and education, and on the proportion of women in positions of responsibility and decision-making positions in the public and private sectors. What measures are envisaged to enhance the status of women in the political area and public service?
25. Please provide information on the situation of domestic personnel, who are not covered by the Labour Code (paragraph 500 of the report).

Dissemination of information relating to the Covenant and the Optional Protocol (art. 2)

26. Please indicate the steps taken to disseminate information on the submission of the periodic reports under article 40 of the Covenant and their consideration by the Committee, in particular on the Committee's concluding observations.
27. Please provide information on training and education on the Covenant and the Optional Protocol procedure provided to public officials.

SAMPLE LIST OF ISSUES OF THE COMMITTEE ON ECONOMIC, SOCIAL AND CULTURAL RIGHTS

FRANCE (2001)

I. GENERAL INFORMATION

A. General legal framework within which human rights are protected

1. Please indicate whether, in addition to any action taken by the State party or at the initiative of the National Advisory Commission on Human Rights itself, an individual can submit a complaint to the Commission directly.
2. The Committee would like to have information on decisions taken by the National Ombudsman and by the ombudsmen of the various departments since the preparation of this report.

B. Information and publicity concerning the rights set forth in the International Covenant on Economic, Social and Cultural Rights and in other international instruments

3. Please indicate whether NGOs have been consulted during the drafting of this report.

II. ISSUES RELATING TO THE GENERAL PROVISIONS OF THE COVENANT (ARTS. 1-5)

Article 1 – Self-determination
4. Please indicate the concrete measures taken to apply the proposed reforms for the autonomy of French Polynesia, in particular with respect to guaranteeing the right concerning employment and real property.
5. Please indicate the position of the State party with regard to the bill on the autonomy of Corsica.

Article 2 – Non-discrimination
6. Please provide information on the situation of aliens who are not citizens of the European Union and of refugees and asylum-seekers with regard to their enjoyment of the rights recognized by the Covenant, and indicate whether there are any restrictions imposed by the State party that affect them.

Article 3 – Equal rights of men and women
7. Please provide information on the policy concerning the equal enjoyment of men and women of economic, social and cultural rights.

III. Issues Relating to Specific Provisions of the Covenant (Arts. 6-15)

Article 6 – Right to work
8. Please provide information on the measures undertaken by the State party to address high levels of unemployment among the least skilled, a high level of long-term unemployment, difficulties in integrating young people in the labour market, and increase in forms of precarious employment such as temporary employment and involuntary part-time employment.
9. Please indicate what steps are being undertaken to reduce unemployment among women.
10. Please provide information on the progress in implementing the youth employment scheme since 1997, as referred to in paragraphs 142-148 of the report.
11. Please provide information on the present situation of women employed in the armed forces.

Article 7 – Right to just and favourable conditions of work
12. Please provide information on the institutional composition of the bodies responsible for overseeing compliance with the occupational health and safety regulations, namely the Higher Council on Occupational Risk Prevention and the committees on health, safety and working conditions, referred to in paragraphs 217-218 of the report.
13. Please describe the procedures of judicial control by industrial tribunals and criminal courts to examine the enforcement of health and safety regulations (paragraph 229 of the report).

Article 8 – Trade union rights
14. Please provide more detailed information on how civil servants exercise their trade union rights, including the right to strike.

Article 9 – Right to social security, including social insurance
15. Please indicate the criteria according to which persons living with HIV/AIDS can obtain 100 per cent health coverage, in the context of Decree No. 93/676, referred to in paragraph 299 (b) of the report.

Article 10 – Protection of the family, mothers and children
16. Please provide more detailed information on the so-called "educational measures" necessary for children and the family, which are ordered by youth courts in cases when "the health, safety and character" of a child are at risk (paragraphs 416-420 of the report).
17. Please provide information on the extent of domestic violence against women, and on the measures taken by the State party to address the problem.

Article 11 – Right to an adequate standard of living
18. Please indicate what measures are being taken to improve the living standards of poor households, and in particular large and single-parent families (paragraphs 460-461 of the report).

180

19. Please provide more detailed information on the requirements for entitlement to RMI (income support), referred to in paragraph 464 of the report.
20. Please indicate what measures have been taken with a view to reducing poverty and extreme poverty, following the reports of France's Economic and Social Council and the National Advisory Commission on Human Rights (paragraphs 462-463 of the report).
21. Please provide information on the extent of homelessness. Please also provide information on measures being taken with regard to temporary or makeshift dwellings (paragraph 512 of the report).
22. Please indicate what specific measures are being taken as part of the plan instituted by Act No. 90-449 of 31 May 1990 to provide housing for the most disadvantaged groups of society (paragraph 534 of the report).
23. Please indicate what specific measures are being taken pursuant to Act No. 94-624 of 21 July 1994, which makes it mandatory for each department to draw up an emergency shelter plan.
24. Please provide more detailed information on the legislation to encourage private owners to rent to people with limited resources, as referred to in paragraph 521 of the report.
25. Please indicate the effects of framework law No. 98-657 of 29 July 1998 addressing the problem of social exclusion (paragraph 522 of the report).

Article 12 – Right to health
26. Please provide more detailed information on the measures being taken to reduce inequalities confronting the health sector, as referred to in paragraph 593 (d) of the report.

Articles 13 and 14 – Right to education
27. Please provide information on the effects of the measures taken to reduce the rate of student drop-out or failure at the university level, in light of the objectives referred to in paragraph 637 of the report. Please also provide information on the results of the policies implemented by the universities (paragraph 638 of the report).

Article 15 – Right to take part in cultural life and to benefit from scientific progress
28. Although the State party, in its third periodic report to the Human Rights Committee (CCPR/C/76/Add.7, para. 94), has declared that "France is a country in which there are no [ethnic, religious or linguistic] minorities", it is obvious that France is characterized by great ethnic and cultural richness. While the Committee recognizes the efforts made by the State party to protect its regional languages and cultures, it would like to have information on the measures taken by the State party to protect the languages and cultures of existing minority groups.

APPENDIX I(C)

SAMPLE LIST OF ISSUES FOR THE COMMITTEE ON THE RIGHTS OF THE CHILD

DENMARK (2001)

IMPLEMENTATION OF THE CONVENTION ON THE RIGHTS OF THE CHILD

PART I

Under this section the State party is requested to submit in writing additional and updated information, if available, before 6 April 2001:

A. Data and statistics, if available
1. Please provide demographic data of the under-18 population, including non-Danish nationals, disaggregated by nationality, sex, and religious or other origin.
2. Please provide specific disaggregated data in percentages on national budgetary allocation and spending for social needs for the period between 1998 and 2000.
   In particular, how much was spent on:

   a) education (including allocations for primary and secondary education, salaries, preservation of school buildings, etc.);
   b) health (including allocations for primary health care, vaccinations, adolescent health care and other health care services for children);
   c) child protection (for example institutional or foster care);
   d) juvenile crime prevention;
   e) programmes and services for child victims of abuse, including sexual abuse and neglect; and
   f) social services (including for minority families).

3. Please provide disaggregated data (by sex, age, nationality, urban or rural areas), covering the period 1997-1999 on the number of children deprived of their family environment:

   a) adopted domestically;
   b) adopted abroad;
   c) living in foster care;
   d) living in institutions; and

e)   living in boarding schools.

4.   Please provide the following statistical data (disaggregated by sex, age, type of crime, type of sanction) concerning children in conflict with the law for the period 1998-2000:

a)   number who were reported to the police for allegedly committing crimes;
b)   number who were sentenced by Courts to sanctions, and the nature of the sanctions imposed (imprisonment; community service; other);
c)   number dealt with outside of criminal proceedings;
d)   number of suspended sentences;
e)   where the sanction is deprivation of liberty, please further specify the period of detention and the nature of the offence;
f)   percentage of recidivism cases; and
g)   children held in solitary confinement and the duration of the confinement.

B. General Measures of Implementation

1.   In light of the Declaration and Plan of Action of the Vienna World Conference on Human Rights (1993), and with reference to information provided in paragraphs 4 and 5 of the report, please indicate whether additional consideration has been given to the withdrawal of the State party's reservation to article 40 (2) (b) (v) of the Convention.
2.   Please provide information concerning the status of the Convention in domestic law. Please specify whether the Convention has been invoked in domestic courts, and if so, please provide examples. Additionally, please indicate areas where law reform is still needed to ensure full conformity with the Convention.
3.   Please provide information on the measures taken to ensure the effective implementation and monitoring of the Convention, including with respect to children belonging to ethnic minority groups and other vulnerable groups. Additionally, please provide information on the system of data collection as well as on the use of statistical data in formulating policies and programmes for children.
4.   Please provide an update of recent measures taken to enhance awareness about the principles and provisions of the Convention, including among professional groups, children and the general public. Please highlight the efforts made to ensure that the Convention is also made available in the principal languages of refugees and migrants. Additionally, please outline the measures taken to disseminate the Initial State party report of Denmark as well as the concluding observations of the Committee on the Rights of the Child concerning this report.

PART II

Please provide the Committee with copies of the text of the Convention on the Rights of the Child in all official languages of the State party as well as in other languages or dialects, when available. If possible, please submit these texts in electronic form.

PART III

Under this section, States parties are invited, whenever appropriate, to briefly (3 pages, maximum) up-date the information provided in their report with regard to:

—   new bills or enacted legislation
—   new institutions

    –   newly implemented policies
    –   newly implemented programmes

PART IV

The following is a preliminary list of major issues that the Committee intends to take-up during the dialogue with the State party – THEY DO NOT REQUIRE WRITTEN RESPONSES. This list is not exhaustive as other issues may be raised in the course of the dialogue.

   The dialogue with the State party might include issues such as:

1. Independent human rights monitoring mechanisms (the possibility for children to directly make complaints).
2. Gender discrimination (in employment impact on children, especially those from single/ female headed households).
3. Discrimination against ethnic minorities, including in schools and through learning materials as well as with respect to housing, employment and economic opportunities.
4. Respect for the views of the child (efforts to promote acceptance of this principle, including for children under the age of 12 years, especially in placement decisions).
5. Article 17 (access to appropriate information and efforts to protect children from racist and other harmful information).
6. Adoptions, including intercountry adoption, placement policies and cultural adoption for minorities.
7. Child abuse and domestic violence (Efforts to promote awareness, preventative and rehabilitative programmes, including for perpetrators of such abuse and violence).
8. Health concerns for young children in institutions, including day care facilities.
9. Adolescent health concerns, including sexually transmitted diseases (STDs), HIV/AIDS, early pregnancy, smoking, drug and alcohol abuse, nutrition concerns (bulimia, anorexia, obesity), violence and bullying in school, physical and sexual abuse, suicide and mental health concerns. (Efforts to promote awareness, preventative and rehabilitative programmes).
10. School dropouts (especially as regards minorities); bullying in school.
11. Children living and/or working on the streets.
12. Commercial sexual exploitation, including child prostitution and pornography (Efforts to strengthen awareness, prevention and rehabilitation, legislative initiatives against perpetrators).
13. Asylum seeking, unaccompanied children (policies and programmes to promote and protect their rights).
14. Trafficking of children (legislative and other initiatives toward prevention).
15. Juvenile justice concerns (separation of children from adults, the holding of children in solitary confinement).

SAMPLE CONCLUDING OBSERVATIONS OF THE HUMAN RIGHTS COMMITTEE

NETHERLANDS (2001)

1. The Committee considered the third periodic report submitted by the Netherlands (CCPR/C/NET/99/3 and Add.1) at its 1928th, 1929th and 1930th meetings, held on 9 and 10 July 2001, and adopted the following concluding observations at its 1943rd and 1947th meetings, held on 19 and 23 July 2001.

A. Introduction

2. The Committee has examined the comprehensive and detailed report of the Netherlands covering events since the submission of its second periodic report in 1988. It regrets the long delay in the submission of the final version of the report. While it appreciates the extensive information provided by the delegation in respect of the European part of the Kingdom, it notes that the delegation was unable to respond to questions raised by Committee members on the human rights situation in the Netherlands Antilles and Aruba. This has unnecessarily complicated the possibility of engaging in a meaningful dialogue on the implementation of the Covenant in these territories. However, the Committee appreciates the timely receipt of the missing responses in writing.

THE EUROPEAN PART OF THE KINGDOM

B. Positive aspects

3. The Committee welcomes the establishment of an independent National Ombudsman, appointed by Parliament, whose authority is constitutionally anchored and whose mandate extends across national, provincial and municipal governments.
4. The Committee also welcomes the establishment of the Equal Treatment Commission, set up by the Equal Treatment Act, as an independent body responsible for investigating and assessing cases of alleged discrimination.

C. Principal subjects of concern and recommendations

5. (a) The Committee discussed the issue of euthanasia and assisted suicide. The Committee acknowledges that the new Act concerning review procedures on the termination of life on request and assisted suicide, which will come into force on 1

January 2002, is the result of extensive public debate addressing a very complex legal and ethical issue. It further recognizes that the new law seeks to provide legal certainty and clarity in a situation which has evolved from case law and medical practice over a number of years. The Committee is well aware that the new Act does not as such decriminalize euthanasia and assisted suicide. However, where a State party seeks to relax legal protection with respect to an act deliberately intended to put an end to human life, the Committee believes that the Covenant obliges it to apply the most rigorous scrutiny to determine whether the State party's obligations to ensure the right to life are being complied with (articles 2 and 6 of the Covenant).

(b) The new Act contains, however, a number of conditions under which the physician is not punishable when he or she terminates the life of a person, inter alia at the "voluntary and well-considered request" of the patient in a situation of "unbearable suffering" offering "no prospect of improvement" and "no other reasonable solution". The Committee is concerned lest such a system may fail to detect and prevent situations where undue pressure could lead to these criteria being circumvented. The Committee is also concerned that, with the passage of time, such a practice may lead to routinization and insensitivity to the strict application of the requirements in a way not anticipated. The Committee learnt with unease that under the present legal system more than 2,000 cases of euthanasia and assisted suicide (or a combination of both) were reported to the review committee in the year 2000 and that the review committee came to a negative assessment only in three cases. The large numbers involved raise doubts whether the present system is only being used in extreme cases in which all the substantive conditions are scrupulously maintained.

(c) The Committee is seriously concerned that the new law is also applicable to minors who have reached the age of 12 years. The Committee notes that the law provides for the consent of parents or guardians of juveniles up to 16 years of age, while for those between 16 and 18 the parents' or guardian's consent may be replaced by the will of the minor, provided that the minor can appropriately assess his or her interests in the matter. The Committee considers it difficult to reconcile a reasoned decision to terminate life with the evolving and maturing capacities of minors. In view of the irreversibility of euthanasia and assisted suicide, the Committee wishes to underline its conviction that minors are in particular need of protection.

(d) The Committee, having taken full note of the monitoring task of the review committee, is also concerned about the fact that it exercises only an ex post control, not being able to prevent the termination of life when the statutory conditions are not fulfilled.

The State party should re-examine its law on euthanasia and assisted suicide in the light of these observations. It must ensure that the procedures employed offer adequate safeguards against abuse or misuse, including undue influence by third parties. The ex ante control mechanism should be strengthened. The application of the law to minors highlights the serious nature of these concerns. The next report should provide detailed information as to what criteria are applied to determine the existence of a "voluntary and well-considered request", "unbearable suffering" and "no other reasonable alternative". It should further include precise information on the number of cases to which the new Act has been applied and on the relevant reports of the review committee. The State party is asked to keep the law and its application under strict monitoring and continuing observation.

6. The Committee is gravely concerned at reports that new-born handicapped infants have had their lives ended by medical personnel.

The State party should scrupulously investigate any such allegations of violations of the right to life (article 6 of the Covenant), which fall outside the law on euthanasia. The State party should further inform the Committee on the number of such cases and on the results of court proceedings arising out of them.

7. While it acknowledges that the State party's Medical Research (Human Subjects) Act 1999 attempts to find a generally acceptable standard and to establish a permanent control system through the Central Committee for Medical Research Involving Human Subjects and the corresponding local committees accredited by the Central Committee, the Human Rights Committee considers aspects of this law to be problematic (article 7 of the Covenant). It is concerned at the general criterion whereby proportionality is assessed by balancing the risks of the research to the subject against the probable value of the research. The Committee considers that this rather subjective criterion must be qualified by a limitation beyond which the risks are so great to the individual that no measure of expected benefit can outweigh them. The Committee is also concerned that minors and other persons unable to give genuine consent may be subject to medical research under certain circumstances.

   The State party should reconsider its Medical Research (Human Subjects) Act in the light of the Committee's concerns, in order to ensure that even high potential value of scientific research is not used to justify severe risks to the subjects of research. The State party should further remove minors and other persons unable to give genuine consent from any medical experiments which do not directly benefit these individuals (non-therapeutic medical research). In its next report, the State party should inform the Committee of the steps taken and provide it with detailed statistics.

8. The Committee remains concerned that, six years after the alleged involvement of members of the State party's peacekeeping forces in the events surrounding the fall of Srebrenica, Bosnia and Herzegovina, in July 1995, the responsibility of the persons concerned has yet to be publicly and finally determined. The Committee considers that in respect of an event of such gravity it is of particular importance that issues relating to the State party's obligation to ensure the right to life be resolved in an expeditious and comprehensive manner (articles 2 and 6 of the Covenant).

   The State party should complete its investigations as to the involvement of its armed forces in Srebrenica as soon as possible, publicize these findings widely and examine the conclusions to determine any appropriate criminal or disciplinary action.

9. While welcoming the establishment of a network of advisory centres to deal with child abuse, the Committee is concerned at the continuing high number of reported incidents (articles 7 and 24).

   The State party should continue to develop strategies designed to prevent child abuse, and investigate where it has occurred. It should also standardize the systems and measures employed by its advisory centres to facilitate these ends.

10. While welcoming the recent appointment of an independent National Rapporteur on Trafficking in Persons endowed with appropriate investigative and research powers, the Committee remains concerned at continuing reports of sexual exploitation of significant numbers of foreign women in the State party (articles 3, 8 and 26 of the Covenant).

    The State party should ensure that the National Rapporteur is equipped with all the means necessary to achieve real and concrete improvement in this area. The State party should inform the Committee of progress made in this respect in the next report.

11. The Committee appreciates the new instructions issued by the Immigration and Naturalization Service aimed at drawing the competent officials' attention to specific aspects of female asylum-seekers' statements peculiar to their gender. However, it

remains concerned that a well-founded fear of genital mutilation or other traditional practices in the country of origin that infringe the physical integrity or health of women (article 7 of the Covenant) does not always result in favourable asylum decisions, for example when genital mutilation, despite a nominal legal prohibition, remains an established practice to which the asylum-seeker would be at risk.

The State party should make the necessary legal adjustments to ensure that the female persons concerned enjoy the required protection under article 7 of the Covenant.

12. The Committee is gravely concerned at the scope afforded for the use of anonymous witnesses in the State party's criminal procedure. The Committee notes that use is made of hearing witnesses in the preliminary examination, prior to the trial, without the accused, counsel or the prosecutor being present. The identity is accordingly known only to the examining magistrate and is subsequently unknown even to the trial judge. While not excluding the use of anonymous witnesses in appropriate instances, the Committee considers that this practice is too broad and that it raises difficulties in terms of article 14 of the Covenant.

The State party should make greater efforts to safeguard the right of a defendant to a fair trial through means which, while protecting witness identity in appropriate and necessary cases, provide a greater opportunity for the evidence to be tested and contested. The State party should also provide further information on how a decision that a witness should be anonymous is reached, and what appeals against or reviews of such a decision are possible. The State party should show why ordinary means of protecting witnesses, such as police security or witness protection and relocation programmes, are considered inadequate in cases where anonymity is allegedly required on account of threats to the witness.

13. The Committee is concerned that the State party's law provides for a maximum of 3 days and 15 hours which may elapse between a suspect's arrest and his or her being brought before a judge. The Committee considers that such a period does not satisfy the requirement in article 9, paragraph 3, of being "promptly" brought before a judicial authority.

The State party should amend this aspect of its criminal procedure to comply with the requirements of the Covenant.

14. The Committee welcomes the State party's recent attempts through legislation and policy to enhance the participation of ethnic minorities in the labour market, including incentives to the private sector to expand the proportion of the workforce made up of ethnic minorities. It notes, however, that these efforts to secure the rights guaranteed under article 27 of the Covenant have yet to show significant results. The Committee is also concerned that children of ethnic minorities are under-represented at higher education levels. The Committee wishes to receive further information concerning the results in practice that the State party's measures in this regard are aimed at achieving.

THE NETHERLANDS ANTILLES

B. Positive aspects

15. The Committee welcomes the comprehensive revision of the Netherlands Antilles Civil Code, removing a large variety of elements discriminating against women. The Committee is also pleased to note the amendments to the Country Ordinances on Income Tax and on Wages and Salaries Tax placing spouses on an equal footing. The Committee notes the establishment of a Prisons Supervisory Board with the power to make binding recommendations on complaints by inmates.

C. Principal subjects of concern and recommendations

16. The Committee is concerned as to the breadth of article 137 of the Constitution, which regulates the imposition of a state of emergency without taking into account the limitation imposed by article 4 of the Covenant for the proclamation of a state of emergency to exceptional circumstances endangering the life of the nation.

    The State party should ensure that its rules on states of emergency are in full conformity with all the requirements of the Covenant.

17. While physical improvements have been made to prison facilities, the Committee remains concerned about unlawful conduct on the part of the staff, combined with their failure to control adequately the behaviour of inmates. These problems threaten the capacity of the competent authorities to administer the penitentiary system properly and to respect the rights of inmates (articles 7 and 10).

    The State party should take the necessary steps to ensure that prison staff act in accordance with the highest professional standards and in a manner that ensures that the rights of all inmates are respected.

18. While welcoming the establishment of the Police Conduct Complaints Committee to receive complaints from members of the public, and the establishment of a committee to monitor the integrity of the police, the Human Rights Committee is concerned that the said authorities do not have the capacity to issue binding determinations. It considers that to act effectively and independently of the executive, of which the police are a part, the authorities should have the competence to issue binding conclusions as to appropriate remedies or disciplinary measures as the case may be.

    The State party should review the limitations on the Authority's powers in the light of the Committee's observations.

19. The Committee is concerned that there is a sizeable backlog in the revision of outdated and obsolete legislation, in particular in the provisions of the Antillean Criminal Code. The Committee considers that, especially in the area of criminal law, legal certainty and clarity are of particular importance in enabling individuals to determine the extent of liability for specific conduct.

    The State party should proceed with the proposed revision of the Criminal Code at the earliest opportunity. In particular, references to the death penalty should be removed.

20. The Committee is equally concerned that the legal rules on the right of peaceful assembly contain a general requirement of prior permission from the local police chief.

    The State party should ensure that the right of peaceful assembly can be exercised by all in strict conformity with the guarantees of article 21 of the Covenant.

21. The Committee notes with regret that the distinctions between legitimate and illegitimate children who have not been recognized by their father, and who accordingly suffer disadvantage under inheritance laws, have not been eliminated.

    The State party should remove all distinctions between legitimate and illegitimate children in compliance with articles 24 and 26 of the Covenant.

ARUBA

B. Positive aspects

22. The Committee commends the State party for the introduction of the State Ordinance Administrative Procedure providing a special objection and judicial appeal mechanism

against any administrative decision. The Committee also welcomes fundamental safeguards against unlawful actions by the authorities contained in the revised Code of Criminal Procedure (1997), notably the availability of legal assistance beginning with a suspect's initial contact with the criminal justice authorities. It appreciates the establishment of universal jurisdiction for the crime of torture. It further welcomes the increased participation of women in Aruba's political life and in the workforce. It also commends the achievement by women of at least as high an educational level as men.

C. Principal subjects of concern and recommendations

23. The Committee is concerned that domestic workers, who are often particularly vulnerable to exploitation as non-Aruban nationals, should be ensured strengthened protection under Aruba's labour laws in order for the State party to be in compliance with the provisions of article 26 of the Covenant. A formal right to sue for breach of contract may well be insufficient in the specific circumstances of the employer-employee relationship.

   The State party should consider the most appropriate way to ensure adequate legal protection for domestic workers, for example by extending the provisions of the Labour Ordinance to cover this class of workers.

24. The Committee is disturbed that the State party has still not put in place an appropriate police complaints authority in Aruba, after the State party admitted that the system established under the Police Complaints Decree did "not function properly in practice" (articles 7 and 26 of the Covenant).

   The State party should ensure that the necessary measures are taken to amend and bring into force the revised Decree.

25. The Committee is concerned that despite the equal protection clause of the Aruban Constitution, the Country Ordinance on Admittance and Deportation still legally distinguishes between the legitimate family of a man born in Aruba with Netherlands nationality and the legitimate family of a woman born in Aruba with Netherlands nationality.

   Although the provision is said not to be applied in practice, the State party should remove this differentiation, which is in breach of article 26 of the Covenant.

26. The State party should widely publicize the text of its third periodic report, the written answers it has provided in responding to the list of issues drawn up by the Committee and, in particular, these concluding observations.

27. The State party is asked, pursuant to rule 70, paragraph 5, of the Committee's rules of procedure, to forward information within 12 months on the implementation of the Committee's recommendations regarding the State party's law on euthanasia (para. 5), the situation on post-natal infanticide (para. 6), the investigation of events surrounding the fall of Srebrenica (para. 7), as well as, for the Netherlands Antilles, the difficulties concerning its prison system (para. 17), and, for Aruba, the implementation of a functioning police complaints authority (para. 24). The Committee requests that information concerning the remainder of its recommendations be included in the fourth periodic report to be presented by 1 August 2006.

SAMPLE CONCLUDING OBSERVATIONS OF THE COMMITTEE ON ECONOMIC, SOCIAL AND CULTURAL RIGHTS

BELGIUM (2000)

1. The Committee considered the second periodic report of Belgium on the implementation of the Covenant on Economic, Social and Cultural Rights (E/1990/6/Add.15) at its 64th, 65th and 66th meetings, held on 17 and 20 November 2000, and adopted, at its 79th meeting, held on 28 November 2000, the following concluding observations.

A. INTRODUCTION

2. The Committee welcomes the submission of the second periodic report of the State party, which was prepared in general in conformity with the Committee's guidelines. A delegation of officials competent in various fields provided extensive written and oral replies to the Committee's list of issues. The Committee welcomes in particular the open and constructive dialogue with the delegation.

B. POSITIVE ASPECTS

3. The Committee notes with satisfaction the positive attitude of the State party towards the active participation of civil society in promoting and protecting economic, social and cultural rights, and the fact that the delegation of the State party invited a representative of a national NGO to address the Committee during the dialogue.
4. The Committee also notes with appreciation the State party's indication of its support for the Committee's work with regard to the draft optional protocol to the Covenant.

C. FACTORS AND DIFFICULTIES IMPEDING THE IMPLEMENTATION OF THE COVENANT

5. The Committee notes with concern that there are not sufficient mechanisms to coordinate and ensure uniformity of compliance, at both the federal and regional levels, with the State party's international human rights obligations.
6. The Committee notes that article 23 of the Constitution represents a step forward in that it incorporates a number of economic, social and cultural rights, leaving the guarantee of such rights to statutes and royal decrees. However, such legislation has so far not been adopted. While article 23, read in conjunction with other fundamental rights guarantees of the Belgian Constitution, could be interpreted to be applicable directly in the domestic

legal order, such interpretation still depends on the exercise of discretion by the national courts.

D. PRINCIPAL SUBJECTS OF CONCERN

7. The Committee regrets that the State party has not established a comprehensive national plan of action for human rights, in accordance with paragraph 71 of the 1993 Vienna Declaration and Programme of Action.
8. The Committee also expresses its concern about the lack of an independent national human rights institution, established in accordance with the Paris Principles of 1991, which would serve to monitor the entire range of human rights in the country.
9. The Committee is deeply concerned that there is no specific legislation which outlaws acts of xenophobia and racism, and in particular the activities of right-wing racist political parties, which are increasingly present on the political scene, especially in Flanders.
10. The Committee expresses its concern about the discriminatory effects against women of the so-called "cohabitation rule" in the unemployment insurance regime of Belgium.
11. The Committee is also concerned about the persistent gap between the unemployment rates of men and women and the discrepancy between them with regard to wages.
12. The Committee expresses its concern about the considerable unemployment among young people and the fact that that State party has not sufficiently addressed the long-term unemployment of persons over 45 years of age, nor the situation of those who have been forced into early retirement.
13. The Committee is also concerned about the phenomena of paedophilia, prostitution of children, child pornography and violence against children.
14. In the light of article 28 of the Covenant, the Committee is concerned about the significant shortage of social housing in Belgium, especially in Flanders. The Committee is also concerned that larger families, as well as single-parent and low-income families, are at a disadvantage in qualifying for such social housing.
15. The Committee is deeply concerned that the State party has not established adequate mechanisms to ensure uniformity in the application of educational standards, including international norms on education, in all regions, owing to the fact that the regional governments have primary responsibility in the formulation of educational policy. The Committee also regrets that the delegation provided uneven information on the implementation of the right to education in the different regions.
16. The Committee notes with concern that, in 1998, Belgium devoted only 0.35 per cent of its gross domestic product (GDP) to international cooperation, while the United Nations recommendation in this regard is 0.7 per cent of GDP for industrialized countries.

E. SUGGESTIONS AND RECOMMENDATIONS

17. The Committee recommends that, in the next periodic report, the State party provide more details on the mechanisms adopted to coordinate and ensure uniformity in activities by the various levels of government aimed at complying with international human rights obligations, in the light of article 28 of the Covenant.
18. The Committee urges the State party to formulate and adopt a comprehensive plan of action for human rights, as called for in paragraph 71 of the 1993 Vienna Declaration and Programme of Action.
19. The Committee also urges the State party to establish an independent national human rights institution, in accordance with the Paris Principles of 1991.

20. The Committee recommends that the State party, having ratified the Covenant, take appropriate steps to guarantee fully the direct applicability of the Covenant in the domestic legal order.

21. The Committee recommends that the State party adopt measures to ensure that xenophobia, racism and activities of racist organizations, groups or political parties are outlawed, with a view to complying with the principle of non-discrimination, set forth in article 2.2 of the Covenant.

22. The Committee urges the State party to revise the "cohabitation rule" in the unemployment insurance regime, in order to eliminate its indirect discriminatory impact on women.

23. The Committee recommends that the State party undertake more active measures to address the inequality of employment between men and women and the discrepancy in wages between them, as well as to promote women's access to all levels of the labour market.

24. The Committee encourages the State party to combat unemployment among young people and the long-term unemployment of workers over the age of 45, through appropriate vocational and technical training. The Committee would welcome more information in the State party's next periodic report on the measures taken and on the results achieved.

25. The Committee urges the State party to take effective measures to combat paedophilia, child prostitution, child pornography and violence against children, and to seek international cooperation in this regard.

26. The Committee urgently requests more detailed information in the State party's next periodic report on the situation of social housing in Belgium, especially in Flanders. The Committee also recommends that the State party take measures to eliminate the disadvantage of larger families, as well as of single-parent and low-income families, in qualifying for such social housing.

27. The Committee recommends that the State party establish an adequate mechanism to monitor and ensure uniformity of educational standards, such as those arising from international legal obligations, throughout the country. In addition, the Committee would welcome information in its next periodic report that reflects adequately and in a balanced manner the situation of education in all regions and communities.

28. The Committee requests more information in the State party's next periodic report concerning the initiative introduced in September 1999 to assist Flemish secondary school students who are in conflict with the educational system and, if the initiative has proved successful, the Committee suggests that consideration be given to its introduction in all the regions.

29. The Committee looks forward to receiving information from the State party in its next periodic report on the enjoyment of the right to participate in and benefit from cultural life, such as access to cultural activities and cultural property, especially by disadvantaged and marginalized groups in society, persons with disabilities and older persons.

30. The Committee recommends that the State party review its budget allocation for international cooperation with a view to increasing its contribution, in accordance with the United Nations recommendation.

31. The Committee encourages the Government of Belgium, as a member of international organizations, in particular the International Monetary Fund and the World Bank, to do all it can to ensure that the policies and decisions of those organizations are in conformity with the obligations of States parties to the Covenant, in particular the obligations contained in article 2.1 concerning international assistance and cooperation.

32. The Committee requests the State party to include in its next periodic report information on how the State party has taken into consideration the suggestions and recommendations contained in the present concluding observations. The Committee looks forward to receiving the third periodic report of Belgium no later than 30 June 2005.

33. The Committee encourages the State party to disseminate widely the present concluding observations.

SAMPLE CONCLUDING OBSERVATIONS OF THE COMMITTEE ON THE ELIMINATION OF RACIAL DISCRIMINATION

NETHERLANDS (2001)

1. The Committee considered the thirteenth and fourteenth periodic reports of the Netherlands, submitted in one document (CERD/C/362/Add.4) at its 1413th and 1414th meetings (CERD/C/SR.1413 and 1414), on 8 and 9 August 2000, and at its 1424th meeting (CERD/C/SR.1424), on 16 August 2000, adopted the following concluding observations.

A. INTRODUCTION

2. The Committee welcomes the very detailed updated report presented by the Government of the Netherlands, containing information on the European part of the Kingdom of the Netherlands, the Netherlands Antilles and Aruba, which follows the Committee's guidelines and contains relevant information about the implementation of the provisions of the Convention. The Committee particularly welcomes the opportunity to be able to continue a constructive and open dialogue with the State party represented by a large delegation and appreciates the detailed answers to questions raised and concerns expressed during the consideration of the report, including valuable written answers from Aruba.

B. POSITIVE ASPECTS

3. The Committee notes that the Netherlands is one of the few countries to refer to minorities without making a distinction between nationals and non-nationals; it welcomes the plan to apply the Framework Convention for the Protection of National Minorities of the Council of Europe without regard to nationality.
4. The Committee notes further progress in the implementation of article 4 of the Convention and welcomes the judicial proceedings that have led to the prohibition of a racist political party. It notes also the creation of the National Discrimination Centre within the prosecution service, the appointment of a national police "discrimination officer", the existence of public prosecutors and advocates general specialized in discrimination cases, and the Partnership Training Project between the police, the public prosecution service and civil society.
5. The Committee welcomes with great satisfaction the establishment of the Reporting

Centre for Discrimination on the Internet which is aimed at combating racism on Internet sites. The Committee considers this initiative a major step forward in the fight against contemporary forms of racism and looks forward to receiving updated information on the work of the Centre.

6. The Committee welcomes the appointment of a Minister for Urban Policy and Integration of Ethnic Minorities.

7. The Committee is also satisfied that its previous request for information on the Frisian-speaking community has been met and that the State party has given satisfactory information on the situation of this community.

8. For the Netherlands Antilles, the Committee welcomes the efforts undertaken – despite huge difficulties – to address the problems of children with language backgrounds different from those of the majority.

9. For Aruba and the Netherlands Antilles, the Committee welcomes the plans to address immigration problems cooperatively in the region.

10. The Committee acknowledges the efforts by the government in Aruba to promote the national language, Papiamento, in the educational system and cultural life.

C. CONCERNS AND RECOMMENDATIONS

11. While the Committee acknowledges the increase in employment among members of minorities, it is concerned that the unemployment rate among minority groups remains four times higher than among the native Dutch population. The Committee therefore hopes to receive information on the results of the "action plan" set up by the Government to reduce that difference by 50 per cent and on the evaluation of the new legal measures (Wet SAMEN).

12. The Committee is concerned about insufficient protection against discrimination in the labour market; it regrets the privatization and the planned dissolution of the Women and Minorities Employment Bureau and wonders what institution is going to fulfil the Bureau's task in the future.

13. While acknowledging the efforts to recruit members of minorities into government service, including the police and armed forces, the Committee is concerned about the disproportionately high number of members of minorities leaving the police forces. It recommends that the State party strengthen its efforts to create a police force reflective of the total population.

14. The Committee expresses concern at de facto school segregation in a number of localities and recommends that the State party undertake further measures to reduce de facto segregation and to promote a multicultural educational system.

15. The State party is invited in its next report to provide further information on the following issues: (a) the revision of the Criminal Code; (b) the living conditions of the Roma minority and the specific measures taken to improve them; (c) the further implementation of the Employment of Minorities (Promotion) Act; (d) the participation of minorities in local elections; (e) the changes brought by the draft new Aliens Act; and (f) statistical data on complaints, indictments and judicial decisions relating to acts of racism.

16. For the Netherlands Antilles, the Committee is concerned that there have been social tensions and problems in the educational system relating to immigration; it recommends that the problems be addressed on a regional level, so as to avoid racial discrimination.

17. While noting the information from the government of Aruba that domestic servants may

change employers though not occupation, it recommends that the government ensure that the status of domestic servants under immigration law is not exploited by employers.

18. The Committee recommends that the State party's reports be made readily available to the public from the time they are submitted and that the Committee's concluding observations on them be similarly publicized.

19. The Committee recommends that the State party's next periodic report, due on 5 January 2001, be an updating report and that it address the points raised in the present.

SAMPLE CONCLUDING COMMENTS OF THE COMMITTEE ON THE ELIMINATION OF DISCRIMINATION AGAINST WOMEN

NETHERLANDS 2001)

1. The Committee considered the second and third periodic reports of the Netherlands (CEDAW/C/NET/2 and Add.1 and 2, CEDAW/C/NET/3 and Add.1 and 2) at its 512th and 513th meetings, on 6 July 2001.

(a) Introduction by the State party

2. In introducing the second and third periodic reports, the representative of the Kingdom of the Netherlands indicated that the Netherlands had fully endorsed the Convention and that, during recent decades, a genuine revolution had taken place in the labour market, whereby while in 1988 only a third of women had paid employment, in 2001 the level of participation had risen to 52 per cent. There was, however, still evidence of a "male breadwinner's model of society", as shown by the low numbers of women in senior positions, in technical professions and the large number of women who had part-time jobs which did not provide economic independence. The representative indicated that the Government would remain firm on accelerating the emancipation process.

3. The representative underscored the fact that paid employment was a prerequisite for economic independence and that women's economic independence contributed to a more equal balance of power, which had proved to be the most effective instrument for preventing and combating violence against women. Participation of women in the labour force was the focus of the Government's recent Multi-year Plan on Emancipation Policy, which involved all government ministries. Concrete targets included that 65 per cent of women would have paid employment by 2010 and that 60 per cent of women who currently had part-time jobs would be fully economically independent.

4. The representative indicated that labour participation by women could be increased only through a reallocation of care tasks between women and men and that a number of measures had been taken in that regard, including doubling the capacity of child-care facilities; the introduction of a Work and Care Bill, which included four weeks' leave for foster parents or parents of adopted children; flexible use of the three-months parental leave provisions; 10 days' leave per year to take care of a sick child, partner or parent; and a law giving employees a right to work more or less hours per week. Additionally, the "Daily Routine" project, which aimed at a better alignment of education, child care and leisure facilities, had been established. The Government would be delineating a "Daily Routine" policy in the near future.

5. The strategy of gender mainstreaming had been accepted by the Government and all departments had a responsibility for gender mainstreaming, with each having formulated measurable emancipation tasks. Examples in this regard included a new tax system, which promoted the economic independence of women; the preparation of a tax measure aimed at facilitating women's re-entry into the labour market; and efforts to increase the number of black, ethnic minority and refugee women in local councils.

6. Domestic violence was still a serious problem in the Netherlands, and the Minister of Justice had submitted to the Parliament a plan of action against domestic violence, which included more severe punishments against the perpetrators of domestic violence. In accordance with European Union policy, the Netherlands had appointed a national rapporteur on trafficking in persons and was the first country of the European Union to do so.

7. The representative of the Netherlands highlighted aspects of the Multi-year Plan on Emancipation Policy, including a life-cycle project, which examined diversity in lifestyles.

8. On behalf of the Government of the Netherlands Antilles, another representative explained the restructuring programme and aggressive economic policy in place and indicated that while obstacles existed, developments in gender equality had taken place. Among these were the coming into force of the first part of a new civil code, which abolished a number of discriminatory laws and granted women equal rights in issues pertaining to marriage and the family. Irretrievable breakdown had been delineated as the only ground for divorce and either spouse could request termination of the marriage on that ground. Differences in status between children born in and out of wedlock had been eliminated; a law had been enacted which provided protection to domestic workers, most of whom were women; and termination of labour contracts on the basis of marriage and pregnancy had been prohibited. In addressing increased sexual violence against women, the penal code had been amended to increase the maximum punishment available for sexual offences and special training had been given to police officers in dealing with victims of domestic violence. Campaigns condemning violence against women had also been carried out in collaboration with local non-governmental organizations. The representative indicated that regional collaboration on gender issues between Aruba, Suriname and the Netherlands Antilles was being expanded.

9. Turning to developments in Aruba on behalf of the Government of Aruba, the representative indicated that a National Bureau of Women's Affairs had been established in 1996, and that had had an important role in raising awareness of women's rights, existing discriminatory laws and traditional attitudes and practices. Owing to limited resources, most of the Bureau's projects had been carried out within the context of the regional collaboration between Aruba, Suriname and the Netherlands Antilles. The three countries had agreed to develop projects on job training for women; gender awareness training for media personnel; sexuality and reproductive health of teenage mothers; and violence against women. A regional meeting would be held on women's participation in leadership and decision-making. The Aruban parliament had approved a new civil code which eliminated existing discriminatory laws, and a medical insurance scheme aimed at providing health care for all persons had been introduced. Efforts were under way to counteract violence against women, including through the establishment of a shelter for battered women and the introduction of draft amendments to the criminal code, which had included marital rape. Also of importance was the establishment of a UNAIDS Theme Group for the prevention and control of HIV/AIDS in Aruba. In closing, the representative mentioned several few remaining areas of concern, including sex-segregation in the labor force, with the employment of women concentrated in the

lower-skilled and lower-paid occupations, and low levels of women's participation in politics and decision-making.

(b) Concluding comments of the Committee

Introduction

10. The Committee commends the Government of the Netherlands on its second and third periodic reports, which are in accordance with the Committee's guidelines for the preparation of periodic reports. It commends the Government for the comprehensive written replies to the questions posed by the Committee's pre-session working group, and the oral presentation of the delegation which sought to clarify the current situation of women in the Kingdom of the Netherlands, including in the Netherlands Antilles and Aruba, and provided additional information on the implementation of the Convention. The Committee also welcomes the written responses to a number of its additional questions posed during constructive dialogue which were provided in the final week of the session.

11. The Committee congratulates the Government for its high-level delegation, headed by the Secretary of State for Social Affairs and Employment. The Committee appreciates the constructive and frank dialogue that took place between the delegation and the members of the Committee, but regrets that no representatives of the Governments of the Netherlands Antilles and Aruba were able to be part of the delegation which presented the reports as this would have enhanced the constructive dialogue.

Positive aspects

12. The Committee commends the Government on its conceptual approach to the implementation of each article of the Convention which incorporates, wherever applicable, three policy levels: achievement of complete equality for women before the law; improvement of the position of women; and efforts to confront the dominant gender-based ideology.

13. The Committee commends the Government on its extensive programme of legislative and administrative reforms which contribute to the implementation of the Convention.

14. The Committee also commends the Government on its programme to combat trafficking, particularly on the appointment of a National Rapporteur on Traffic in Persons, whose aim is to provide the Government with recommendations on how best to tackle the problem of trafficking, and for its commitment to combat this phenomenon at the European Union level.

15. The Committee commends that Government for its willingness to place objections to reservations entered by other States parties that it considers incompatible with the object and purpose of the Convention.

16. The Committee also commends the Government for having accepted the amendment to article 20, paragraph 1, of the Convention.

17. The Committee welcomes the establishment in Aruba in 1996, in accordance with the Committee's recommendations, of a National Bureau on Women's Affairs. Factors and difficulties affecting the implementation of the Convention

18. The Committee notes that there are no significant factors or difficulties which prevent the effective implementation of the Convention in the Kingdom of the Netherlands.

Principal areas of concern and recommendations

19. The Committee expresses concern that the Netherlands' policy of balanced division of paid work and unpaid care has not produced expected results, as the burden of unpaid care still falls mainly on women. The Committee is also concerned that women who work outside the home devote twice as much time as men to unpaid work, and that there are still insufficient child-care places.

20. The Committee recommends that the policy of balanced division of paid work and unpaid care be reviewed. It also recommends that greater efforts be devoted to the development of additional programmes and policies to encourage men to share family and caring responsibilities. The Committee also recommends that the Government ensure the availability of sufficient child-care places, and an uninterrupted long school day.

21. Despite efforts to combat discrimination in the Netherlands, the Committee expresses concern at the continuing discrimination against immigrant, refugee and minority women who suffer from multiple discrimination, based on their sex and ethnic background in society at large as well as in their own communities, particularly with respect to education, employment and violence against women. The Committee is also concerned about manifestations of racism and xenophobia in the Netherlands.

22. The Committee urges the Government to take effective measures to eliminate discrimination against immigrant, refugee and minority women, both within their communities and society at large. It urges the Government to respect and promote the human rights of women over discriminatory cultural practices, and take effective and proactive measures, including awareness-raising and community sensitizing programmes, to combat patriarchal attitudes, practices and stereotypical roles and to eliminate discrimination and violence against women in immigrant and minority communities. The Committee also urges the Government to eliminate xenophobia and racism in the Netherlands by strengthening its efforts to combat the activities of racist and xenophobic groups based in the Kingdom of the Netherlands.

23. The Committee is concerned about the lack of information in the reports on the de facto situation of women of ethnic and minority communities in respect to their access to education, employment and health services. It is also concerned at the limited information on their freedom from violence, including through female genital mutilation, domestic violence and honour crimes, as well as other discriminatory practices such as polygamy, early marriage and forced pregnancy.

24. The Committee urges the Government to provide in its next report detailed information, including statistics disaggregated by sex and ethnicity on the implementation of the Convention with respect to different ethnic and minority groups resident in the territory of the State party.

25. Noting the recent legislation on the abolition of the ban on brothels, which came into effect in October 2000, the Committee underlines the fact that prostitution poses risks for women of exploitation and violence.

26. The Committee urges the Government to begin monitoring this law immediately and provide, in its next report, an assessment of the intended, as well as unintended effects of the law, including with respect to risks of violence and to health, in particular in regard to those women without residence permits who are engaged in prostitution. The Committee also urges the Government to increase its efforts to provide training and education for prostitutes inorder to ensure that they have a full range of options for earning their livelihood.

27. The Committee is concerned about non-European women who have been trafficked who fear expulsion to their countries of origin and who might lack the effective protection of their Government on their return.

28. The Committee urges the Government of the Kingdom of the Netherlands to ensure that trafficked women are provided with full protection in their countries of origin or grant them asylum/refugee status.

29. Although acknowledging the efforts undertaken by the Government in solving the problem of discrimination faced by women at the work place through all the legislative measures aimed at improving women's economic status, including, inter alia, the Work and Care Bill, the Flexibility and Security Act, the Working Conditions Act and the Working Hours (Adjustment) Act, the Committee expresses concern over continuing discrimination in employment and business enterprises. The Committee is also concerned with the "horizontal" and "vertical" gender segregation of the labour market, and the concentration of women in part-time employment. The Committee is concerned that in the private sector women earn on average 23% less than men, although when "corrected" in light of the work they do and their personal characteristics, this differential is reduced to 7%.

30. The Committee urges the Government to increase its efforts to eliminate stereotypes relating to traditional areas of employment and education for women. The Committee recommends efforts to improve the conditions for working women so as to enable them to choose full-time, rather than part-time employment, in which they are currently overrepresented. It also urges the Government to eliminate the discrimination part-time workers face in relation to overtime.

31. The Committee is concerned that elderly women might be marginalized within, as well as insufficiently covered by, the health insurance and pension systems and urges the Government to pay special attention to the needs of elderly women in Daily Routine programmes.

32. The Committee is concerned about the low presence of women in high-ranking posts in all areas, and particularly in academia where, according to 1996 figures, women hold only 5 per cent of professorships. The Committee is also concerned about the low participation of women in political and public life. In the present Government, women hold 26.75 per cent of posts in ministries whereas, according to 1998 figures, only 7.5 per cent of posts at the level of ambassadors, permanent representatives and consuls-general are filled by women.

33. The Committee urges the Government to make efforts to facilitate an increase of the numbers of women in high-ranking posts. It recommends the adoption of proactive measures to encourage more women to apply for these positions, as well as through the implementation of temporary special measures in accordance with article 4, paragraph 1, of the Convention, where necessary including in decision-making in politics, the economy and academia.

34. The Committee notes with concern that in the Netherlands there is a political party represented in the Parliament which excludes women from membership which is a violation of article 7c of the Convention.

35. The Committee recommends that the State party take urgent measure to address this situation, including through the adoption of legislation that brings the membership of political parties into conformity with the obligations under article 7.

36. The Committee is concerned that there is insufficient information on the issue of HIV/AIDS is included in the reports and requests the Government to provide such information in its next periodic report in accordance with the Committee's general recommendation 15.

37. The Committee is concerned at the absence of information in the reports of tobacco and alcohol addiction among women. It is also concerned at the absence of information on

drug addiction among women, particularly in light of the decriminalization of the use of certain drugs. The Committee requests that information on these areas be provided in the next report, and taking account of paragraph 10 of its general recommendation 24 on women and health, on any meaures to address these issues.

38. The Committee is concerned that the new Law on Names provides that where the parents cannot reach an agreement as to the name of a child, the father has the ultimate decision. The Committee considers that this contravenes the basic principle of equality in the Convention and, in particular, article 16 (g).

39. The Committee recommends that the Government review the Law on Names and amend it to comply with the Convention.

40. The Committee found it difficult to evaluate the implementation of the Convention in the Netherlands Antilles and Aruba because no representatives of the Governments of those territories were part of the delegation which presented their reports.

41. The Committee urges the Government of the Netherlands to ensure that the Governments of the Netherlands Antilles and Aruba are sufficiently supported so that they can be part of the delegation of the Kingdom of the Netherlands when it presents its next periodic report to the Committee.

42. Based on the information provided, the Committee expresses concern about the status of women in the Netherlands Antilles and Aruba where, despite the strides that have been made towards strengthening women's legal position, gender equality is far from being achieved, and gender-based stereotypes persist. The Committee is particularly concerned about the negative effects which the Structural Adjustment Programmes might have on women in the Netherlands Antilles as well as on the limited resources available to the National Bureau of Women's Affairs in Aruba, which might prevent the effective implementation of projects aimed at empowering women.

43. The Committee urges the Government of the Netherlands to strengthen its economic support to the Netherlands Antilles and Aruba, particularly support for programmes on capacity-building to better achieve gender equality, including support for the implementation of the Convention.

44. Noting the positive contributions of the Netherlands to the process of elaboration of the Optional Protocol, the Committee urges the Government to ratify that instrument as soon as possible.

45. The Committee requests the Government to respond to the concerns expressed in the present concluding comments in its next periodic report under article 18 of the Convention.

46. The Committee requests the wide dissemination in the Kingdom of the Netherlands, including the Netherlands Antilles and Aruba, of the present concluding comments in order to make the people of the Kingdom of the Netherlands, and particularly government administrators and politicians, aware of the steps that have been taken to ensure de jure and de facto equality for women and the future steps required in that regard. It also requests the Government to continue to disseminate widely, in particular to women's and human rights organizations, the Convention and its Optional Protocol, the Committee's general recommendations, the Beijing Declaration and Platform for Action, and the results of the twenty-third special session of the General Assembly entitled "Women 2000: gender equality, development and peace in the twenty-first century".

SAMPLE CONCLUSIONS AND RECOMMENDATIONS OF THE COMMITTEE AGAINST TORTURE

NETHERLANDS (2000)

181. The Committee considered the third periodic report of the Netherlands (CAT/C/44/ Add.4 and 8) at its 426th, 429th and 433rd meetings on 11, 12 and 16 May 2000 (CAT/C/ SR.426, 429 and 433), and adopted the following conclusions and recommendations.

1. INTRODUCTION

182. The Committee notes with satisfaction the third periodic report of the Netherlands (European part of the Kingdom, Antilles and Aruba), which conforms to the general guidelines for the preparation of periodic reports as to content and form.
183. The Committee thanks the three Governments concerned for their comprehensive reports as well as for the oral reports and clarifications made by the delegations, which displayed a spirit of openness and cooperation.
184. The Committee welcomes the three accompanying core documents which, although not submitted within the prescribed time, facilitated the examination of the reports.
185. The Committee regrets that no Aruba delegation could be present during the examination of the reports. However, the Committee appreciates the written information and answers provided by Aruba to the Committee.

2. POSITIVE ASPECTS

186. The Committee particularly notes with satisfaction the following:

(a) That it has received no information about allegations of torture in the State party;
(b) As of early 1999, a special National War Criminals Investigation Team has been set up and made operational in the Netherlands (European part), to facilitate the investigation and prosecution of war crimes, which can include torture as specified in the Convention;
(c) The State party's contributions to the United Nations Voluntary Fund for the Victims of Torture;
(d) Clarifications by the representative of the State party with regard to the non-prosecution of General Pinochet when he was on the territory of the Netherlands. While regretting the lack of prosecution, on the grounds of non-feasibility, the Committee notes with satisfaction that the State party representative has affirmed that immunity from prosecution does not at present hold under international human rights law;

(e) The Netherlands Antilles and Aruba have both recently made the act of torture punishable in criminal legislation, as a separate criminal offence, and have also established the principle of universal jurisdiction;

(f) The Netherlands Antilles has established a National Investigation Department to investigate allegations of breach of authority by public servants and a public Complaints Committee on police brutality. In addition, several short and medium-term measures have been taken to ameliorate conditions in prisons;

(g) The assurances that, despite privatization of prisons in the Netherlands Antilles, the State's obligations under the Convention continue to apply;

(h) Measures taken in the Netherlands Antilles to ensure that officials visit the prisons once a week.

3. SUBJECTS OF CONCERN

187. The Committee expresses its concern about:

(a) Allegations of police actions in the Netherlands (European part), involving illegitimate body searches, inadequate deployment of female officers, and some excessive use of force by the police in connection with crowd control;

(b) Allegations of inter-prisoner violence, including sexual assault in Koraal Specht prison in the Netherlands Antilles;

(c) The daily use of a riot squad as a means of prisoner control in Koraal Specht prison in the Netherlands Antilles;

(d) Some allegations of police brutality in Aruba and the absence of information, including statistics, regarding the prison population.

4. RECOMMENDATIONS

188. The Committee recommends that:

(a) Measures be taken in the Netherlands (European part) to fully incorporate the Convention in domestic law, including adopting the definition of torture contained in article 1 of the Convention;

(b) Despite improvement already made in the Netherlands Antilles, effective measures should continue to be taken to bring to an end the deplorable conditions of detention at Koraal Specht prison;

(c) The practice of controlling prison discipline by the use, on a virtually daily basis, of riot squads, in the Netherlands Antilles should be reviewed and, in particular, efforts should be made to develop alternative means to prevent inter-prisoner violence. Such means should include the proper training of prison personnel;

(d) Relevant statistics should be provided to the Committee, disaggregated by gender and geography.

SAMPLE CONCLUDING OBSERVATIONS OF THE COMMITTEE ON THE RIGHTS OF THE CHILD

NETHERLANDS (1999)

1. The Committee considered the initial report of the Netherlands (CRC/C/51/Add.1) at its 578th to 580th meetings (see CRC/C/SR.578-580), held on 4 and 5 October 1999 and adopted, at the 586th meeting, held on 8 October 1999, the following concluding observations.

A. INTRODUCTION

2. The Committee expresses its appreciation for the clear and comprehensive nature of the report, which follows the Committee's guidelines. The report, however, focuses heavily on legislation, programmes and policy at the expense of information on the actual enjoyment of the rights of the child. While regretting their late submission, the Committee takes note of the detailed and informative written answers to the list of issues (CRC/C/Q/NETH.1) and some additional information provided to it during the course of the meetings, which enabled the Committee to assess the situation of the rights of the child in the State party. The Committee regrets the limitations placed on the State party's delegation by the unavailability of appropriate information to answer some of the questions during the discussion, which imposed constraints on a productive dialogue.

B. POSITIVE ASPECTS

3. The Committee welcomes the commitment and efforts of the State party in achieving a commendable degree of enjoyment by children in the State party of their rights through the establishment of infrastructure, comprehensive policies, legislation and administrative and other measures.
4. Moreover, the Committee commends the State party for its continued commitment to the rights of the child in its development assistance programmes and notes with satisfaction that the State party has exceeded the United Nations target of 0.7 per cent of GDP for development assistance.
5. The Committee commends the State party's efforts to combat the phenomenon of child-sex tourism.
6. The Committee notes with satisfaction the State party's ratification of the Hague Convention of 1980, on the Civil Aspects of International Child Abduction, and the Hague Convention of 1993 on the Protection of Children and Co-operation in Respect of Intercountry Adoption.

C. PRINCIPAL SUBJECTS OF CONCERN AND THE COMMITTEE'S RECOMMENDATIONS

C.1 General measures of implementation

7. The Committee is encouraged that the State party has indicated its willingness to reconsider its reservation to article 10 of the International Covenant on Civil and Political Rights. However, it notes with concern the reservations to articles 26, 37 and 40 of the Convention made by the State party. In the light of the Vienna Declaration and Programme of Action (1993), the Committee encourages the State party to consider withdrawing all of its reservations.

8. The Committee notes that cooperation with and the involvement of non-governmental organizations in the implementation of the Convention, including the preparation of the report, remain limited. The Committee encourages the State party to consider a more systematic approach to involve NGOs, and civil society in general, throughout all stages of the implementation of the Convention.

9. While acknowledging the initial efforts made to disseminate the Convention, the Committee regrets that the State party's report was not made widely available, or disseminated. Furthermore, the Committee is concerned that the State party is not undertaking information and awareness-raising activities on an ongoing basis. In this regard, the Committee recommends that the State party develop an ongoing programme for the dissemination of information regarding the implementation of the Convention, in order to maintain a high level of awareness of the importance of the Convention among children and parents, civil society and all sectors and levels of government. Moreover, the Committee recommends that the State party develop systematic and ongoing training programmes on the provisions of the Convention for all professional groups working for and with children, such as judges, lawyers, law enforcement officials, civil servants, personnel working in institutions and places of detention for children, teachers, health personnel, including psychologists, and social workers.

10. The Committee expresses its concern that measures and policies developed by the State party for implementation at the provincial and municipal levels are not sufficiently child rights-based. The Committee is concerned that compartmentalization of policy sectors often leads to fragmentation and overlap in respect of the implementation of the Convention. In this regard, the Committee recommends that the State party adopt a comprehensive national plan of action to implement the Convention, and give increased attention to intersectoral coordination and cooperation at and between the central, provincial and municipal levels of government.

11. While noting the positive aspects of decentralization in the implementation of child policies, the Committee is nevertheless concerned that it may contribute to bottlenecks in the implementation of provisions of the Convention. The State party is encouraged to provide support to local authorities for implementation of the principles and provisions of the Convention.

12. While acknowledging the role played by the Council for Child Protection and the "children's law polyclinics" in offering legal advice and information to children and in promoting their interests, the Committee remains concerned about the lack of an independent mechanism to monitor the implementation of the Convention. The Committee recommends that consideration be given to the establishment of a fully independent ombudsman for children to monitor and assess the full implementation of the Convention.

13. The Committee is concerned about the lack of information regarding the implementation of article 4 of the Convention and the use to the "maximum extent" of available resources to implement the economic, social and cultural rights of children. The Committee urges the State party to develop ways to establish a systematic assessment of the impact of budgetary allocations and macroeconomic policies on the implementation of children's rights and to collect and disseminate information in this regard.

C.2 General principles

14. The Committee welcomes the generally good levels of participation of children, particularly in secondary schools and at the local level. The Committee encourages the State party to continue promoting such participation, in particular in decision-making processes in all matters affecting children themselves. In this regard, the Committee recommends that the State party develop training programmes for local officials and other decision-makers to enable them to take adequately into consideration the opinions of children presented to them, with particular emphasis on involving and reaching vulnerable groups, such as children of ethnic minorities. The Committee also recommends that more attention be given to the promotion of child participation in primary schools.

C.3 Family environment and alternative care

15. In relation to article 11 of the Convention, the Committee notes that the Netherlands is a party to the Hague Convention of 1993, on the Protection of Children and Cooperation in Respect of Intercountry Adoption and to the Hague Convention of 1980 on the Civil Aspects of International Child Abduction. The Committee encourages the State party to consider concluding bilateral agreements with States that are not parties to the two above-mentioned conventions.

16. The Committee is concerned about the long waiting periods for placement in residential care. The Committee encourages the State party to increase the number of places available in residential facilities, while giving increased attention to alternatives to placement in residential facilities, in particular foster family care services, bearing in mind the principles and provisions of the Convention, especially the best interests of the child.

17. The Committee welcomes the recent efforts to establish a network of child abuse reporting and counselling centres and the plans to strengthen child abuse monitoring and reporting systems. However, the Committee remains concerned about the growth in reported cases of child abuse and about the level of protection available to children. The Committee urges the State party to give increased priority to the prompt implementation and support of monitoring and reporting systems based on the position paper of the Ministries of Justice, and Health, Welfare and Sport concerning the prevention of child abuse and the protection and rehabilitation offered to victims of child abuse. Furthermore, the Committee recommends that the State party, in line with developments in other European countries, take legislative measures to prohibit the use of all forms of mental and physical violence against children, including corporal punishment, within the family.

C.4 Basic health and welfare

18. The Committee welcomes the efforts made and understands the difficulties faced by the State party in protecting girls within its jurisdiction from female genital mutilation carried out outside its territory. Nevertheless, the Committee urges the State party to undertake strong and effectively targeted information campaigns to combat this phenomenon, and to consider adopting legislation with extraterritorial reach which could improve the protection of children within its jurisdiction from such harmful traditional practices.

19. The Committee remains concerned that the right of access to medical advice and treatment without parental consent, such as testing for HIV/AIDS, may be compromised in instances where the bill for such services is sent to the parents, violating the confidentiality of the doctor-child relationship. The Committee recommends that the State party take adequate measures to ensure that medical advice and treatment remain confidential for children of appropriate age and maturity, in accordance with articles 12 and 16 of the Convention.

20. The Committee is concerned at the low rates of breastfeeding. The Committee encourages the State party to undertake breastfeeding promotion campaigns, stressing its advantages and the negative impact of substitutes, while providing counselling to HIV/AIDS-infected mothers about the risk of transmission of HIV/AIDS through breastfeeding.

C.5 Education, leisure and cultural activities

21. The Committee is concerned that not enough attention has been given to the inclusion of human rights education in the school curricula, particularly at the primary level. The Committee urges the State party to consider introducing human rights issues into the school curricula at earlier ages and to ensure that the Convention on the Rights of the Child and its provisions are adequately covered in the existing curricula for older children and in new curricula for primary school pupils.

22. The Committee welcomes the efforts being made to address the problem of bullying in schools, including the "Safe schools" campaign. The Committee encourages the State party to continue its efforts to prevent bullying in schools, to collect information on the extent of this phenomenon and, in particular, to strengthen structures to enable children to participate in adequately addressing and resolving this problem.

C.6 Special protection measures

23. While noting the efforts to deal with unaccompanied asylum-seeking minors, the Committee is concerned that they may need to receive increased attention. The Committee recommends that the State party strengthen measures so as to provide immediate counselling and prompt and full access to education and other services for refugee and asylum-seeking children. Furthermore, the Committee recommends that the State party take effective measures for the integration of these children into its society.

24. The Committee takes note of the efforts made to raise steadily the age of recruitment into the armed forces and involvement in hostilities. It also notes the declaration stating the intention of the State party to apply a higher standard than that required by the Convention, and its commitment to international efforts in this regard. Nevertheless, the

Committee urges the State party to reconsider its present recruitment policies, with a view to setting the age of recruitment into the armed forces at 18 years.

25. The Committee welcomes the information provided on the improvements that the Youth Custodial Institutions Act will introduce to deal, as quickly as possible, with complaints regarding ill-treatment. Nonetheless, the Committee recommends that due attention be given to ensuring that efforts to settle such complaints promptly through a mediation procedure will not result in less than thorough investigations.

26. The Committee is concerned about the delays faced by juvenile offenders in need of psychological and psychiatric treatment. The Committee recommends that the State party increase the availability of places in institutions in order to provide these juvenile offenders with timely and appropriate treatment.

27. On the protection of children from sexual abuse, the Committee welcomes the attention given by the State party to the impact of the "complaint requirement" for prosecuting offences committed against children between 12 and 16 years. However, the Committee remains concerned that the balance sought between protecting children against sexual abuse and protecting their sexual freedom may still unduly limit protection from abuse. The Committee also remains concerned that efforts to increase the protection of children against exploitation in the production of pornography have not made further progress. The Committee encourages the State party to continue reviewing its legislation and policies so as to modify the "complaint requirement" for prosecution of sexual offences committed against children over 12. Furthermore, the Committee encourages the State party to change its legislation with a view to improving the protection of all children from inducement to participate in the production of pornographic shows or materials, and from other forms of commercial sexual exploitation. While welcoming the introduction of such legislation, the Committee also encourages the State party to consider reviewing the "dual criminality" requirement in legislation establishing extraterritorial jurisdiction for cases of sexual abuse of children.

28. The Committee notes the concern of the State party with respect to the problem of the sexual exploitation of children, often victims of trafficking, including the disappearance of unaccompanied minor asylum-seekers from reception centres. The Committee, however, remains concerned that no specific policies and measures appear to be contemplated at this point to address the problem as a matter of urgency. The Committee urges the State party to give prompt and serious attention to the need to ensure that children are not used as prostitutes and that asylum-seeking procedures, while fully respecting the rights of unaccompanied minor asylum-seekers, effectively protect children from involvement in trafficking for sexual exploitation. Further, the Committee recommends that the State party adopt a comprehensive national plan of action to prevent and combat commercial sexual exploitation of children, taking into account the recommendations formulated in the Agenda for Action adopted at the 1996 Stockholm World Congress Against Commercial Sexual Exploitation of Children.

29. The Committee notes the monitoring of the educational performance of children from ethnic minorities, but it remains concerned that the results continue to show noticeable disparities. The Committee urges the State party to review its efforts closely and to consider the possibility of providing further assistance to children at risk and the need to provide assistance to families from ethnic minorities with socioeconomic problems, thus addressing the root causes of poor educational performance.

30. The Committee is seriously concerned about the implications of the reservation entered by the State party on the applicability of adult criminal law to children over 16 years of age. The Committee is also seriously concerned at information provided which indicates

that children aged 12 to 15 are also sometimes tried under adult criminal law. The Committee urges the State party to ensure that under the existing law no child under the age of 16 at the time of the commission of a crime is tried under adult criminal law, and to review the reservation mentioned above with a view to withdrawing it. The Committee further recommends that the State party takes legislative steps to ensure that a life sentence cannot be imposed on children who are tried under adult criminal law.

31. Finally, in the light of article 44, paragraph 6, of the Convention, the Committee recommends that the initial report and written replies submitted by the State party be made widely available to the public, along with the summary records of the relevant meetings and concluding observations adopted by the Committee. Such wide distribution should generate debate and awareness of the Convention and the state of its implementation, particularly within the Government, the relevant ministries, the Parliament and non-governmental organizations.

MODEL COMMUNICATION

Date: . . . .

Communication to:
    The Human Rights Committee
    OHCHR
    United Nations Office
    8–14 avenue de la Paix
    1211 Geneva 10, Switzerland,
submitted for consideration under the Optional Protocol to the International Covenant on Civil and Political Rights.

I. Information concerning the author of the communication

Name . . . .   First name(s) . . . .

Nationality . . . .   Profession . . . .

Date and place of birth. . . . .

Present address . . . .

. . . .

Address for exchange of confidential correspondence (if other than present address) . . . . .

. . . .

. . . .

Submitting the communication as:

    (a)   Victim of the violation or violations set forth below . . . . ☐

    (b)   Appointed representative/legal counsel of the alleged victim(s). . . . . ☐

    (c)   Other . . . . ☐

If box *(c)* is marked, the author should explain:

(i)   In what capacity he is acting on behalf of the victim(s) (e.g. family relationship or other personal links with the alleged victim(s)):

    . . . .

(ii)   Why the victim(s) is (are) unable to submit the communication himself (themselves):

    . . . .

An unrelated third party having no link to the victim(s) cannot submit a communication on his (their) behalf.

II. Information concerning the alleged victim(s) (if other than author)

Name . . . . First name(s) . . . .

Nationality . . . . Profession . . . .

Date and place of birth. . . . .

Present address or whereabouts . . . .

. . . .

III. State concerned/articles violated/domestic remedies

Name of the State party (country) to the International Covenant and the Optional Protocol against which the communication is directed:

. . . .

Articles of the International Covenant on Civil and Political Rights allegedly violated:

. . . .

Steps taken by or on behalf of the alleged victim(s) to exhaust domestic remedies – recourse to the courts or other public authorities, when and with what results (if possible, enclose copies of all relevant judicial or administrative decisions):

. . . .

If domestic remedies have not been exhausted, explain why:

. . . .

IV. Other international procedures

Has the same matter been submitted for examination under another procedure of international investigation or settlement (e.g. the Inter-American Commission on Human Rights, the European Commission on Human Rights)? If so, when and with what results?

. . . .

V. Facts of the claim

Detailed description of the facts of the alleged violation or violations (including relevant dates)*

. . . .

Author's signature:. . . . .

*Add as many pages as needed for this description.

213

MODEL COMMUNICATION

Date: . . . .

Communication to:
    The Committee against Torture
    OHCHR
    United Nations Office
    8–14 avenue de la Paix
    1211 Geneva 10, Switzerland,
submitted for consideration under the Convention against Torture and other Cruel, Inhuman or Degrading Treatment or Punishment.

I. Information concerning the author of the communication

Name . . . . First name(s) . . . .

Nationality . . . . Profession . . . .

Date and place of birth . . . .

Present address . . . .

. . . .

Address for exchange of confidential correspondence (if other than present address) . . . . .

. . . .

. . . .

Submitting the communication as:

    (a)   Victim of the violation or violations set forth below . . . . ☐

    (b)   Appointed representative/legal counsel of the alleged victim(s). . . . . ☐

    (c)   Other . . . . ☐

If box *(c)* is marked, the author should explain:

(i)   In what capacity he is acting on behalf of the victim(s) (e.g. family relationship or other personal links with the alleged victim(s)):

    . . . .

(ii)   Why the victim(s) is (are) unable to submit the communication himself (themselves):

    . . . .

An unrelated third party having no link to the victim(s) cannot submit a communication on his (their) behalf.

II. Information concerning the alleged victim(s) (if other than author)

Name . . . . First name(s) . . . .

Nationality . . . . Profession . . . .

Date and place of birth. . . . .

Present address or whereabouts . . . .

. . . .

III. State concerned/articles violated/domestic remedies

Name of the State party (country) to the Convention against Torture and Other Cruel, Inhuman or Degrading Treatment or Punishment against which the communication is directed:

. . . .

Articles of the Convention against Torture allegedly violated:

. . . .

Steps taken by or on behalf of the alleged victim(s) to exhaust domestic remedies – recourse to the courts or other public authorities, when and with what results (if possible, enclose copies of all relevant judicial or administrative decisions):

. . . .

If domestic remedies have not been exhausted, explain why:

. . . .

IV. Other international procedures

Has the same matter been submitted for examination under another procedure of international investigation or settlement (e.g. the Inter-American Commission on Human Rights, the European Commission on Human Rights)? If so, when and with what results?

. . . .

V. Facts of the claim

Detailed description of the facts of the alleged violation or violations (including relevant dates)*

. . . .

Author's signature:. . . . .

*Add as many pages as needed for this description.

INDEX

NIJHOFF LAW SPECIALS

23. E.-U. Petersmann: *The GATT/WTO Dispute Settlement System*. International Law, International Organizations and Dispute Settlement. 1996   ISBN 90-411-0933-1
24. G. de Nooy (ed.): *Cooperative Security, the OSCE, and its Code of Conduct*. 1996   ISBN 90-411-0316-3
25. M. Bertrand: *The United Nations*. Past, Present and Future. 1997   ISBN 90-411-0337-6
26. D. Dijkzeul: *The Management of Multilateral Organizations*. 1997   ISBN 90-411-0356-2
27. G. de Nooy (ed.): *The Role of European Ground and Air Forces after the Cold War*. 1997   ISBN 90-411-0397-X
28. M. Hilaire: *International Law and the United States Military Intervention in the Western Hemisphere*. 1997   ISBN 90-411-0399-6
29. D. Warner (ed.): *Human Rights and Humanitarian Law*. The Guest for Universality. 1997   ISBN 90-411-0407-0
30. J.C. Hathaway (ed.): *Reconceiving International Refugee Law*. 1997   ISBN 90-411-0418-6
31. G. de Nooy (ed.): *The Clausewitzian Dictum and the Future of Western Military Strategy*. 1997   ISBN 90-411-0455-0
32. Canadian Council on International Law and The Markland Group (ed.): *Treaty Compliance: Some Concerns and Remedies*. 1997   ISBN 90-411-0732-0
33. B. de Rossanet: *War and Peace in the Former Yugoslavia*. 1998   ISBN 90-411-0499-2
34. C.M. Mazzoni (ed.): *A Legal Framework for Bioethics*. 1998   ISBN 90-411-0523-9
35. M. Marín-Bosch: *Votes in the UN General Assembly*. 1998   ISBN 90-411-0564-6
36. L. Caflisch: *The Peaceful Settlement of Disputes between States: Universal and European Perspectives. Règlement pacifique des différends entre États: Perspectives universelle et européenne*. 1998   ISBN 90-411-0461-5
37. R. Wazir and N. van Oudenhoven (eds.): *Child Sexual Abuse: What can Governments do?* A Comparative Investigation into Policy Instruments Used in Belgium, Britain, Germany, the Netherlands and Norway. 1998   ISBN 90-411-1034-8
38. E.M. Barron and I. Nielsen (eds.): *Agriculture and Sustainable Land Use in Europe*. 1998   ISBN 90-411-9691-9
39. K. van Walraven (ed.): *Early Warning and Conflict Prevention*. 1998   ISBN 90-411-1064-X
40. S. Shubber: *The International Code of Marketing of Breast-milk Substitutes*. An International Measure to Protect and Promote Breast-feeding. 1999   ISBN 90-411-1100-X
41. G. Prins and H. Tromp (eds.): *The Future of War*. 2000   ISBN 90-411-1196-4
42. Choung Il Chee: *Korean Perspectives on Ocean Law Issues for the 21st Century*. 2000   ISBN 90-411-1301-0
43. K. Idris and M. Bartolo: *A Better United Nations for the New Millennium*. The United Nations System – How it is now and how it should be in the future. 2000   ISBN 90-411-1344-4

NIJHOFF LAW SPECIALS

MARTINUS NIJHOFF PUBLISHERS – THE HAGUE / BOSTON / LONDON